T0094743

Opposing the Crusader State

More Praise for *Opposing the Crusader State*

"Can America effectively export Democracy through military intervention? *Opposing the Crusader State* is a thought-provoking and highly readable book that will help you shape your answer to this question, outlining a disappointing history of America's past military forays into democracy building, heated discussions of the role of democracy and property rights in mitigating warfare, and a policy of reducing foreign intervention and promoting world-wide free trade."

—**PRICE V. FISHBACK**, Frank and Clara Kramer Professor
of Economics, University of Arizona

"Contemporary public discourse on U.S. foreign policy has become largely a battle of sound bites, with even our government's highest ranking officials addressing complex security and diplomatic matters in slogans and simplistic propositions. 24-7 news coverage only exacerbates this dumbing-down of foreign policy. Lost in all this is any deep understanding of either the principles of non-intervention (a policy that served America so well for so long) or of the aggressively interventionist foreign policy that has become the hallmark of recent administrations (both Republican and Democratic). *Opposing the Crusader State* pulls together in one volume enough substantive and timely writings on why current American foreign policy is so disjointed, costly, and self-destructive as to make even the most die-hard interventionists think twice before applauding Washington's next foreign invasion or nation-building folly."

—**BOB BARR**, former U.S. Congressman and senior member,
House Judiciary Committee

"One need not agree with all of views on intervention found in the thoughtful book, *Opposing the Crusader State*, to recognize that it provides a tremendously useful survey of the history, rationales, and contemporary relevance of opponents of military activism. Higgs and Close have brought commentaries on the past and present together in a clear and cogent way that will challenge even skeptical readers."

—**RICHARD K. BETTS**, Director, Arnold A. Saltzman Institute of War and Peace Studies, Columbia University

Opposing the Crusader State

Alternatives to Global Interventionism

Edited by
Robert Higgs and Carl P. Close

The INDEPENDENT INSTITUTE

Oakland, California

The Independent Institute
100 Swan Way, Oakland, CA 94621-1428
Telephone: 510-632-1366 · Fax: 510-568-6040
Email: info@independent.org
Website: www.independent.org

Cover Photo: © Peter Turnley/Corbis
Cover Design: Gail Saari

Library of Congress Cataloging-in-Publication Data
Opposing the crusader state : alternatives to global interventionism / edited by
Robert Higgs and Carl P. Close.
    p. cm.
  Includes bibliographical references and index.
  ISBN-13: 978-1-59813-015-7 (alk. paper)
  ISBN-10: 1-59813-015-3 (alk. paper)
  1. Isolationism--United States--History. 2. Nonalignment--United States--
History. 3. United States--Foreign relations--History. I. Higgs, Robert. II.
Close, Carl P.,
  JZ1313.3.O77 2007
  327.1'170973--dc22
                                        2007024660
Printed in the United States of America

11 10 09 08 07   1 2 3 4 5

Contents

Introduction

ROBERT HIGGS AND CARL P. CLOSE

To attain a peaceful and prosperous world, we must reconsider current approaches to international security and economic development. For many countries, the first step toward the realization of this goal is to treat trade policy as seriously as issues of war and peace. This step is imperative because commerce tends to strengthen the bonds of peace between trading countries as it enriches them economically. For the United States, improving national security and promoting international harmony requires the reinstatement of foreign-policy traditions that fell out of favor long ago.

For more than a century, U.S. foreign policy, whether conducted by Democrats or Republicans, liberals or conservatives, has rested on the assumption that Americans' interests are served best by intervening abroad militarily to secure markets for U.S. exports, fight potential enemies far from American shores, support security alliances, or engage in democratic nation-building. Before 1898, however, an opposite approach to foreign policy was widely considered to be more desirable and more consistent with the principles of the American Revolution. This approach—whether called neutrality, noninterventionism, or isolationism (the latter a smear word used by its critics)—boiled down to refraining from the use of military forces except to defend the nation against attack. Colloquially, one might call it "minding one's own business," but this shorthand expression may obscure the political, economic, and geo-strategic reasons that prompted the country's leaders and citizens to favor this approach for so long.

The seeds of nonintervention were planted early in the life of the republic. In his farewell address as president, George Washington famously advised his countrymen to steer clear of entangling alliances: "The great rule of conduct for us in regard to foreign nations is, in tending our commercial relations, to have with them as little political connection as possible." Thomas Jefferson proposed at his first inaugural to extend "peace, commerce, and honest friendship with all nations, entangling alliances with none." Amplifying those sentiments, John Quincy Adams, while serving as Secretary of State, told Congress: "[The United States] goes not abroad, in search of monsters to destroy. She is the well-wisher to the freedom and independence of all. She is the champion and vindicator only of her own."

These words, so foreign-sounding to today's ears, reflected a shared sense of American self-identity that had been forged years earlier (McDougall 1997). The colonists and their descendants believed that the moral calling of their blessed "city on a hill" was to lead by example, to enshrine (however imperfectly) individual rights at home and thereby to commence a New Order of the Ages (*novus ordo seclorum*), not to liberate others abroad and thereby to forge a New World Order (*novus ordo mundi*). The new republic was to be distinguished from its European counterparts by sending goods and ideas, not soldiers and decrees, to foreign shores. Except for the territorial expansion across North America, which was indeed aided by soldiers and decrees, this norm was generally followed. In the mid-nineteenth century, U.S. policymakers, to avoid setting a precedent, refused to send arms, funds, or even official letters of protest at the request of Hungarian and Polish freedom fighters who were struggling against their Hapsburg and Czarist overlords (Raico 1995). Avoidance of entangling alliances and military commitments helped to keep federal taxation and spending relatively limited and thereby contributed to the rapid growth of the civilian economy.

Nevertheless, at the end of the nineteenth century, the United States joined the European powers in playing the imperial game. Victory in the Spanish-American War brought the United States control over not only nearby Cuba and Puerto Rico, but also faraway Guam and the Philippine Islands. The U.S. occupation of the Philippines was especially troubling because the brutal counterinsurgency campaign that supported it hardly resembled the benevolent liberation that President William McKinley had promised "our little brown brothers." Sociologist William Graham Sumner, one of a dwindling number of influential classical liberals, told an audience at Yale at the time that the takeover of Spain's possessions revealed a supreme irony: despite the U.S. military victory, Spain had achieved a "conquest" of the United States in the sense that European-style imperialism, not small-government republicanism, had prevailed. Henceforth, the stage was set for an endless series of interventions in the Caribbean islands, Latin America, the Pacific islands, east Asia, and elsewhere.

The new foreign-policy posture gained bold rhetorical support when Woodrow Wilson promised a foreign war to "make the world safe for democracy." Franklin D. Roosevelt polished this rhetoric by promising to secure "the four freedoms"—freedom of speech and expression, freedom of worship, freedom from want, and freedom from armed aggression—"everywhere in the world." Thus, the inwardly ambitious but outwardly humble "city on a hill" had become the global crusader state. The foreign-policy premises of McKinley, Theodore Roosevelt, Wilson, and Franklin D. Roosevelt were carried forward, with only marginal modifications, into the Cold War. America's leaders presumed, more or less unilaterally, that the benefits of freedom for people in other countries were worth the sacrifice of American lives and resources. But securing the blessings of liberty for others entailed sacrificing them at home.

Despite brief periods of retrenchment, the transformation from a noninterventionist republic to a crusader state tended to be self-reinforcing in the long run. The end of the Cold War brought no significant curtailment of U.S. interventionism, nor did any organized political movement call for one. Neoconservatives in the 1990s even lamented that the United States was not crusading enough (Ledeen 1996). Americans seemed for the most part to have lost an awareness and an understanding of their country's noninterventionist past. Although some commentators and activists protested various military interventions, they did so increasingly on an ad hoc basis, rather than as exponents of a principle embraced by generations past. (For an exception during this era, see Nordlinger 1995.) A foreign-policy observer might have said with only slight exaggeration, "We're all interventionists now; we simply don't agree on which interventions are the most desirable."

Some writers have argued that the U.S. empire differs in kind from the traditional variety (Odom and Dujarric 2004). Regardless of the motivations for America's global hegemony or its net effects on others, however, the abandonment of the nonintervention principle has imposed large costs on Americans in terms of constitutional integrity, domestic tranquility, and economic progress. The power to make war has been shifted from Congress to the president—an unconstitutional and especially troubling transfer of authority because presidents have often invoked exaggerations or falsehoods about national security threats to bring the country into war (Astor 2006; Higgs 2002, 2005, 2007). In domestic political life, foreign-policy interventionism has often fostered a divisiveness that has contributed to the polarization of society; especially disheartening are cases in which policy differences have led to official and unofficial harassment and the suspension of civil liberties (Linfield 1990, Cole and Dempsey 2002). Economically, the rise of the American empire has required a military buildup that has diverted labor and capital away from production for the civilian economy, reduced the rate of saving, diverted technological brainpower into military channels, and thereby reduced private investment and economic growth (Higgs 1987, 2004, 2006).

Many have assumed that these costs are more than offset by security benefits, but this view has been met with new challenges. Ivan Eland concisely summarizes the argument that interventionism has pushed Americans closer to the red on the national-security ledger: "In a post-cold war world, taking into account only the security of American citizens, their property, and U.S. territory, the benefits of an interventionist foreign policy have declined and the costs have escalated dramatically. Americans are being put at risk for catastrophic terrorism, perhaps even from an attack with chemical, biological, or nuclear weapons, just so the American government can conduct imperial wars in remote regions of the world that have little to do with U.S. security—except to undermine it" (2004, 219–20).

Foreign-policy debates, of course, are seldom determined by strictly practical concerns. Many critics of a noninterventionist approach to foreign policy have been quick to impugn it on ethical grounds, equating "isolationism" (their term) with willful evasion, cowardly appeasement, dogmatic pacifism, shirking of global responsibilities, stinginess, and xenophobia. Noninterventionism, we are told, stands in opposition to America's core values, and Americans reject the "false comfort" it provides. William Graham Sumner anticipated some of these objections. In the same speech in which he lamented the United States' succumbing to the doctrines of European imperialism, he attempted to answer those who warn us against the terrors of "isolation":

> Our ancestors all came here to isolate themselves from the social burdens and inherited errors of the old world. When the others are all over ears in trouble, who would not be isolated in freedom from

care? When the others are crushed under the burden of militarism, who would not be isolated in peace and industry? When the others are all struggling under debt and taxes, who would not be isolated in the enjoyment of his own earnings for the benefit of his own family? When the rest are all in a quiver of anxiety, lest at a day's notice they may be involved in a social cataclysm, who would not be isolated out of reach of the disaster? What we are doing is that we are abandoning this blessed isolation to run after a share in the trouble. (qtd. in Bannister 1992, 292)

Sumner could take for granted that his audience was familiar with the pro-trade precepts of classical liberalism and therefore would not equate "isolation" with economic nationalism or autarky. Today, however, after years of activism by populists à la Patrick Buchanan, who champion both noninterventionism and economic nationalism, it is important to emphasize that noninterventionism is fully compatible with free-trade, pro-immigration views. Classical liberals have long argued that the free movement of goods, money, capital, and labor is a key ingredient for a lasting peace. Clearly, the time is ripe for a reconsideration of noninterventionism.

Opposing the Crusader State: Alternatives to Global Interventionism examines the historical and contemporary relevance of noninterventionism, particularly for U.S. foreign policy. The questions it considers are longstanding ones, but they are especially relevant today: How have Americans viewed the relationship between noninterventionism and republican government—and between interventionism and empire? Why did the United States abandon its tradition of noninterventionism? What is the success record of democratic nation-building? What are the best arguments for and against the claim that democracies, by their nature, do not go to war with each other? Why do some observers believe that the cause of peace and freedom is best served by promoting globalization and unfettered international commerce?

After having read this book, readers will come away with a richer understanding of the noninterventionist movements in American history. More important, they will better understand the complexities surrounding democratic nation-building and democratic-peace theory. This understanding will enable them to evaluate better not only recent U.S. foreign interventions, but also legislative efforts to promote freedom abroad, such as the Advance Democracy Act of 2005. Most important, perhaps, readers will have a firmer understanding of why many classical liberals embrace the strengthening of commercial ties among all countries as a means of avoiding war.

OVERVIEW OF THE BOOK

American Noninterventionism

Because history is written by the victors, the people who would benefit the most from understanding the noninterventionist tradition are ignorant of its history and relevance. The contributors to Part I, "American Non-interventionism," examine noninterventionist thinkers and movements in American history from the post-Revolutionary era through the Cold War. They shed light on the relationship between noninterventionism and republican government and show the continuity and interrelations of classical liberalism and various antiwar movements.

Joseph Stromberg provides a historical overview in the chapter on "Imperialism, Noninterventionism, and Revolution: Opponents of the Modern American Empire." Although nonintervention was the seldom-questioned premise of U.S. relations with established European nations until the late nineteenth century, clues that an alternative perspective would later emerge may be detected in the Republic's early years. Both James Madison's theory of territorial expansion and the Monroe Doctrine, for example, provided intellectual ammunition to those who sought to direct America's messianic inclinations outward. Nevertheless, the urge to project American power overseas was still held in check by republican ideals until the emergence of the Progressive movement in the late nineteenth century.

Progressivism constituted a major reorientation of intellectuals and policymakers toward the growth of the state. Fulfilling the promise of American life, the Progressives argued, required the use of the state's coercive apparatus not only to promote economic planning and social reform at home, but also to export Progressive aspirations overseas, beginning with the Spanish-American War and the subsequent occupations of Cuba, Puerto Rico, and the Philippine Islands.

Joining the "humanitarian" crusade were "practical" economists, such as Charles Conant, John Bates Clark, and Jeremiah Jenks, who argued that unless the government helped to open up markets overseas, the American economy would suffer a crisis of "overproduction" and falling profits. Thus, the embrace of interventionism coincided with the move away from classical free-market economic theory. The classical liberals of the era saw ominous implications, arguing that the pursuit of empire would erode republican government and weaken individual liberty. Two world wars and the Cold War would help to empower further the imperial presidency and to marginalize the remaining noninterventionists.

In the chapter on "New Deal Nemesis: The 'Old Right' Jeffersonians," Sheldon Richman examines those who criticized both Franklin Roosevelt's domestic policy and his foreign policy. Fearful of Roosevelt's unprecedented accretion of executive power, this diverse group of politicians, writers, and activists saw Roosevelt as a threat to private-property rights and economic recovery, as well as a threat to American interests on the world stage. The only clear victor of a war in which the United States fought on the same side as the Soviet Union, many of them argued, would be the latter.

Neither truly right-wing nor conservative, the Old Right drew from the ranks of "Progressive" isolationists (Senator William Borah, John T. Flynn), Republican "conservative" isolationists (Senator Robert Taft), libertarian iconoclasts regarded as leftist radicals in the 1920s (H. L. Mencken, Albert Jay Nock), conservative Democrats (Senator Bennett Champ Clark), social democratic historians (Charles Beard), a trio of individualist women writers (Ayn Rand, Rose Wilder Lane, and Isabel Patterson), and free-market journalists and economists (Frank Chodorov, Garet Garrett, Leonard Read, F. A. Harper). Unlike the New Right that emerged in the early days of the Cold War, the Old Right was united by a deep-seated suspicion of concentrated political power, and in that sense it exemplified the Jeffersonian tradition.

Ralph Raico explores the pre-war noninterventionist movement further in the chapter titled "On the Brink of World War II: Justus Doenecke's *Storm on the Horizon.*" From 1939 until the Japanese attack on Pearl Harbor, dozens of events across the globe fanned intense public debate about U.S. entry into the war. Many of these episodes (including the destroyers-for-bases agreement, aid to Finland after the Soviet attack, and Roosevelt's bogus claim to have possessed a "secret map" showing Hitler's plan to invade the United States via Latin America) have been nearly forgotten. This historical amnesia is unfortunate because an understanding of these numerous and often complex events would help contemporary readers to appreciate better the challenges that confronted partisans on both sides of the debate.

Closer scrutiny of events that were often obscured by the "fog of war" (and by deliberate misrepresentations) allows a fairer assessment of the noninterventionist movement than it has usually received.

Opponents of U.S. entry into World War II have been stereotyped as ignorant dupes or worse, but the anti-war movement was extremely diverse, and its sympathizers included well-known men and women of letters, such as W. H. Auden, e. e. cummings, Sherwood Anderson, Edward Lee Masters, Kathleen Norris, Pearl Buck, Theodore Dreiser, Henry Miller, and Sinclair Lewis. The young John F. Kennedy and Gore Vidal were among the eight hundred thousand members of the maligned but mainstream America First Committee. Years before "McCarthyism" would become an oft-hurled epithet, anti-war activists found themselves out of work, owing to their politically incorrect opinions.

In the chapter on "The Republican Road Not Taken: The Foreign-Policy Vision of Robert A. Taft," Michael Hayes considers one of the most important opponents of the crusader state in American politics. Whereas the foreign policies of the Roosevelt, Truman, and Eisenhower administrations primarily emphasized supporting other governments, securing access to raw materials, and ensuring overseas markets for U.S. exports, Senator Taft—known as "Mr. Republican"—held that the primary objectives of U.S. foreign policy should be, first, to protect the liberty of Americans, and, second, to maintain peace. An advocate of democracy founded on universal human rights, Taft opposed the use of force to impose democracy on other countries.

Critical of the United Nations for its structural weaknesses, Taft proposed the creation of an international tribunal that would settle disputes between countries according to the rule of law and enforce its findings with an international police force. At the same time, he explicitly opposed a world government. In parallel with his approach to domestic policy, he held that the global society should be organized not as a purposive association, in which it is assumed that members share a multitude of aspirations, but as a civic association, whose members' autonomy is honored unless they aggress against others. Though derided in his day as ostrich-like, Taft showed a prescience that suggests he was the opposite of an idealist blinded by his own principles: he foresaw that the U.S. emphasis on maintaining regime stability abroad would make Americans vulnerable to a backlash of resentment from people suffering under the yoke of their own (U.S.-supported) governments.

The Case Against Nation Building

Democratic nation-building has become a commonly expressed goal of U.S. foreign-policy leaders and pundits. Wishful nation-builders often present their case in a manner easily caricatured. Because aspirations to liberty and self-government beat in everyone's breast, the would-be builders seem to suggest, undemocratic countries need little more than a nudge from outsiders to help them start the democratic construction project. Part II, "The Case Against Nation Building," presents theoretical and empirical arguments against this presumption.

Scholarly critics of nation-building typically argue that although a yearning for self-government is a necessary condition for liberal democracy to arise and take root, scores of other prerequisites must be met. In the chapter on "The Prospects for Democracy in High-Violence Societies," James L. Payne argues that these critics also make too many assumptions and neglect the most essential ingredient. Unless a society has made a thoroughgoing commitment to eschew political violence, democratic politics cannot take root or persist. Recognizing the importance of culture and political violence helps us to steer clear of the false dichotomy of naïve optimism and fatalism.

This recognition also helps to explain the frequent failure of efforts to export democracy, the subject of the chapter titled "Does Nation Building Work?" According to Payne, from 1850 to 2006 Great Britain and the United States sent military forces abroad fifty-one times to engage in democratic nation building (as distinct from purely peacekeeping or punitive missions and the establishment of military outposts without interfering significantly in local politics), but they left behind a lasting democracy in only fourteen of the countries—a success rate of 27 percent. Moreover, even this low rate overstates the effectiveness of nation-building, Payne argues, because it includes instances in which a country probably would have become democratic without the military intervention of other countries.

Two countries widely believed to be success stories of U.S. nation-building are postwar Japan and West Germany. Payne examines the German case in the chapter titled "Did the United States Create Democracy in Germany?" The title of a September 1949 *Commentary* magazine article—"Why Democracy Is Losing in Germany"—reminds us that postwar policy had its share of troubles. As Payne explains, U.S. policy during the occupation from 1945 to 1952 consisted of measures to eliminate Germany's war-making potential, denazify German society, and penalize ordinary Germans.

The Joint Chiefs of Staff never gave serious attention to the goal of preparing Germany for democracy. Directive JCS 1067, in force from May 1945 to July 1947, forbade the occupation authority to take steps that would improve the Germany economy and even went so far as to order Americans in occupied Germany not to fraternize with the locals. "If anything, the U.S. occupation harassed and delayed the formation and functioning of political parties," Payne concludes.

Encouraging fledgling democracies has not always ranked high on the list of U.S. foreign-policy goals, of course. Some policies have been blatantly at odds with democratic nation-building, as Jerry K. Sweeney argues in the chapter on "A Matter of Small Consequence: U.S. Foreign Policy and the Tragedy in East Timor." In the mid-1970s, as Portugal's rule over this southeast Asian colony was coming to an end, U.S. policymakers favored not the popular East Timorese independence movement, but a takeover by neighboring Indonesia. Evidently President Gerald Ford and Secretary of State Henry Kissinger deemed Indonesia's President Suharto to be a more reliable friend of the goal of retaining U.S. submarine access to the deepwater channel north of East Timor, and they personally assured him that his invasion of East Timor would not jeopardize U.S. aid to his regime.

Debating the Democratic Peace

The relationship between liberal democracy and peace has been a hot topic in academia in recent years, although it was first discussed in theoretical terms during the Enlightenment. The academic literature seems finally to have reached policymakers. In February 2005, reportedly after having read Natan Sharansky's book *The Case for Democracy: The Power of Freedom to Overcome Tyranny and Terror*, President George W. Bush told an audience in Brussels, "America supports Europe's democratic unity for the same reason we support the spread of democracy in the Middle East: because freedom leads to peace."

The claim that democratic-peace theorists commonly make today is not that democracies rarely go to war, but rather that democracies rarely, if ever, go to war against each other. If true, this claim would lend support to the goal of promoting democratic nation-building. Even if the record of democratic nation-building is dismal, one might argue that such projects are nevertheless worthwhile if someday more democracies will result from such attempts (because practice makes perfect) and the world will thereby become more pacific. Of course, the desirability of democratic regime-change (or pro-democracy financial and technical assistance) need not hinge on the validity of democratic-peace theory, but the topic has understandably provoked intense interest and has prompted two obvious questions: How strong is the evidence that supports the democratic-peace theory? And, if democracies rarely make war against each other, is this condition owing to their character as democracies or is it owing to other factors not directly related to their type of government?

Considering the vigorousness of the disagreement evident in Part III, "Debating the Democratic Peace," these and related questions remain unsettled even among classical liberals and libertarians. Most of this section is devoted to an exchange between Cato Institute foreign-policy analyst Ted Galen Carpenter, a foreign-policy realist who sees democratic-peace theory as mere wishful thinking, and University of Hawaii political scientist R. J. Rummel, a leading scholar of the violence committed by governments (and a nominee for the Nobel Peace Prize). Rummel's empirical studies have led him to conclude that democracies do not make war against each other and are less warlike and more peaceful internally than undemocratic governments. He theorizes that democracy's relative peacefulness reflects the influence of democratic institutions and culture and, most important, the decentralization of political power in this form of government.

In the chapter on "Democracy and War," Carpenter criticizes the version of democratic-peace theory found in Rummel's 1997 book *Power Kills: Democracy as a Method of Nonviolence*, a summary of decades of research. Like the work of other democratic-peace theorists, Rummel's book exhibits, according to Carpenter, a "tendency to minimize or ignore factors other than the existence of democracy as an explanation for the apparent lack of wars among democratic states." To Carpenter, Rummel and others of like mind seem too enamored with their own theory to examine the possibility that realist strategic calculations or balance-of-power considerations may explain the so-called democratic peace. Carpenter also chides Rummel for, among other things, a tendency to "avoid 'hard cases' that might cast doubt on the peaceful democracies thesis," such as the U.S. War Between the States, the Boer War, and World War I.

Rummel returns fire in the chapter titled "Democracy and War: Reply," offering rebuttals of a dozen of Carpenter's criticisms. (No one has said that democratic-peace scholars never go to war against each other!) World War I does not contradict democratic-peace theory, Rummel argues, because Germany was not a democracy: the Chancellor served at the pleasure of the Kaiser, and the democratically elected Reichstag had no control of the army. As for his supposed failure to consider alternative explanations for the peace observed among democracies, Rummel maintains that he (and the authorities he cites) considered and ruled out far more possibilities than those Carpenter raises.

Given the last word in this exchange, in the chapter titled "Democracy and War: Rejoinder," Carpenter argues that Rummel and others can explain away counterexamples to their theory in part because their designation of which countries are truly democratic is arbitrary. He also charges that their insistence on firmly distinguishing between hot wars and cold wars enables them to downplay the democracies' many proxy wars, covert operations, and close calls that risked breaking out into open warfare.

Rummel's book argues that liberal democracy is the cure not only for war, but also for "democide," the genocide or mass murder of civilians by their own government. The latter form of mass killing, not considered in Carpenter's critiques, took even more lives during the twentieth century than did war. (Rummel, the first scholar to attempt a complete accounting of that century's democides, currently puts the toll of those killed in this way at 262 million.) Stephen W. Carson outlines an alternative to Rummel's regime-type theory of democide in the chapter on "Stealing and Killing: A Property-Rights Theory of Mass Murder."

Among other advantages of his approach, Carson argues, focusing on private-property violations rather than regime type as the most important factor common to democides helps us to understand cycles of mass murder under the same regime type (e.g., democide intensifies when property is collectivized and lessens during retreats from collectivization, as the Soviet experience illustrates). This view also provides insights into how governments obtain the power to inflict democide (e.g., massive violations of property rights rob citizens of the resources needed to help them defend themselves). The cure for democide, Carson concludes, lies in strengthening the protection of private-property rights, not in spreading democracy, which tends toward a weakening of private-property rights.

In fairness to Rummel, we must note that he stipulates in his book that by "democracy" he means a liberal democracy, which includes "a constitutional framework of law to which the government is subordinate and that guarantees equal rights" (Rummel 1997, 11). Although he does not say so explicitly, this condition would seem to bar the especially egregious property-rights violations characteristic of countries that have experienced democide. Fortunately, the attractiveness of Carson's theory does not depend on interpreting Rummel as willing to sacrifice private-property rights to the will of the majority.

Free Trade as a Peace Strategy

The message of most of the chapters described so far is negative: their authors challenge the assumption that interventionism is an appropriate default-setting for U.S. foreign policy; they criticize common misunderstandings of U.S. noninterventionism; and they question the effectiveness of democratic nation-building. The contributors to Part IV, "Free Trade as a Peace Strategy," make a positive case for an often-vilified economic policy. They also offer approaches that complement in many ways the findings of the democratic-peace theorists, foreign-policy realists, and private-property advocates presented in Part III.

According to Edward P. Stringham, modern liberals and conservatives alike can learn much about fostering peace (and prosperity) from the nineteenth-century classical-liberal writer and British parliamentarian Richard Cobden (1804–1865). In the chapter on "Commerce, Markets, and Peace: Richard Cobden's Enduring Lessons," Stringham explains that Cobden, unlike many conservative advocates of market economies, viewed the military and the market not as complements but as substitutes: more military entails less market. The military spending undertaken to secure the jewels in the crown of the British empire required relatively high taxation, which made civilians worse off directly and indirectly (through reduced saving and investment in the private, civilian economy).

Just as advocates of the market should in principle also be strong advocates of peace and opponents of military adventurism, so friends of peace and foes of imperialism should in principle be strongly committed to market economics. Mercantilism, with its government-established monopolies, made the economics of imperialism sound plausible. "Because the government maintained these commercial monopolies with armed forces, the discussion of commerce and the military [in Cobden's day] went hand in hand," Stringham writes. Thus, for Cobden, mercantilist economic policies not only conflict with free trade, but also feed military spending, foreign-policy interventionism, militarism, and imperialism. Whereas mercantilism requires a navy to protect a monopoly trader from the competition of other traders, free trade requires no extra military forces to discourage competition, and its security requirements are much less because it encourages peaceful relations between nations. As Cobden put it, "the more any nation traffics abroad upon free and honest principles, the less it will be in danger of wars."

In one of the most important contributions to this volume, the chapter on "The Diffusion of Prosperity and Peace by Globalization," Erich Weede argues that open markets and foreign direct investment not only bring economic benefits to the people in the countries involved, but also have a strong tendency to bring peace. Scholars have examined several competing hypotheses as to why trade fosters peace: war between trading partners would be disruptive economically, so leaders try to avoid it; commerce may foster broader values of cooperation and harmony within a society; and trade promotes prosperity and therefore democracy in the trading countries (the democratic-peace theory). Regardless of its cause, the international-security benefit of trade and globalization is firmly established by quantitative research, according to Weede, although it remains unknown to the critics of globalization.

What can be done to promote a "capitalist peace," as Weede calls it? The process is simple: encourage, both at home and abroad, economic freedom (including the establishment and maintenance of private-property rights, contract enforcement, and the rule of law); provide open markets for exports from poor countries; make direct private investments in poor countries; abolish subsidies to agricultural producers in rich countries; and discourage price controls and similar interventions in the market system throughout the world.

TOWARD AN INTEGRATED STUDY OF PEACE

No single book can adequately cover the many issues related to foreign policy and the promotion of peace, and in offering the present volume we do not pretend to do so. Our ambition has been simply to bring together contributions that offer important perspectives that are relatively neglected by current books on foreign policy. In addition, the chapters in this book, like those in two earlier books we co-edited, *Re-Thinking Green: Alternatives to Environmental Bureaucracy* (2005) and *The Challenge of Liberty: Classical Liberalism Today* (2006), share the trait of having been drawn from a single source, *The Independent Review: A Journal of Political Economy*, a quarterly publication of the Independent Institute edited by Robert Higgs. Although collections compiled from a single periodical may have limitations, we hope that we have selected contributions with the right combination of form and substance to create a worthwhile anthology.

We have been pleased that so many talented researchers have submitted their work for publication in our journal since its inception in 1996. We owe special thanks not only to the scholars whose work appears in *Opposing the Crusader State*, but also to the many referees whose anonymous input helped to strengthen each of these chapters. In working with these scholars, we have gained a greater appreciation of the need to speak to an audience beyond the narrow confines that constrain a strictly academic journal—in language accessible to nonspecialists. *The Independent Review's* accessibility is unusual for a serious journal devoted primarily to political economy. Besides making the final product more interesting to the general reader, it has enabled our contributors to draw on literature from diverse fields of inquiry, not only from economics and political science, but also from history, law, philosophy, and sociology. This multidisciplinary approach is especially important for understanding complex issues such as peace and foreign policy. We hope these examples will encourage more scholars to take an integrated, multidisciplinary approach. When their research involves the study of war and peace, a great deal may turn on their doing so.

REFERENCES AND SUGGESTIONS FOR FURTHER READING

Astor, Gerald. 2006. *Presidents at War: From Truman to Bush, The Gathering of Military Powers to Our Commanders in Chief.* Hoboken, N.J.: Wiley.

Bacevich, Andrew J. 2002. *American Empire: The Realities and Consequences of U.S. Diplomacy.* Cambridge, Mass.: Harvard University Press.

———. 2005. *The New American Militarism: How Americans Are Seduced by War.* New York: Oxford University Press.

Bannister, Robert C. 1992. *On Liberty, Society, and Politics: The Essential Essays of William Graham Sumner.* Indianapolis: Liberty Fund.

Bovard, James. 2003. *Terrorism and Tyranny: Trampling Freedom, Justice, and Peace to Rid the World of Evil.* New York: Palgrave Macmillan.

Cole, David, and James X. Dempsey. 2002. *Terrorism and the Constitution: Sacrificing Civil Liberties in the Name of National Security,* 2d ed. New York: Norton.

Dempsey, Gary, and Roger Fontaine. 2001. *Fool's Errands: America's Recent Encounters with Nation Building.* Washington, D.C.: Cato.

Denson, John V., ed. 1999. *The Costs of War: America's Pyrrhic Victories,* 2d ed. New Brunswick, N.J.: Transaction.

———. 2001. *Reassessing the Presidency: The Rise of the Executive State and the Decline of Freedom.* Auburn, Ala.: Ludwig von Mises Institute.

Doenecke, Justus D. 2000. *Storm on the Horizon: The Challenge to American Intervention, 1939–1941.* Lanham, Md.: Rowman and Littlefield.

Ebeling, Richard M., and Jacob G. Hornberger, eds. 1996. *The Failure of America's Foreign Wars.* Fairfax, Va.: Future of Freedom Foundation.

———. 2003. *Liberty, Security, and the War on Terrorism.* Fairfax, Va.: Future of Freedom Foundation.

Eland, Ivan. 2001. *Putting "Defense" Back into U.S. Defense Policy: Rethinking U.S. Security in the Post–Cold War World.* Westport, Conn.: Praeger.

———. 2004. *The Empire Has No Clothes: U.S. Foreign Policy Exposed.* Oakland, Calif.: The Independent Institute.

Higgs, Robert. 1987. *Crisis and Leviathan: Critical Episodes in the Growth of American Government.* New York: Oxford University Press.

———. 2002. The Oval Office Liar's Club. *San Francisco Chronicle,* November 24.

———. 2004. *Against Leviathan: Government Power and a Free Society.* Oakland, Calif.: The Independent Institute.

———. 2005. *Resurgence of the Warfare State: The Crisis since 9/11.* Oakland, Calif.: The Independent Institute.

———. 2006. *Depression, War, and Cold War: Studies in Political Economy.* New York: Oxford University Press for the Independent Institute.

———. 2007. *Neither Liberty nor Safety: Fear, Ideology, and the Growth of Government.* Oakland, Calif.: The Independent Institute.

Higgs, Robert, and Carl P. Close, eds. 2005. *Re-Thinking Green: Alternatives to Environmental Bureaucracy.* Oakland, Calif.: The Independent Institute.

———. 2006. *The Challenge of Liberty: Classical Liberalism Today.* Oakland, Calif.: The Independent Institute.

Isaacson, Walter, and Evan Thomas. 1986. *The Wise Men: Six Friends and the World They Made. Acheson, Bohlen, Harriman, Kennan, Lovett, McCloy.* New York: Simon and Schuster.

Johnson, Chalmers. 2004. *The Sorrows of Empire: Militarism, Secrecy, and the End of the Republic.* New York: Metropolitan.

Kwitney, Jonathan. 1984. *Endless Enemies: The Making of an Unfriendly World.* New York: Penguin.

Ledeen, Michael A. 1996. *Freedom Betrayed: How America Led a Global Democratic Revolution, Won the Cold War, and Walked Away.* Washington, D.C.: AEI Press.

Leebaert, Derek. 2002. *The Fifty-Year Wound: The True Price of America's Cold War Victory.* Boston: Little, Brown.

Linfield, Michael. 1990. *Freedom Under Fire: U.S. Civil Liberties in Times of War.* Boston: South End Press.

MacDonagh, Oliver. 1962. The Anti-Imperialism of Free Trade. *Economic History Review,* 2d ser., 14, no. 3: 489–501.

McDougall, Walter A. 1997. *Promised Land, Crusader State: The American Encounter with the World Since 1776*. Boston and New York: Houghton Mifflin.

Nisbet, Robert. 1988. *The Present Age: Progress and Anarchy in Modern America*. New York: Harper & Row.

Nordlinger, Eric. 1995. *Isolationism Reconsidered: American Foreign Policy for a New Century*. Princeton, N.J.: Princeton University Press.

Odom, William E., and Robert Dujarric. 2004. *America's Inadvertent Empire*. New Haven: Yale University Press.

Olsen, Edward A. 2002. *U.S. National Defense for the Twenty-First Century: The Grand Exit Strategy*. London: Frank Cass.

Perret, Geoffrey. 1989. *A Country Made by War: From the Revolution to Vietnam: The Story of America's Rise to Power*. New York: Random House.

Porter, Bruce. 1994. *War and the Rise of the State: The Military Foundations of Modern Politics*. New York: Free Press.

Raico, Ralph. 1995. American Foreign Policy: The Turning Point, 1898–1919. Fairfax, Va.: The Future of Freedom Foundation. Available at: www.independent.org/newsroom/article.asp?id=1345.

Reisman, George. 2006. Globalization: The Long-Run Big Picture. November 18. Available at: www.mises.org/story/2361.

Rummel, R. J. 1994. *Death by Government*. New Brunswick, N.J.: Transaction.

———. 1997. *Power Kills: Democracy as a Method of Nonviolence*. New Brunswick, N.J.: Transaction.

Steel, Ronald. 1980. *Walter Lippmann and the American Century*. Boston: Little, Brown.

Stromberg, Joseph R. 2001. War, Peace, and the State. Available at: www.mises.org/empire.asp.

Sumner, William Graham. 1899. The Conquest of the United States by Spain. Available at: http://praxeology.net/WGS-CUS.htm.

PART I

American Noninterventionism

1

Imperialism, Noninterventionism, and Revolution
Opponents of the Modern American Empire

JOSEPH R. STROMBERG

From one angle of vision, nonintervention is *the* essential American perspective on foreign affairs. Honored in the breach more than in practice, nonintervention may nevertheless be the foreign-policy option most consistent with the broadly libertarian values of the liberal republicanism that characterized the American Revolution (Arieli 1964, Bailyn 1967). It is the application of that libertarian heritage to foreign affairs.

Libertarianism, as a full-wrought ideological system, rests on every individual's self-ownership. On this axiom, no one can own another, and all possess equal liberty by virtue of their self-ownership. Equal liberty entails everyone's right to acquire and exchange property, along with a right to defend person and property. Hence, it follows that no one may *initiate* the use of force. It is legitimate to use force only in self-defense, and it is possible to establish firm criteria for what constitutes genuine self-defense (Rothbard 1998, esp. 161–97).

It serves ethical consistency, as well as certain practical results, if the standards that apply between individuals are applied as far as possible to the actions of states, armies, and bureaucracies. Nonintervention, sometimes miscalled "isolationism," is thus the application of classical liberal (libertarian) principles to foreign policy. Hence, libertarians typically wish that the U.S. government restrict its use of force to repelling actual attacks on the territory of the United States (Rothbard 2000, 115–32). Unlike liberals, conservatives, and even some radicals, who argue over how much—and what kinds of—aid to send to which oppressive regimes abroad, or exactly where to apply American military might, libertarians reject the imperial path and all arguments for empire: economic, power-political, or "humanitarian."[1]

Of course, not everyone arrives at nonintervention by such an organized, ideological route. There are other paths and differing degrees of theoretical rigor. Nevertheless, nonintervention reflects a number of basic themes in American cultural history. One of these is the Puritan, and later typically American, notion of America as a "City on a Hill," aloof from the Old World's quarrels yet able to influence the world through the good example of a successful, free, and prosperous commonwealth eschewing militarism and imperial expansion. In the original Puritan view, of course, the example involved a particular kind of Calvinist piety, and this theme could slide over into sundry secular, liberal, or republican missions of wielding state power and armed force to right the world's wrongs (see Tuveson 1968, Hatch 1977). A recent writer uses the term "exemplarism" for the City-on-a-Hill ideal and sees a tendency for its adherents to turn toward "vindicationism" (armed intervention) when the American example is not embraced (Monten 2005).

Many statesmen of our revolutionary era espoused the cause of nonintervention. George Washington, in his celebrated Farewell Address to the American people in 1796, urged Americans to avoid taking sides in foreign quarrels. America, he said, should maintain liberal and impartial commercial relations with the rest of the world, but "have with them as little political connection as possible." President John Adams practiced successful nonintervention by maneuvering to avoid war with France in spite of strong pressures from within his own Federalist Party. His successor, Thomas Jefferson, also advocated nonintervention, despite partisan differences with the Federalists on other issues. In his First Inaugural, Jefferson called for "peace, commerce, and honest friendships with all nations, entangling alliances with none" (quotations from Washington and Jefferson from Commager 1963, 174, 188, emphasis in original).

Reinforced by geographical isolation from the rest of the world, the traditions of British insularity, and public preoccupation with expansion into contiguous land areas,[2] nonintervention became the seldom-questioned premise of U.S. relations with established European powers and their empires. Nearer to home, in 1823, the Monroe Doctrine signaled U.S. pretensions to hegemony over the Western Hemisphere, although few interventions came of it until the late nineteenth century.

Despite some lapses, nonintervention was still the accepted rhetorical standard of traditional U.S. foreign policy, and the lapses were deviations *from it*. This is an important point because today's *overseas* interventions enjoy the blessings of the political-intellectual establishment at the outset.

John Quincy Adams summed up the noninterventionist creed in his justly famous Fourth of July Address in 1821:

> America goes not abroad in search of monsters to destroy. She is the well-wisher to the freedom and independence of all. She is the champion and vindicator only of her own. She will recommend the general cause by the countenance of her voice, and the benignant sympathy of her example. She well knows that by once enlisting under other banners than her own, were they even the banners of foreign independence, she would involve herself beyond the power of extrication in all the wars of interest and intrigue, of individual avarice, envy and ambition, which assume the colors and usurp the standards of freedom. The fundamental maxims of her policy would insensibly change from liberty to force.[3]

As expressed by Adams and others, nonintervention, or strict noninterference in the internal affairs of other nations as well as strict neutrality in conflicts between nations, remained a key force in U.S. public opinion and actual policy up to 1898 and even to 1917. After the disillusioning experience of World War I, nonintervention enjoyed a strong revival in the 1920s and 1930s, only to be buried by World War II and subsequent events.

Already in the early nineteenth century, despite U.S. adherence to nonintervention in overseas territories, there existed a consensus that saw the gradual absorption of contiguous land areas as desirable, convenient, and even imperative for any number of reasons. As historian William Appleman Williams has written, James Madison, "father of the Constitution," was an especially persuasive and influential theorist of expansion.[4] According to classical republican political theory, territorial expansion necessarily weakens free, representative institutions, but Madison stood this argument on its head, reasoning that larger territory would diminish the evils of "faction" and thereby make constitutional government safer (Williams 1973, 157–65).[5]

The implications of territorial expansion were not lost on several generations of Americans bent on grabbing the land adjoining their own. Territorial expansion as such does not immediately involve a nation in the problems of empire in quite the same way that "saltwater," or overseas, expansion does; and expansion into neighboring lands can in principle be accomplished by peaceful means, such as the (probably unconstitutional) Louisiana Purchase. Nonetheless, the characteristic use of force to take land, as in the Seminole War, other Indian wars, and the Mexican War, began to stretch the republic's institutional balance early on. Thus, although James Polk set a precedent for "presidential war" by maneuvering U.S. troops into an incident with Mexico, historian William Earl Weeks has argued that U.S. diplomacy with regard to Florida and Oregon had already shifted power away from Congress and into the hands of the executive branch two decades earlier (1992, esp. 181–85).

The bitter struggle between North and South over the status of slavery in the western territories led directly to the War for Southern Independence, revealing the downside of Madison's expansionist rationale. Northern victory in turn drastically shifted the institutional balance away from that of the original union. As classical-liberal historian Arthur A. Ekirch describes the process in *The Decline of American Liberalism* (1969) and *Ideas, Ideals, and American Diplomacy* (1966), the "agricultural imperialism" of Manifest Destiny helped to engender "civil war," which in turn strengthened the hand of mercantilism in federal policy—for example, in tariffs, excises, conscription (the supreme violation of individual liberty), paper money, and the like—and weakened localism or "states rights."[6]

Powerful ideas accompanied this practical retreat from American liberal, pacific ideals. One of these ideas was Manifest Destiny, the doctrine of inherent necessity and righteousness in U.S. territorial aggrandizement by whatever means. Another significant idea was a sense of the superiority of U.S. republican institutions; Madison's belief that expansion was a positive good led to the view that U.S. ideals and forms of government could usefully be extended by force of arms. This view ironically is similar to later Soviet rhetoric, which held that the extension of the USSR's influence was the expansion of the area of freedom.[7]

This messianic sense of American mission survived into the late nineteenth and early twentieth centuries. Combined with it was a newer strategic formulation of U.S. "interest," supposedly "economic" in character. As historians William Appleman Williams and Walter LaFeber have shown in *The Roots of the Modern American Empire* (1969) and *The New Empire* (1963), respectively, some U.S. statesmen and businessmen toward the turn of the century came to believe that American prosperity hinged on access to foreign markets for the "surplus" products of American farms and factories, as well as for "surplus" capital. Economic depressions in the 1870s and 1890s were taken as proof of that analysis (see also Gardner 1966; McCormick 1967). Libertarians, stressing Austrian economic analysis and Say's Law of Markets, would of course dispute this "overproduction" hypothesis, and some would argue that a prior inflation of the money supply by federal policies was at fault. Depressions are not inherent in a market economy, though; they are caused by the state's disruptive monetary policies.[8] Hence, the demand for foreign markets to be secured by a vigorous—ultimately imperial—foreign policy came out of faulty analysis, exporters' self-interested claims, and later, the coherent *weltanschauung* of corporate liberalism advanced by reformers and business groups.

It is especially important to grasp that the same Progressive reformers who sought broad departures from (relative) economic liberty at home likewise sought a more vigorous, imperial foreign policy. Very close in spirit and analysis to English and European "social imperialists,"[9] the Progressive activists (who overlapped with the businessmen they were supposedly going to regulate for the common good) sought the strong state at home and abroad as the instrument of power and social justice.[10] This point is important because later usage of political labels has thoroughly confused the identities of the contending factions. That the modern liberals' policies ultimately strengthened a great many objectively (situationally) conservative social groups—Big Business, Big Labor, Big Government, the military, defense contractors, and the like—should never be allowed to obscure the newer liberalism's ideological role in blessing the policies.

With the increasing acceptance of the theory that the U.S. economy had to expand *as a system* into foreign markets, America's leaders pushed the country more and more into hemispheric interference and finally into "world leadership." The supposed expansionist logic was ably articulated by such publicists and statesmen as Frederick Jackson Turner in "The Significance of the Frontier in American History" ([1893] 1920), Brooks Adams in *America's Economic Supremacy* (1900), Theodore Roosevelt in numerous essays and speeches, and many others of the then "best and brightest."[11]

Economists chimed in, especially Charles Conant, John Bates Clark, and Jeremiah W. Jenks, who proclaimed that a general crisis of "overproduction" and falling profits menaced American economic life—a crisis so severe, according to them, that only state-assisted engrossment of overseas markets could allay it.[12]

The Spanish-American War (1898) was the first important conflict occasioned by the new strategy of economic empire. By containing the Cuban Revolution and rendering Cuba a virtual U.S. colony, policymakers secured markets there. Cuba also proved useful as a "laboratory" for Progressive reformers (Pérez 1985, 1988; see also Gillette 1973). In addition, the war allowed the acquisition of the Philippine Islands from Spain; the added territory, like the earlier acquisition of Hawaii, was seen as an important stepping-stone to the markets of Asia. In a foretaste of things to come, this adventure in formal colonial imperialism soon led to a guerrilla war—the Philippine Insurrection—in which U.S. forces ultimately prevailed by means of overwhelming firepower and atrocities. By the end, some 220,000 Filipinos had perished.

The subsequent *Open Door Notes* (1899, 1900) represented a statement of American determination to have access to world markets, whether the peoples of the world willed it or not. Directed at the problem of exclusive European spheres of trade in China, the notes nonetheless reflected U.S. official policy toward the world as a whole. Hence, U.S. policy since the notes can conveniently be referred to as Open Door Imperialism. It is worth pointing out that the supposed "open door" swung mostly one way and did not imply equal access to U.S. markets for foreign companies and countries; it was to be imposed by force if necessary—another indication of how far the Open Door was (and remains) from true free trade.

Firmly convinced of the need for foreign markets, the rightness of gaining them by force, and the "liberalism" of their aims, American administrations from the late nineteenth century to today have subsidized exporters, lobbied abroad for business, brought down "unfriendly" governments by pressure and force, and ultimately gone to war in pursuit of the Open Door and against all apparent threats to its realization. This multifaceted program has composed the essence of U.S. "liberal internationalism" in the twentieth century and into the twenty-first. First the Central Powers, then the Japanese and Germans in the 1930s and 1940s, then the USSR, the People's Republic of China, and most recently revolutionary movements in small Third World countries have all somehow failed to play a U.S.-defined economic role and had to be met head on, "contained," and shown the error of their ways.[13] World War I, World War II, and the conflicts of the past sixty years display great continuity upon examination of the record.

By the same token, the domestic opposition to U.S. interventionism has shown a moral and ideological continuity that derives from old liberal ideas of laissez-faire, peace, and nonintervention. Although the antiwar forces have allowed themselves to be divided by labels and the loss, at times, of historical self-consciousness, nonetheless a rough tradition has persisted from the opponents of the War of 1812, the Mexican War, and the Spanish-American War (who were in this case, more properly, the Anti-Imperialist League, which heroically sought to expose massacres in the Philippines) to the opponents of World War I, World War II, the Cold War, Vietnam, and all the wars since then. The continuity and tradition of the antiwar forces concern me here. I begin with a summary of some early antiwar movements.

EARLY WARS, EARLY CRITICS, AND OPPONENTS

Most American wars have generated dissent well beyond the ranks of traditional pacifist groups, which should not be surprising in view of the cosmopolitan neutrality and pacific inclinations of our original individualist liberalism. These tendencies cut across party lines and narrower concerns. Thus, the supposedly pro-peace Jeffersonians shortsightedly embroiled America in the War of 1812, partly through mercantilist measures of economic warfare (Stagg 1981) that were intended to "coerce" Britain and France and thereby to achieve U.S. aims short of war. The war itself proved to be extremely unpopular in New England, and remnants of the moribund Federalist Party rallied much of New England in opposition to it, even keeping local militia out of the conflict. Denounced as "traitors," these Federalist activists met in the much-maligned Hartford Convention (1814) and proposed an interesting series of amendments to the Constitution that would have greatly limited the ability of U.S. administrations to wage aggressive and unpopular wars. A high point in the struggle over carrying out the war came with the *defeat* of a conscription bill in 1812—an interesting and neglected precedent!

The Mexican War, too, provoked considerable opposition. Many Northerners viewed the war as simply a means to extend slavery, and they opposed it on that ground. Therefore, opposition tended once again to center in the Northeast. Henry David Thoreau was only one of many protesters, and Congressman Abraham Lincoln's opposition is well known.[14] Opposition was not confined to the North. Some Southerners, including Alexander H. Stephens, Robert Toombs, John Archibald Campbell, and John C. Calhoun, worried that the war would damage the fabric of the Union.[15]

Ultimately, acquisition of new territories contributed to the conflict between North and South and the War for Southern Independence (or "Civil War"). The war brought about the triumph of statism and militarism on both sides of the lines. In many ways the prototype of a modern "total war," the Civil War generated varying degrees and types of opposition on both sides, from draft resistance to illegal peace movements, a fact almost universally deplored by the majority of (pro-war) historians North and South. In the North, one wing of the Democratic Party, symbolized by the much-reviled (and only recently reevaluated) Clement L. Vallandigham, spoke out against the institutional, moral, and economic costs of the war and took at least a hesitant pro-peace line. The administration responded by resorting to martial law and other violations of civil liberty where these so-called "Copperheads" were strongest. In the South, a sort of Confederate opposition developed, made up of those as concerned about despotism in Richmond as about that in Washington. Confederate vice president Alexander H. Stephens, Robert Toombs, Georgia governor Joe Brown, and North Carolina governor Zebulon Vance were among those notable for opposition to carrying on the war on the basis of centralized methods. In a sense, men such as Vallandigham and Stephens were the last of the Anglo-American True Whigs, asserting the validity of reserved rights and constitutional procedures even in wartime. (As a result, they have gone down in most accounts as narrow doctrinaires, men of small vision incapable of great feats of "nation building.")[16]

The War of 1861–65 established numerous dangerous and illiberal precedents, including conscription, suppression of dissent, and inflationary war finance. Taken as a whole, the Lincoln administration's actions, based on Lincoln's invention of special executive "war powers" out of whole cloth and the rationale of "emergency," amounted to the "presidential dictatorship" that Edward S. Corwin describes so well in *Total War and the Constitution* (1947).[17] Thus, a host of wartime powers and "exceptions" to the apparent meaning of the Constitution became available for use by later presidents who chose to lead the United States into major wars.

After 1865, American attention shifted to the internal "reconstruction" of the union, economic development, and westward expansion. The latter involved the familiar series of Indian wars, broken promises, and unrelenting pressure against resisting tribal peoples; it likewise provided another reason for maintaining a regular standing army in a period (for the United States) of international tranquility. In fighting the Indians, defined from the outset as undifferentiated "savages," officers and men acquired attitudes that would carry over into the Philippine Insurrection and other interventions. Except in the West itself, the Indian wars were regarded as marginal affairs, and they attracted little protest save that by humanitarian groups, especially in New England.

1898: COLONIALISTS, INFORMAL IMPERIALISTS, AND THE ANTI-IMPERIALIST LEAGUE

Mainstream historians have tended to present the Spanish-American War as a sort of "youthful fling," an atypical and aberrant adventure in imperialism, as the United States was getting on the path of constructive world leadership. Other historians, including Charles A. Beard and William Appleman Williams, see 1898 as a major turning point in U.S. diplomatic history and the first important result of a foreign-policy consensus that emerged in the late nineteenth century. For the revisionists, the war with Spain was the first war for the informal Open Door Empire. Certainly it seemed so to foreign observers, including Rudyard Kipling, the poet laureate of British imperialism, who urged the Americans to "take up the white man's burden."

Represented by the McKinley administration as an altruistic crusade to relieve Cuba from the oppressions of the corrupt and decrepit Spanish Empire, the war was initially quite popular. Later, as the fighting died down and the administration's intentions became clear, public opinion became much less unified. U.S. official determination to establish a protectorate over Cuba, make a formal colony of the Philippines, and maintain a more "forward" posture in Asia raised the issue of republic versus empire in many minds (see, for example, British-Canadian liberal Goldwin Smith [1902]). But it was the desire of the Filipinos, not consulted by the Americans and Spaniards, to achieve self-rule that had the most adverse effects on popular perceptions of U.S. policy. Reports of the ugly, brutal counterinsurgency could not be kept from getting back to the United States. The issue of annexation of the Philippines stirred the most important opposition to McKinley's imperial program (for an overview, see Stromberg 1999, 169–201, and 2001).

In June 1898, a small group of old-line liberals and reformers met at Boston's famed Faneuil Hall and founded the Anti-Imperialist League; veterans of abolitionism, liberal Republicans, and civil service reformers, these men brought their uncompromising classical liberalism to bear on the issues raised by overseas imperialism. Well-known members of the league included the retired Boston textile manufacturer Edward Atkinson, former secretary of the Treasury George S. Boutwell, writer Mark Twain, industrialist Andrew Carnegie, philosopher William James, and others. The league quickly began to distribute cheaply printed propaganda against U.S. policy, especially in the Philippines. By the end of the year, its activity was beginning to have an effect.

Atkinson, perhaps the league's most radical and active figure, proceeded to mail antiwar pamphlets to the soldiers in the islands. The War Department denounced the action as "seditious" and had the material seized in transit. In interesting contrast to more recent times, at least some of the press defended Atkinson's right to print and mail his pamphlets. Unfortunately, although the league had a clear and consistent critique of war and empire, its leaders, as Leonard Liggio has noted, "were paralyzed by their upper social position from bringing forward and educating those who sympathized with their views" (1966b, 22).

As a result, no mass-based anti-imperialist movement was built up. Opposition to empire was, of course, broader than the league; it also included rank-and-file Democrats and Populists. In the election of 1900, however, William Jennings Bryan, as Democratic presidential candidate and symbol of populism, failed to turn the administration's imperialist ventures into a real campaign issue. The election was fought and lost by Bryan largely over economic issues; hence, contrary to many historians' judgment, McKinley's reelection was *not* a "popular mandate" for imperialism.[18]

Even if Bryan was unable or unwilling to exploit the issue, he did remark the analogy between two contemporaneous counterinsurgencies—British suppression of the Boer Republics in South Africa and what Americans were doing in the Philippine Islands—and the McKinley administration made no secret of its support for the British side in South Africa (Noer 1978, 87).[19]

In addition, misleading epithets as well as failure to recognize divisions within the imperialist camp have obscured what was at issue in 1900 and thereafter. Writing as if "*imperialism*" means only the formal annexation of colonial territories, many historians conclude that, with the exception of the Philippines, U.S. policy has not been imperial. Because the advocates of formal colonialism were eventually defeated after the Spanish-American War, it has been easy to think that imperialism in general was repudiated. Hence, "the splendid little war" has been seen as a mere aberration from the U.S. norm.

Informal empire, synonymous with the Open Door, involved bringing to bear U.S. power everywhere in the world, especially against weaker, less-developed countries in the interest of keeping markets open (whatever the natives' wishes).[20] This practice was, in effect, an attempt to have the political and economic benefits of empire without paying the full costs (conquest, war, and colonial administration) and without, it was thought, seriously compromising American ideals of self-determination. As Williams writes, within a few years after 1898, the imperialists who had favored outright colonialism had largely been won over to the informal Open Door view of empire; and the "anti-imperialists" who in fact opposed only colonies had likewise coalesced with the informal empire men. This consensus on a moderate, even anticolonial strategy of empire accounts for such frequent mistakes as the view that Bryan "shifted" dramatically in his position upon becoming secretary of state. For libertarians and other revisionists, the key is *not* whether a policymaker or businessman favored mere expansion into foreign markets, but whether or not he favored state actions (subsidies, loans to exporters, military intervention, and ultimately war) to penetrate and secure such markets. The critical distinction is that between a mercantilist policy favoring certain exporters, manufacturers, and contractors (at the expense of the people who are taxed to sustain unnatural expansion) and the policy of genuine free trade, which eschews both hindrances and supports. It is important to keep this distinction in mind because much of the literature speaks of "expansion" and "expansionists" without discussing clearly the actors' ideas of the role that the state should (or should not) play.[21]

In any event, the imperialists prevailed, using a combination of arguments that today seems bizarre, even ludicrous. The then in-vogue Anglo-Saxon racism and an imperialist interpretation of social Darwinism were given as evidence that the United States, in hardy racial tandem with Great Britain, was destined to give order to a chaotic world in line with our perfect *and therefore exportable* republican institutions (on this theme, see Horsman 1981). Missionaries foresaw hordes of new converts being brought within their grasp by the extension of U.S. influence. Last but not least, exporters, manufacturers, and investors continued to argue that U.S. prosperity depended on foreign markets. Spread-eagle orators such as Senator Albert Beveridge and President Theodore Roosevelt tended to use all these expansionist theses interchangeably.

The anti-imperialists responded with a restatement of the classical-liberal position. The sociologist William Graham Sumner, known for his strong laissez-faire and social Darwinist views, wrote *The Conquest of the United States by Spain* ([1899] 1965) to show how the crusade against the ramshackle Spanish Empire was leading America down the un-American path of conscription, taxation, conquest—the very evils that Spain had exemplified. For Sumner, Atkinson, and other anti-empire men, the fundamental issue was that imperialist foreign policy would necessarily undermine freedom at home in addition to the harm that might be done abroad. Unfortunately, no one vigorously pushed such views in the election of 1900 and afterward. Because empire had not yet proved very expensive, struggle could not yet take shape around the issue of costs.

DEVELOPMENTS UP TO 1914

After McKinley's assassination in 1901, the archimperialist Theodore Roosevelt as president sought the expansion of U.S. political and commercial influence in Asia, Latin America, and even the Mediterranean. The Roosevelt Corollary to the Monroe Doctrine, for example, envisioned regular American interventions to "keep order" in the Americas. Roosevelt's mediation of the Russo-Japanese War helped establish Japan as the major Far Eastern power, something his successors may have regretted. U.S. backing of the Panamanian Revolution in order to secure territory for the canal, U.S. participation in the Algeciras Conference called to settle the first Moroccan crisis, and Roosevelt's sending of the Great White Fleet around the world reflected an aggressive policy of Open Door Empire, expressed with a special belligerent exuberance.

The administration of Roosevelt's hand-picked (and later repudiated) successor, William Howard Taft, was known for the concrete, if less flashy, imperialism of "dollar diplomacy." When Woodrow Wilson came into the White House in 1912, as the beneficiary of the Republican Party split, foreign policy underwent little change. Wilson, on record many times as believing in the "righteous conquest of foreign markets," differed from his predecessors only in minor matters of tactics. From an anti-imperialist standpoint, the only hopeful development was the appointment of William Jennings Bryan as secretary of state. Bryan's reputation as a "pacifist" held out some hope for a change of emphasis. In 1915–16, however, Wilson's intervention in the Mexican Revolution dispelled such illusions.

THE "GREAT WAR" AND ITS OPPONENTS, 1914–1920

The outbreak of the general European War in August 1914 caught Americans by surprise. The administration pledged U.S. neutrality in word and deed, and Americans congratulated themselves on not being involved. Unfortunately, numerous ideological and material forces worked against consistent nonintervention from the start. One of these forces was the pervasive Anglophilia of leading northeastern political and commercial circles. This Anglophilia extended deep into the administration, strongly influencing Wilson himself (with his admiration of the British political system). Anglophilia, Anglo-Saxon racism (the opiate of the northeastern elite of the day), and the idea of the United States and Great Britain as joint guarantors of an orderly world predisposed many influential Americans to the English side. Ties of kinship, culture, and political ideas allowed pro-British elements to depict the war as a heroic struggle of "democracies" against the autocratic Central Powers and obscured the imperialist rivalries that had actually caused the debacle.[22]

Great Britain's blockade of Germany and its interference with neutral shipping led to U.S. protest, as did the German countermeasure—the U-boat. Unhappily, the administration's response to these events was less than neutral. It protested mildly and ineffectually against British violations, but held the German Reich "strictly accountable." Bryan resigned in June 1915 rather than sign an especially strong note to Germany. Ironically, U.S.

"stretching" of blockade rules during the War for Southern Independence gave color of law to the current British violations (see Baxter 1928). Anglophile feeling likewise contributed to an unbalanced policy. In addition, Germany's U-boats directly took the lives of civilians of both belligerent and neutral countries, making for more emotion against Germany. (The Allied starvation blockade of Germany—continued out of sheer vindictiveness for months after Germany's surrender—was less dramatic [see Raico 1989].) American acquiescence in British sea-warfare rules left the Germans increasingly unable to get supplies of all kinds; in this situation, advocates of unrestricted submarine warfare carried the day in the German cabinet. The sinking of the *Lusitania* was simply the most dramatic incident in the new style of seaborne warfare for which Great Britain and Germany shared responsibility.[23]

It is probably worth noting in passing that those who sailed into the "war zone" at least had the choice not to do so, whereas those sent later to the trenches of northern France, supposedly in response to U-boat excesses, had no choice—an important fact to keep in mind in evaluating the U.S. decision to go to war, over U-boats or anything else.

It was not fundamentally German "atrocities" in Belgium or on the high seas (matched, we must recall, by Allied deeds), however, that led U.S. leaders to choose war; it was their very definition of U.S. political and economic welfare as a function of foreign trade. German victory and Allied defeat seemed, in several ways, to preclude an orderly "liberal-capitalist" world. In the short run, U.S. recovery from a prewar recession had been boosted by Allied war orders (because the British blockade prevented Germany from placing significant orders). When Allied cash ran low, the bankers, including the very influential J. P. Morgan, brought pressure on the administration to reverse its position and allow large loans to the Allies. Once this reversal had taken place, the fortunes of the bankers and many exporters required Allied victory; and they, in turn, could make the persuasive, if uneconomic, argument that the health of the "nation" depended on Allied victory. This belief was very important inside the administration (see Williams [1962] 1972).

In a broader sense, however, the administration saw Allied victory as essential. "Free-trading" imperial Britain was for Anglophile U.S. statesmen a model power with which cooperation was quite possible. The German Reich, in contrast, seemed autocratic and irresponsibly and erratically imperialist, bent on exclusive spheres of influence (the antithesis of the Open Door), and willing to use unconventional weapons such as U-boats (which were less "acceptable," somehow, than mass slaughter on land). Victory of the Central Powers, with Germany at their head, might forever block access to foreign markets necessary for U.S. prosperity and therefore for U.S. political stability. Identifying state-subsidized and state-defended export markets with national well-being and the federal government with liberalism, Wilson and others easily persuaded themselves to crusade for "democracy," prosperity, and the Open Door, all at once. (Real personal and economic losses suffered by the citizenry were compatible with this definition of economic well-being.)

The whole set of German actions, as seen through the weltanschauung of Open Door Empire, led Wilson to ask for war; German actions, however remote, were seen as threatening an ambitious conception of U.S. welfare.[24] Opponents of U.S. entry into the war understood and attacked these motives at the time. Liberal and socialist "isolationists" pointed out the antisocial character of war to save bankers' investments and to continue the profits of munitions makers.[25] These critics differed among themselves on many points, but they did agree that the European war was not our affair; for them, U.S. participation would only add American lives and treasure to those already being senselessly wasted. Drawing on the popular "isolationism," which had survived intact the beginnings of Open Door Empire, and appealing to the nineteenth-century tradition of continentalism, antiwar spokesmen had a potentially much larger constituency than the Anti-Imperialist League had in 1900. The obvious scale of possible involvement in the world war ensured that entry into it, unlike entry into the marginal war in the Philippines, would be strongly contested.

The war issue cut across ideological and class lines. Of the liberals, those closest to the administration, such as Herbert Croly of *The New Republic*, backed the war as a crusade compatible with liberalism and reform, only to see—as the antiwar radical Randolph Bourne caustically remarked—their reasons for supporting the war disappear one by one. (Certainly, *classical-liberal* values were undermined.) Other liberals, such as Oswald Garrison Villard of *The Nation*, Bourne, and the radical libertarian writer Albert Jay Nock, consistently opposed the war, its conduct, and its repressive aftermath. Not surprisingly, these liberal critics held pronounced laissez-faire views on foreign and domestic policy. Likewise opposed to entry into the war and close in spirit to these publicists was a small group of Progressives in Congress, including Senators Robert A. LaFollette of Wisconsin and George W. Norris of Nebraska, Congresswoman Jeannette Rankin of Montana, and former senator Richard F. Pettigrew of South Dakota (later indicted by a federal grand jury for speaking out against the war). These latter-day Progressives were concentrated in midwestern and western farm states, the major mass base of the country's "isolationist" voters.

One reason for strong noninterventionist sentiment in the Midwest was the presence of great numbers of German Americans there. Since the mid-nineteenth century, German immigrants and their descendants had strongly embraced liberal values of peace and antimilitarism. Many of their forebears had fled Europe to avoid the war system, and in 1914–17 they constituted a significant force for peace, especially as regarded a war that would pit German Americans against Germany, whatever the Reich's alleged misdeeds. Opposition to British imperialism as a world system and support for the impending Irish Revolution led another large mass into the pro-peace camp. (The identification of German Americans and Irish Americans as "isolationists" persisted until the virtual effacement of pro-peace forces during and after World War II.) Certain prominent pro-British "100 percent Americans," such as Theodore Roosevelt, raised a great hue and cry about "hyphenates" (British Americans apparently suffered no such handicap) and their potential "disloyalty" to pro-British interventionist policy.

When the vote on war came in early April 1917, six senators stood against the pro-war tide: Asle J. Gronna, LaFollette, Harry Lane, William J. Stone, James K. Vardaman, and George Norris, along with fifty representatives, including Jeannette Rankin, Majority Leader Claude Kitchin, and Meyer London (the only Socialist member). Following rapidly on the declaration of war, the administration, realizing the continuing unpopularity of the war with many Americans, enacted the most repressive "espionage" and "sedition" laws since 1798 (or since Lincoln). The mildest criticism soon became criminal, and the executive branch launched a virtual terror campaign against "pro-German," antiwar, radical, and even liberal elements. The wave of repression embraced strict press censorship, suppression of speech, and "war socialism" (that is, government-sponsored cartelization, conscription, and sacrifice of everything to the state—in a word, the very evils that classical liberals had always associated with war). As Bourne famously wrote at the time, "War is the health of the state."

Once the war had begun, politics split along the lines of the war itself, with "war liberals" and "war socialists" opposing antiwar liberals and socialists. The Wilson administration used the "emergency" as an excuse to crush the radical left generally (socialists, the Industrial Workers of the World, and so forth), as did local governments and vigilante groups. (Most of our numskull state "criminal anarchosyndicalism" laws and loyalty oaths date from World War I.) The war strengthened statism in all respects and created a "know-nothing" mass base of hysterical "patriots," many of whom later flocked into the American Legion and the so-called Ku Klux Klan (KKK), which dated from 1915.

The antiwar socialists, symbolized by Eugene V. Debs (sentenced to ten years in prison for denouncing the war), were especially vocal dissenters from war policies, counseling draft refusal and stressing economic motives for the war. Along with the socialists, the radical liberals (Bourne, Nock, Villard) and traditional pacifists also maintained the dangerous posture of "disloyal" opposition.

THE INTERWAR YEARS: HEYDAY OF "ISOLATIONISM"

As Bourne predicted, the great crusade for democracy, "the war to end war," soon ran up against harsh reality, and the outcome was a general disillusionment that had many facets (some negative, such as the "revived" KKK). The most important reaction was a general revulsion against war and grand crusades that was to last for two decades and that required the Franklin Roosevelt administration's most extreme duplicity to overcome in 1940–41. The immediate result was a vast broadening of the pre-1917 antiwar coalition. Disillusioned "war liberals" and other former Wilson supporters now joined the loose aggregation of pro-peace "ethnics," midwestern and western Progressives, laissez-faire liberals, and socialists to scuttle the imperialist Treaty of Versailles and to keep the United States out of the League of Nations.

Because this debate was crucial and its character is often misapprehended in the literature, it is important to acquire a revisionist view of its contours. Rather than accepting the conventional "isolationist versus internationalist" dichotomy, it is more instructive to divide the 1919-20 debaters into at least four camps.[26] Of these, "pure pacifists" held the least political clout. At the political center stood the corporate-liberal advocates of Open

Door Empire, many of whom, like Wilson, now espoused great-power co-operation through the League of Nations to make "stability" possible (that is, to preserve an unjust status quo in the face of revisionist powers and colonial revolutions). To their "right" and "left" stood two distinct sets of anti-League, anti-"internationalist" figures usually lumped together as bitter-end "isolationists" out of step with the necessities of twentieth-century life. On the right were unilateral imperialists, such as Senator Henry Cabot Lodge, who fully accepted the political-economic program of empire, but thought that the United States could dominate the world economy better by acting alone as much as possible. On the left were the laissez-faire liberals and Progressives, who, as Williams emphasizes strongly, were genuinely committed to the self-determination of all peoples, embracing the right of revolution. Senator William E. Borah of Idaho, who had been a moderate supporter of war in 1917, emerged as the chief spokesman of the anti-imperial "isolationists" in the debate over the League of Nations and the Treaty of Versailles.[27]

Heirs of the Anti-Imperialist League, the true "isolationist" critics opposed the treaty for its perpetuation of Western imperialism, including U.S. imperialism, and its establishment of the groundwork for a new world war by its treatment of Germany and other nations. In this analysis, the whole point of the League of Nations was the use of collective force by imperial powers against change in the status quo (stigmatized as "Communist" revolutions on the Bolshevik model, whatever the local focus and causes, or as simple "aggression" by unreformed autocracies). Wilson's interventions in Mexico, in the world war, and—perhaps most revealing—against the Bolsheviks in Russia were of a piece, designed to preserve and extend the Open Door (on Russia, see, for example, Williams 1967).

"Isolationist" spokesmen such as Senators LaFollette and Borah bitterly attacked the concert of imperialist powers involved in Russia as wrong in practice and in principle. The attack on the Versailles settlement was another aspect of the battle for nonintervention and peace. Senator Borah was especially outspoken on this whole set of issues.

The defeat of the treaty reflected public reaction against the "oversold" world war, which had failed to create a better world, as did the election of President William G. Harding, who pledged to return America to "normalcy." In this climate, scholars and publicists alike took a closer look at the war's causes, course, and consequences. Focusing on economic and power motives, the "literature of disillusionment" was the intellectual counterpart of the struggle against the diktat of Versailles waged by the congressional "Battalion of Death." The extreme libertarian essayist Albert Jay Nock wrote *The Myth of a Guilty Nation* (1922), assailing the war's official theory, which was published originally as a series in *LaFollette's Magazine*, published by the senator. Throughout the 1920s and 1930s, a continuing barrage of "revisionist" literature came out in a fairly favorable intellectual climate.

Among the more important works were Harry Elmer Barnes's *The Genesis of the World War* (1929); Sidney B. Fay's *The Origins of the World War*, 2 vols. ([1928] 1966); C.H. Grattan's *Why We Fought* (1929); Walter Millis's popularly written and much-read *Road to War* (1935); H.C. Engelbrecht and Frank Hanighen's *Merchants of Death* (1934); English economist J.M. Keynes's very influential work *Economic Consequences of the Peace* (1920); and Charles Callan Tansill's *America Goes to War* (1938). Liberal and radical journals such as Nock's *Freeman*, H.L. Mencken's *American Mercury*, Oswald Garrison Villard's *Nation*, and the formerly pro-Wilson *New Republic* opened their doors to all manner of "revisionist" and "isolationist" writers. In addition, illustrating the continuity of "isolationism" and anti-imperialism, Barnes, probably the most indefatigable and hardest hitting of the revisionists, was associated with the interwar Vanguard series of books dealing with growing U.S. political-economic dominance of undeveloped nations.

The net effect of the revisionist literature and resurgent "isolationist" opinion was a climate favorable to lower military spending and nonintervention. A large section of the public now saw World War I as a "European" power struggle and viewed U.S. entry as brought about by special economic interests, very effective British propaganda, and irrational ideologies. The revisionist literature shifted at least part of the "war guilt" from Germany and Austria-Hungary to France and Russia and, secondarily, to England (some were not so kind to Britain!). With wartime hysteria and myths dispelled (including the myth of unique German diabolism), it was easier to maintain that the United States *could* and should have remained neutral. The implications for future policy were clear.

Concern that practical nonneutrality had helped to embroil the United States in World War I led to renewed scholarly work on neutrality in international law and to legislation designed to make the U.S. neutral in fact in the event of another sea struggle between rival empires. With the failure of the feeble official arms-limitations efforts of the 1920s, "isolationists" and pacifists turned their attention to neutrality. The famous Nye Committee of the mid-1930s investigated the munitions industry, providing much intellectual ammunition for those who held that the arms firms had been a major force for getting the United States into the war. Senator Gerald P. Nye himself supported legislation to curb arms sales and other intercourse with belligerents potentially dangerous to neutrality. The Neutrality Act of 1935 was in line with such "timid isolationist" reasoning and allowed the executive to proclaim the existence of a state of war, after which an embargo automatically applied to the warring powers. Despite good intentions, such provisions were probably inappropriate means to preserve neutrality.

"Belligerent isolationists," such as Senators Borah and Hiram Johnson and Representative Hamilton Fish, stood for strict neutrality but opposed any embargo, relying instead on international law and American power to protect our genuine neutral rights.[28] In this quest, they drew on the writings of Edwin M. Borchard and William Potter Lage (1937), leading authorities on international law, who believed neutrality to be both a desirable and a practical pursuit. Unfortunately, true neutrality was to prove inconsistent with the premises that presidents and policymakers embraced, and mere legislative tinkering could not forever restrain a president bent on risking intervention for the Open Door.

Besides neutrality, other causes reflected the American public's peaceful inclinations. One of these causes was the partially successful campaign by the pacifists, liberals, and liberal clergymen to eliminate the compulsory Reserve Officers Training Corps (ROTC) on American college campuses (see Ekirch 1972, 217–33). Even more expressive was the campaign for the Ludlow Amendment, which would have required a popular referendum on war, except in case of actual invasion of the United States. Rejected on a close vote in Congress in January 1938 after the administration put great pressure on the members, this proposed constitutional amendment (ridiculed as unwieldy and unrealistic) eloquently bespoke the current state of opinion on intervention (on the Ludlow Amendment, see Jonas 1966 and Ekirch 1972, 248).

"Isolationist" feeling pervaded the country, but it was concentrated in a broad belt consisting of the new Northwest and a large part of the old Northwest (or "Middle West"). The "isolationist" stronghold consisted especially of Ohio, Michigan, Minnesota, Wisconsin, Iowa, North and

South Dakota, Nebraska, Kansas, Wyoming, and Idaho. According to one study, not only did "isolationist" voting patterns correlate fairly well with German and Irish ancestry, they also reflected better education (see Smuckler 1953).

THE COMING OF WORLD WAR II AND AMERICA FIRST

Despite the popular "isolationist" mood of the 1920s and 1930s, U.S. policymakers continued to think within the weltanschauung of Open Door Empire and the (related) frontier-expansionist philosophy of history. So strong was government support for extension of U.S. business abroad that Williams writes of "the legend of isolationism" ([1962] 1972, chap. 4). Certainly, at the level of policymaking, little support existed for principled nonintervention. Herbert Hoover, first as secretary of commerce under Presidents Harding and Coolidge and then as president, vigorously pushed U.S. foreign trade and investment while pursuing a proto–New Dealish program of economic cartelization wherever possible at home (on Hoover, see Rothbard 1970).

Although routine interventions took place in Latin America and the U.S. military roamed as far away as China, some advocates of Open Door Empire attempted to pursue their goals as peacefully as possible. Hoover was particularly moderate and finally chose peace over war in Asia, even at the risk of losing the "China market," the traditional mirage of Open Door enthusiasts. (He later found himself in the "isolationist" coalition, opposing New Deal foreign and domestic policies.) The Great Depression retired Hoover and brought into office an administration pledged to restoring prosperity.

As the New Deal's domestic failures became evident, policymakers turned more and more to foreign markets as a panacea. By the late 1930s, concern with keeping markets open in the face of Japanese competition, as well as that of Germany and Italy (whose businesses were penetrating even Latin America), predisposed Roosevelt to military solutions. In addition, the "shot in the arm" of increased military spending doubtless appealed to an administration whose recovery programs had hardly dented the Depression. Roosevelt's request for increased naval spending in 1937 thus reflected a growing anxiety over domestic recovery, foreign markets, and the possible necessity of war to sustain both. Rapidly abandoning his semi-"isolationist" posture once war broke out in Europe in September 1939, Roosevelt moved gradually but purposefully to involve America in the war on the British side. Constrained by the climate of opinion, he ran as a virtual "peace candidate" in 1940 (as had Wilson in 1916). Once reelected, however, he sought one pretext after another to enter the war (or wars, inasmuch as the Sino-Japanese War and the European War were still only tangentially connected) and put great pressure on Japan in the Pacific.[29]

Alarmed by "peace candidate" Roosevelt's behind-the-scenes moves toward intervention, concerned citizens, including Yale students influenced by Borchard (the theorist of pure neutrality), founded the America First Committee (AFC) in September 1940 to counter the drift into war. By bringing the issues into open debate through the printed word, radio, and mass rallies, the AFC sought to nullify the propaganda of such well-financed pro-interventionist groups as the Committee to Defend America by Aiding the Allies (widely regarded as an administration "front").[30] Although the AFC failed in its stated objective of preventing U.S. entry into World War II, it was a significant movement in several respects. It attempted to fight an anticipated intervention on the basis of historical lessons from a previous war. It was a broad coalition of antiwar forces, liberal and conservative, united on a few principles (analogous to Students for a Democratic Society from about 1965 to 1970); it rested on a genuine popular base, unlike the religious, pacifist, and left-wing groups that also opposed war in 1940–41. As a mass-based movement consciously in the American noninterventionist tradition, the AFC substantially slowed the Roosevelt administration's interventionist course and provoked public debate (a so-called great debate) over foreign policy. Despite failures of strategic vision and leadership, the AFC deepened Roosevelt's dilemma of how to intervene against the wishes of a large segment of the people, a dilemma from which only an event such as the attack on Pearl Harbor could have delivered him.

For its part, the administration did its best to avoid presenting the war issue squarely to the citizenry and pictured each stage of intervention as a last-ditch measure to keep out of war. The AFC—in cooperation with liberal "isolationist" groups such as the Keep America Out of War Congress (which was supported by such notables as Oswald Garrison Villard, Charles Beard, Harry Elmer Barnes, Senator Burton K. Wheeler of Montana, and Senator Nye of North Dakota)—tried to alert the public to the interventionist character of such successive measures as Lend-Lease, "neutrality patrols" (actually secret convoys), convoys, repeal of the Neutrality Law, and the draft extension bill. Thus, in early 1941, Amos Pinchot and Charles Lindbergh testified against Lend-Lease in congressional hearings. (Beard and Norman Thomas also testified against it.). When Roosevelt announced his "neutrality patrols" in April 1941, the AFC held two mass anticonvoy rallies in New York, each attended by forty thousand people. Another such rally in Philadelphia was addressed by John T. Flynn, Thomas, Lindbergh, and Senator Wheeler.

Interventionist moves accumulated quickly. In May, FDR announced more "neutrality patrols" and proclaimed an "unlimited state of national emergency." In July, full convoys began, and U.S. forces occupied Iceland. By September, an undeclared naval war was beginning in the North Atlantic, bearing out the "isolationists'" claims that supplying the Allies would lead to convoying the supply ships, which in turn would lead to shooting and bring war that much closer. Shooting incidents involving the *Greer*, the *Kearsarge*, and the *Reuben James* failed to bring the pro-war fervor the administration apparently hoped for, but they did underscore the seriousness of the situation in the North Atlantic.[31]

Unfortunately, the national AFC leadership in Chicago took increasingly weak stands in the face of Roosevelt's initiatives and thereby undercut the hopes of the movement's mass base in the old and new Midwest and of the "isolationist" intellectuals. The AFC leadership was replete with retired officers and businessmen such as General Robert Wood, a Sears-Roebuck executive, who were conventional, unimaginative, and conservative; those qualities carried over into the AFC's strategy and tactics. Thus, for example, the AFC's failure to take a principled stand against conscription and militarism allowed extension of the draft in August 1941 by only one vote; this extension in turn enabled the administration to pursue confidently a collision course with Japan (see Liggio 1966b, 24).

Despite the weaknesses of the national office, the AFC possessed intelligent and articulate spokesmen. Of these "liberal isolationists," perhaps none was as tireless an activist or as perceptive a critic as John T. Flynn, the political writer who headed the New York City chapter of the AFC. An anti-imperialist since 1900, Flynn, like Barnes, shows the unity of noninterventionist movements. As head of the New York City AFC, Flynn developed a very "forward" strategy involving congressional lobbying, use of media, and analysis of the interventionist forces.

In his neglected books *Country Squire in the White House* (1940) and *As We Go Marching* (1944), Flynn insightfully analyzed the support for foreign war. *As We Go Marching*, possibly the single most prophetic American political book of the mid-twentieth century, dealt with the New Deal's marriage of welfare and warfare as America's coming "genteel fascism," openly comparing the New Deal with Italy's fascist corporative-state economy. Flynn stressed the temptation of "democratic" politicians to save the economy from depression through military spending and even war, a motive he saw as propelling Roosevelt's interventionist coalition. He sagely noted that "defense" was the one "pump-priming" boondoggle that powerful anti–New Deal congressional conservatives would back unthinkingly. Thus, Flynn developed a revisionist analysis of the connections between power, economics, and war similar to later new left discussions.[32] Other "isolationists" were aware of and responded to the administration's concern with access to foreign markets, which they knew to be an important motive for intervention (see Doenecke 1976).

War came finally at Pearl Harbor after months of U.S. pressure on Japan, and it came from a quarter that the "isolationists" and the general public had tended to underestimate, leading to charges that the government had consciously sought war in the Pacific as a "back door" to the war in Europe (see Tansill 1952). Shortly after Pearl Harbor, the national board of the AFC voted to dissolve the committee and to support the war now that it had come. With the major mass-based antiwar front done in by its residual "patriotism" and nonradical leaders, antiwar forces generally were buried by wartime emotions and by firm, if "moderate" repression (which fell hardest on West Coast residents of Japanese ancestry).

A number of circumstances contributed to the failure of nonintervention in 1940–41. The defection of liberals was a major blow. Disillusioned with World WarI, liberals, exemplified by *The Nation* and *The New Republic*, had become strongly noninterventionist. With the outbreak of war in Europe, however, and the propensity to follow Roosevelt, whose domestic New Deal many liberals supported, perhaps the majority of these liberals reenlisted as Wilsonian interventionists.[33] Soon such staunch liberals as Flynn and Barnes found themselves excluded from the liberal press for their noninterventionist views. As the major national media came to support intervention, the lack of respectable outlets soon greatly handicapped the "isolationist" cause. In addition, the existence of small "fascist" and pro-Nazi groups, such as the German-American Bund, the Silver Shirts, and the Coughlinites, played up by the interventionist press, hurt the AFC by their attempts to infiltrate it. These attempts lent color to the interventionists' charge (inevitable anyway) that to oppose intervention was to be "pro-Nazi" (just as opposition to the war in Vietnam was stigmatized as "Communist").[34] Finally, in 1940, Senator Borah's death deprived "isolationism" of the spokesman best equipped to deal with a wide range of issues from within a conscious framework of anti-imperialism.

Even in defeat, however, the "isolationists" had raised once again the fundamental questions of freedom versus empire. In addition, Roosevelt's duplicity, which pro–New Deal historians later admitted and justified, presented still relevant issues of democratic procedure and ethics (for a short discussion of such issues, see Radosh 1967). Lyndon Johnson's "credibility gap" was very much in an established tradition. Use of the Federal Bureau of Investigation (FBI) for political spying dates back at least to Franklin Roosevelt's presidency, however much his successors emulated him. In focusing attention and debate on such abuses along with the larger issues of war and peace and republic versus empire, the much-maligned "isolationists" remained true to a vital American tradition. Unhappily, they lived to see some of their direst predictions come true as World War II and the Cold War fastened on the United States the features of a garrison state, even in "peacetime."

Because the attack on Pearl Harbor rallied the nation behind the government, open antiwar activity ceased almost completely, in contrast to its continued presence during World War I. Traditional pacifists maintained witness against the war, serving as forced laborers in conscientious objector (CO) camps or doing time in prison. (At least two COs gained prominence later as revisionist historians.) One of the few important wartime protests was the Peace Now movement, led by George Hartmann.[35] Peace Now called for serious negotiations toward a cease-fire, as opposed to the official Allied goal of "unconditional surrender," in order to end the massive destruction, especially through terror bombing, that continued war would bring. The pro-war media—liberal, conservative, and Stalinist—roundly denounced Peace Now as "seditious" and "fascist," as did even some pacifist leaders who disliked Peace Now's "impure" coalition of pacifist and "isolationist" elements. (For A. J. Muste, "right-wing" activists could not possibly really be for peace.)

Aside from draft resistance and Peace Now, some opponents of the war and its actual conduct managed to express themselves in obscure "little magazines"; notable were Frank Chodorov's *analysis*, Felix Morley and Frank C. Hanighen's *Human Events*, and Dwight MacDonald' *Politics*, for overlap of right-wing and left-wing antiwar critiques. In addition, World War II revisionism began even before the war's end, as pamphlets and more complete critical histories came out in the late 1940s and early 1950s (Flynn 1944; Neumann 1945). These works raised the question of whether or not the "isolationists" had been right, but unlike the situation for the World War I revisionists, the new wave of revisionism worked in a completely hostile climate.

COLD WARS AND HOT WARS: NONINTERVENTION'S NADIR

Having successfully overcome fascist threats to the Open Door, the U.S. government focused attention on the remaining threats to American hegemony and the Open Door; these threats were the Soviet Union, whose expansion into eastern Europe might close those countries to U.S. economic penetration, and the revolutionary movements in the colonial possessions of the Western empires. These movements, including the Chinese Revolution, were conveniently grouped together as "communism" by U.S. policymakers, who blamed the USSR for them.[36]

The new Truman administration, which had unleashed the atom bomb with no second thoughts at all, now proceeded to push for encirclement of the USSR with bases around the world, a mass standing army sustained by peacetime conscription, greater air power, and a host of other "defense" measures designed to maximize the Open Door Empire.[37] Presenting its power-political, economic, and ideological crusade as purely a reaction to Communist "aggression," the administration asked Congress and the people to support a set of warlike policies in peacetime in supposed defense of a rather nebulous "free world" (meaning *all* states, however oppressive, that did not profess to be Marxist).

This program took some doing, even though Pearl Harbor and the whole war experience had discredited nonintervention seemingly forever. Americans had elected a Republican Congress in 1946; some of these men were unrepentant "isolationists," and a great many more were simply reluctant to spend their constituents' money on new crusades. Thus, the administration had to "oversell" its program as a great crusade for liberty and as part of a life-and-death struggle against "communism," and thus the Truman Doctrine was born. In a paradoxical reversal of recent ideological stereotypes, such opposition as there was to the early Cold War program came from a rough coalition of "old right" noninterventionists and (numerically fewer) left liberals such as Henry Wallace (Stromberg 1976).

Fighting a clearly losing battle, the noninterventionists opposed the Greek-Turkish aid bill of 1947, the Marshall Plan, the North Atlantic Treaty Organization (NATO), and, finally, the Korean escapade, but they dwindled in numbers as events unfolded, until no one in politics upheld nonintervention. "Isolationism" became the cause of a handful of despairing writers and revisionist historians on the fringes of American politics. Nonetheless, as they went down to defeat, the "isolationist" remnant articulated a position that in hindsight seems prophetic.

Congressmen Howard Buffett (R., Nebraska), Frederic Smith (R., Ohio), and Lawrence Smith (R., Wisconsin) vied with one another in denouncing the Truman Doctrine as "imperialism." Radical libertarian publicist Frank Chodorov wrote that the Truman policies would turn the United States into a "Byzantine empire of the West"; the country would become a fully statized society in which educational and social policies would ultimately be geared to creating a garrison state. Senator Taft, arguing against NATO, asserted that it would promote war in the long run and would immediately obligate the United States to arm western Europe. Felix Morley, one of the most persistent critics, offered the mid-1950s warning of an economy dangerously addicted to "defense" spending to create full employment (Stromberg 1978).

Somewhere between 1947, when the right-wing "isolationists" largely opposed the Truman Doctrine's interventionism (while the China lobby section of the right supported it), and 1953, when Robert Taft died, a series of changes occurred that, taken together, compose what Rothbard has called the "transformation" of the right wing. The years 1949–51 were especially critical for the decline of "isolationist" ideas and spokesmen. The so-called "fall" of China, the rise of Joe McCarthy (who made a career out of turning the Cold War liberals' anti-Communist crusade against them), and the Korean War convinced the politically active public, including Congress itself, that communism was indeed a monolithic menace and that reasonable men could debate only the means and degree of intervention, not the principle.

Although Congressman Buffett and Senator Taft denounced Truman for initiating an unconstitutional presidential war, the right was divided on the war. One wing, represented by Hoover and Joe Kennedy, called for immediate withdrawal and for reduction of U.S. "defense" perimeters to modest dimensions. Another wing adopted the imperialist position of General Douglas MacArthur, the China lobbyists (loyal chiefly to Chiang Kai-shek), and McCarthyites. Sundry patriots, confused by official claims that U.S. survival was at stake, demanded military solutions at any price. Finally, many right-wing figures, including Taft himself, wavered confusedly or opportunistically between the "isolationist" and the unilateral imperialist positions. (The latter took inspiration from Theodore Roosevelt and Henry Cabot Lodge Sr.)

The evaporation of the "isolationist" remnant during the Korean War meant that the last significant group that stood for nonintervention was now gone from American politics. Just as mainstream liberals had embraced intervention in 1940–41, they enthusiastically supported the new war, which liberal policymakers had initiated and which seemed to embody the interventionist ideal of "collective security." As Carl Oglesby has written with regard to Vietnam, the dissembling of the Cold War liberals, in and out of the administration, led many onetime "isolationists" (who failed to develop a critique of the political description of the war) to demand "victory." The problem, then, lay in the premises of policy, but by the 1950s only a few marginal commentators such as Flynn and Lawrence Dennis kept up anything like a consistent "isolationist" critique.

From 1950 until the mid-1960s, the noninterventionist cause seemed completely discredited. Save for the much-persecuted Communist Party itself and a few isolated noninterventionists, the entire political spectrum embraced Cold War policies. Blaming Cold War setbacks, such as the "fall" of China and the stalemate in Korea, on internal Communist subversion, the New Right dissented from establishment policy and demanded greater military intervention abroad and greater police power at home. Thus, on the face of it, an opportunity to limit U.S. globalism was lost when Taft failed to win the Republican presidential nomination in 1952.

The Eisenhower administration, in practice, was more moderately interventionist than its predecessors or successors. Influenced by the former Taft supporters in his administration, Eisenhower restrained Secretary of State Dulles and Vice President Nixon, who advocated direct U.S. military involvement to aid French imperialists in Vietnam, and submitted the matter to Congress, where caution prevailed. Despite this moderation, "defense" budgets stayed well above "normal" peacetime levels, interventions took place across the globe, and the premises of foreign policy remained the same. Indeed, the strategy adopted by the Eisenhower government seems profoundly immoral because it relied on atomic bombs as the key to budgetary "savings" under such slogans as "the New Look" and "more bang for a buck" (see Gaddis 1982, 127–63).

Domestically, the Eisenhower years saw great advances in state-fostered corporatism, in which the new "military-industrial" culture played a major role.[38]

NEW FRONTIERS, NEW WARS, AND A NEW OPPOSITION

On the left, dissent was limited to a self-restricted sort of liberal and liberal-pacifist campaign to ban future nuclear testing as opposed to a radical questioning of overkill or interventionism on principle (for a summary, see Wittner 1969). The election of John Kennedy, a youthful, "vigorous" leader pledged to moderate reform, created a situation in which liberals felt they could serve their consciences and the state. Kennedy would "get things done"—lots of them—in contrast to the "do-nothing" Eisenhower presidency.

Even foreign-policy matters failed to spoil this cozy social-democratic idyll because Kennedy's concern with counterinsurgency, efficiency, and adolescent competition with the Soviets seemed simply the export, albeit sometimes by force, of American liberal ideas and institutions. Even the Cuban Missile Crisis, itself ultimately the result of U.S. unwillingness to accept the Cuban Revolution, failed to curb the crusading fervor of Cold Warriors, liberal and conservative, though it may have added to an already strong emphasis on "winning" in the undeveloped countries or Third World.[39]

Significantly, the new administration called itself the "New Frontier"; unfortunately, even the choice of slogan reflected continued commitment to the by-now-traditional policies of Open Door Empire and the frontier-expansionist philosophy of history. By the 1960s, the peacetime garrison state predicted and feared by the last "isolationists" had become a functioning reality. The interpenetration of government and favored corporations had become so thorough that to separate the personnel of the state and the corporations at the highest level became well-nigh impossible. As C. Wright Mills (1956) put it, top leadership was in the hands of a "power elite" whose economic and bureaucratic interests pointed in the direction of further interventions.[40]

Barnes had predicted in 1953 that only a major foreign-policy disaster could reopen public debate and force Americans to reconsider revisionist history and noninterventionist alternatives. Vietnam was that disaster. It is crucial to understand that that ugly conflict grew out of established policy and was in no sense a "mistake" or well-intentioned blunder, any more than 1898 was a foreign-policy "aberration" with no long-range consequences. Begun by Kennedy, carried on and escalated by Johnson, clung to for dear life by Nixon, the Vietnam War ironically proved so costly that even its would-be political and economic beneficiaries came to regret it.

At the same time that the national-security managers were preparing and implementing intervention in Indochina, a new opposition was emerging outside the Cold War consensus. Beginning in the late 1950s and early 1960s, more as a radical "mood" and style than as a body of doctrine, this new left, at its best, raised issues of individual autonomy and responsibility and rejected the social-democratic old left policy of accommodation with big government. The new left had also begun to question U.S. Cold War policies when the war in Vietnam confronted it with a need for thoroughly *radical* revision of inherited establishment-liberal views.[41]

Left liberals, pacifists, and even radicals had focused so much attention on nuclear weapons and great-power conflict that the "brushfire war" in Southeast Asia caught them without a ready analysis and political response. When Lyndon Johnson, long a dedicated interventionist (after the school of Franklin Roosevelt), ran as a virtual "peace candidate" against the overtly warlike Barry Goldwater in 1964, the nation and many intellectuals as well voted for Johnson and imagined in doing so they served the cause of peace. As Johnson widened the war with ground troops and massive bombing, war critics failed to assess matters radically and got bogged down in side issues.

The university and college teach-ins, which began in 1965, were side-tracked by pseudo-issues of stopping the bombing and engaging in negotiations. As a result, the administration was able to confuse and silence its critics by making ultimately meaningless gestures such as Johnson's "bombing pause" and the Paris "peace" talks. In this situation, the old right "isolationist" remnant could play a vanguard role by educating the incipient antiwar movement regarding the continuity of U.S. imperialism and its tactics, from the bloody Philippine Insurrection to World War II terror bombing of German and Japanese civilians, and regarding the consequent necessity for radical and total opposition to the U.S. presence in Vietnam.[42]

This relearning process took place especially in the brilliant new left journal Studies on the Left and the radical libertarian journal *Left and Right* (edited by Rothbard, Liggio, and H. George Resch), both of which dealt extensively with politics and revisionist history. In these two journals and in *Liberation*, *Viet-Report*, *Ramparts*, and elsewhere, radical activists made clear to the broader "movement" the reasons for demanding unconditional U.S. withdrawal from Indochina. In one of the dialectical ironies of the corporate-state system, the universities became the center of opposition to the military-industrial-university complex. As great masses of American youth were "channeled" into expanding universities by the threat of the draft, the very precariousness of their temporary student deferments forced them to take the war and the draft seriously. Designed to produce technicians and bureaucrats for the state and the military, the system of channeling at the same time helped to generate a base for antiwar activity.[43]

Infusing antiwar activity with the spirit and tactics used by the Student Non-Violent Coordinating Committee in the struggle for blacks' voting rights in the South, Students for a Democratic Society (SDS) emerged in the mid-1960s as the major hub of actual antiwar action. Scorning the ritualistic "anti-Communist" rhetoric of the old left, SDS focused on the war as a moral evil to be opposed and fought it with demonstrations, sit-ins, direct confrontation, and propaganda. By 1967, SDS had adopted the radical and libertarian stance of draft resistance; supposedly "nonideological," it was instinctively operating out of a highly libertarian, native American radicalism.[44]

By March 1968, the broad antiwar movement had begun to constrain policymakers. Faced with mounting opposition at home and a major setback in Vietnam—the Tet Offensive—Johnson announced he would not seek reelection. Unfortunately, the antiwar movement remained altogether too campus bound and did not appeal to ordinary Americans in American terms, as had the AFC. The nomination of two look-alike pro-war centrists, Nixon and Humphrey, offered little choice anyway on the chief issue of the decade.

Nixon won, in part, on the strength of a pledge to end the war by means of his "secret plan." The secret apparently was that Nixon intended to prolong the war as long as possible and become a Great Statesman. Still confined largely to the universities, unable to communicate to the mass of Americans, the antiwar movement became increasingly divided. The vacuum left by early new left nonideological looseness was filled by warring varieties of Marxism because a theory, *any* theory, seemed necessary to explain the war and its continuation. (The disciplined, doctrinaire, and wrongheaded Progressive Labor Party did more than its share to destroy SDS as a viable antiwar organization.)

Mass marches in Washington, D.C., especially in 1970, met with mass arrests by the government, but helped corner the war makers morally. Along with the news media, which now shed some of their Cold War complacency and "patriotic" self-censorship, the marches dramatized the war issue effectively. Unfortunately, with SDS split into multiple groups, the mass of antiwar activists lost direction and cohesiveness. A madness and "paranoia" descended on the movement, exemplified by the bombings and the suicidal tactics of the Weathermen. The contributions made to this state of mind by agents provocateurs and the serious campaign of repression undertaken by FBI, Army Intelligence, and other agents under Nixon have received less discussion than they deserve.

Watergate is perhaps best understood as an attempted internal coup by Nixon and his circle intended to crush all real opposition in the name of national security. The exposure of Watergate, the Huston Plan for police surveillance of everything, and the cover-up served to illustrate eloquently the potential for totalitarianism inherent in the imperial presidency. The war and Watergate together constitute irrefutable evidence that noninterventionists have correctly apprehended the dangers of statism and empire almost from the founding of the republic. Although it may be too early to assess properly the long-run accomplishments of the anti-Vietnam War movement, we can see that a generation was educated to the nature of war, the dishonesty of its leaders, and the corruptions of power.

CONCLUSION: LEFT AND RIGHT, THE PROSPECTS FOR NONINTERVENTION

Whatever the lessons of Vietnam, they were insufficient to overcome the institutionalization of the war party in the state, academe, and economic life that accompanied the highly artificial Cold War political consensus. From the caretaker administration of Gerald Ford to the administration of George H. W. Bush, the same assumptions reigned—a broad and ambitious conception of "national security," coupled with geopolitics, atomic cultism, and an abiding interest in applying the latest technologies to war.

The Soviet implosion widened the field in which U.S. policymakers could play, and few cared to admit that if anyone had "won" the Cold War, it was *state power*, plain and simple. The first Gulf War, coming after the Soviet collapse, did not define a new foreign policy. From the early 1990s to the present, policymakers and policy advocates have offered Americans basically two choices: either liberal imperialism, with humanitarian intervention, transparency, and a new conception of "openness" far surpassing a mere open door, or the proactive, routine intervention advocated by neoconservatives proposing big historical gambles and American-led world revolution.

The broader public cannot afford, however, to leave such matters to historical gamblers. A "neo-isolationist" critique, combining the "right-wing" insight that U.S. intervention corrupts America with the "left-wing" insight that U.S. intervention corrupts the world, might engender a powerful ideological front, forcing a political realignment and a real debate on foreign policy. This debate would involve a searching critique of all standing American ideas of destiny, world mission, and the like; a similar critique of the whole problem of American security in the world; and finally, a thorough critique of the allegedly compulsive nature of overseas trade.

Fortunately, there exist foundations on which to build. One is the survival, despite a half century of mobilization, of a genuine American civil society (Porter 1994, 293). Further, historian Leonard P. Liggio has stressed the continuity—obscured by divisions into left and right—of the social support for peace and nonintervention. War and empire present much the same issues over the long haul, and a homegrown American radicalism, a broad libertarianism, and "isolationism" have reasserted themselves at crisis points in our history (Liggio 1966).

As noted, antiwar forces of left and right have failed to block or even to slow the institutional growth of the entrenched war party. The lack of cooperation between antiwar forces across lines of left and right has compounded this failure. One cause of such disaffection is that peace activists often insist on defining peace in terms of a "just" world (Mueller 1991, 25). This strains communication between them and right-wing noninterventionists, who either believe that the world cannot be changed so fundamentally or oppose the particular changes proposed by left-wing peace advocates. Short-run agreement on a pragmatic definition of peace as the absence of war might improve communication between different sorts of antiwar activists.

It is likewise important that those opposed to empire and its attendant wars understand their own heritage and predecessors. Here, for example, is Senator Calhoun, addressing the Democratic Party on its embrace of President Polk's unitary-executive war with Mexico:

> I, then, opposed the war, not only because it might have been easily avoided; not only because the President had no authority to order a part of the disputed territory in possession of the Mexicans to be occupied by our troops; not only because I believed *the allegations upon which Congress sanctioned the war untrue*; but from high considerations of policy—because I believed it would lead to many and serious evils to the country, and greatly endanger its free institutions. (2003, 642, emphasis added)

Calhoun went on to decry the increase of executive patronage and power resulting from the war, as well as the imperial spirit, and he explained to the Democrats, point by point, how their support for this war undermined their professed political principles (2003, 642). The points are well taken, and whether or not most moderns like Calhoun, his statement of the issues remains trenchant. It could as easily be the statement of a contemporary senator with some sense of the constitutional tradition—perhaps Robert Byrd (D., W.Va.)—addressing George Bush's Republicans in 2005.

Thus, we arrive at the conclusion that it does not matter much at this point who takes up noninterventionist ideas as the basis of policy. If today's Democratic Party should happen, any time soon, to take up the ideas of Borah and Taft, it would be all to the good. That way, at least, we would indeed have a choice and not an echo.

NOTES

1. For a general introduction to libertarianism, see Rothbard [1973] 1978; for an important essay dealing with war and "isolationism" from a libertarian perspective, see Rothbard [1963] 2000b. For the ethical foundations of Rothbard's views, see Rothbard [1982] 1998, esp. 161–97.
2. Whether or not continued expansion into neighboring territories shaped an imperial psychology cannot be dealt with here, but see Vevier 1960.
3. Printed as frontispiece in Barnes 1953. Adams, of course, did not see anything wrong with ongoing U.S. territorial aggrandizement in the Western Hemisphere, until such territorial increase seemed to benefit excessively the slaveholding South.
4. Editor's note: As president, Madison practiced what he preached; see Higgs 2005 for a little-known example.
5. For Madison's core argument, see *Federalist No. 10* in any edition.
6. On continental expansion, see Wilson 1974 and Williams 1973, 180–342.
7. "Extending the area of freedom": Andrew Jackson, 1843, quoted in Weinberg [1935] 1963, 109.
8. On the cause of depressions, see Rothbard [1963] 2000a, 3–36.
9. On the reformers' imperialism, see Semmel 1968 and Ekirch 1969, chap. 11, "The Progressives as Nationalists."
10. On the practical conservatism of reformers, see Kolko 1967 and Weinstein 1968.
11. For deeper background of Turner's thesis, see Benson 1960.
12. On the economists' contribution to the expansionist creed, see "The Origins of the Federal Reserve," part 2 of Rothbard 2002, 208–34.
13. William Appleman Williams's *The Tragedy of American Diplomacy* ([1962] 1972) probably remains the best one-volume summary. In the post–Cold War world, the issue remains the same, as shown by U.S. targeting of "nationalist" regimes that get in the way of the full realization of the Open Door.
14. Here Lincoln was acting within the Whig policy of measured and somewhat state-directed expansion. Many in the Democratic Party, by contrast, favored grabbing new land as fast as possible and then declaring a general free-for-all for yeoman farmers to settle it. On these contrasting styles of expansion, see Wilson 1974.
15. Southern opponents were usually Whigs. Calhoun had wanted Texas, but he feared the consequences of wider territorial acquisitions. For John Archibald Campbell's views, see his letter to John C. Calhoun, November 20, 1847, in Duncan 1905, 138–40.
16. On "Civil War" dissent, see Ekirch 1972, 90–106. On state building—North and South—during the war, see Bensel 1990.
17. For the U.S. military's longstanding commitment to waging total war, see Weigley 1977.
18. Bailey calls it a "spurious mandate" (1974, 478–79).
19. On U.S. support for Britain in South Africa, see Clymer 1975, 158–61.
20. For the British experience with informal empire, see the classic article by Gallagher and Robinson, "The Imperialism of Free Trade" (1953). For a reply that stresses the difference between "free-trade" imperialism and mere free trade, see MacDonagh 1962.
21. Even Williams tends to be a bit unclear on this point, as is McCormick (1967), who otherwise has written a very useful and important book. Marina notes that "it is a mistake to consider anyone who believed in developing American commercial interests as an imperialist" (1968, 100).
22. For a good summary of U.S. policies in World War I, see Raico 1999b.
23. For British prewar plans to outfit Cunard liners as auxiliary cruisers (secretly armed) and for the argument that Churchill and others at the Admiralty connived at the sinking of the

Lusitania to bring America into the war, see Simpson 1972. For more on Churchill's role, see Raico 1999a.

24. Williams defines *weltanschauung* as a "definition of the world combined with an explanation of how it works" (1973, 20).
25. For a postwar example of the literature against munitions makers, see Engelbrecht and Hanighen 1934.
26. Williams rightly observes that the use of the term *isolationists* to characterize opponents of intervention has "crippled American thought about foreign policy for forty years" ([1962] 1972, 107). The term is used here solely for convenience.
27. On Borah, see Pinckney 1960. Williams explicitly refers to Borah and his associates as "laissez-faire liberals" ([1962] 1972, 122–27), and, relatively speaking, this description is true enough.
28. For a discussion of "timid" versus "belligerent" isolationists," see Jonas 1966, 42–69.
29. See Williams [1962] 1972, chap. 5. Important critical studies include Beard 1948; Tansill 1952; Barnes 1953; and Russett 1972.
30. On the AFC, see the classic study by Cole (1953) and the excellent study by Stenehjem (1976). For an unfriendly account of the AFC from which, nonetheless, useful facts can be extracted, see Adler 1961, 273–80. See also Doenecke 1972.
31. For an account of the naval incidents, see Beard 1948, chap. 5, and Russett 1972, 77–83. Russett makes an explicit comparison with President Johnson's Gulf of Tonkin incident.
32. On Flynn, see Stenehjem 1976 and Radosh 1975, 197–229 ("John T. Flynn and the Coming of World War II"). See also Flynn 1940 and [1944] 1973.
33. On this metamorphosis, the best study is Martin 1964.
34. For accounts that lay to rest the myth of AFC "fascism," see Jonas 1967 and Stenehjem 1976, chap. 7, "Anti-Semitism and Profascism in the NYC-AFC: Fact and Fiction," 121–41.
35. Martin has rescued Peace Now from oblivion in "The Bombing and Negotiated Peace Questions—in 1944" (1971, 71–124).
36. On the nonrevolutionary character of Stalin's foreign policy, see Kolko 1970.
37. For background on the Truman Doctrine, see Barnet 1972, 119–45.
38. For Eisenhower's corporatism, see Griffith 1982; for the "galloping" corporatism of the period, see Wiarda 1997, 139–40; and for the politics of defense spending, see Lotchin 1992.
39. For a critical review of Kennedy's foreign policies, see Walton 1973. For JFK's primary responsibility for the Cuban crisis, see chap. 7, 103–42. For more on the Kennedy administration's enthusiasm for a proactive strategy of counterinsurgency, see Miroff 1976.
40. On the "new class" of national-security managers, see Barnet 1972, 36–50, and 1973; and Liggio 1972.
41. For early examples of a new left mood, see Mills 1958, where Mills calls attention to World War II and Korean War atrocities, including terror bombing, and presents a noninterventionist alternative; see also Lens 1964 and the many works of Paul Goodman.
42. On the "vanguard role" of the old right, see Liggio 1970. On teach-ins, see Menashe and Radosh 1967.
43. On Selective Service, see Hess and Reeves 1970; for the infamous Selective Service System memo on "channeling," see 193–200.
44. On SDS, see Sale 1973 and the article "SDS: The New Turn" (1967). Also see Miller 1987.

REFERENCES

Adams, Brooks. [1900] 1947. *America's Economic Supremacy*. New York: Harper.

Adler, Selig. 1961. *The Isolationist Impulse*. New York: Collier Books.

Arieli, Yehoshua. 1964. *Individualism and Nationalism in American Ideology*. Baltimore: Penguin.

Bailey, Thomas A. 1974. *A Diplomatic History of the American People*. 9th ed. Englewood Cliffs, N.J.: Prentice-Hall.

Bailyn, Bernard. 1967. *The Ideological Origins of the American Revolution*. Cambridge, Mass.: Harvard University Press.

Barnes, Harry Elmer. 1929. *The Genesis of the World War: An Introduction to the Problem of War Guilt*. New York: Alfred A. Knopf.

———, ed. 1953. Perpetual War for Perpetual Peace. Caldwell, Idaho: Caxton Printers.

Barnet, Richard J. 1972. *Intervention and Revolution*. New York: New American Library.

———. 1973. *Roots of War*. Baltimore: Penguin.

Baxter, James P. 1928. The British Government and Neutral Rights, 1861–1865. *American Historical Review* 34, no. 1 (October): 9–29.

Beard, Charles A. 1948. *President Roosevelt and the Coming of the War, 1941*. New Haven, Conn.: Yale University Press.

Bensel, Richard Franklin. 1990. *Yankee Leviathan: The Origins of Central State Authority in America, 1859–1877*. Cambridge, U.K.: Cambridge University Press.

Benson, Lee. 1960. *Turner and Beard: American Historical Writing Reconsidered*. New York: Free Press.

Borchard, Edwin M., and William P. Lage. 1937. *Neutrality for the United States*. New Haven, Conn.: Yale University Press.

Calhoun, John C. 2003. Speech on the War with Mexico. In *John C. Calhoun: Selected Writings and Speeches*, edited by H. Lee Cheek, Washington, D.C.: Regnery.

Clymer, Kenton J. 1975. *John Hay: The Gentleman as Diplomat*. Ann Arbor: University of Michigan Press.

Cole, Wayne S. 1953. *America First: The Battle Against Intervention*. Madison: University of Wisconsin Press.

Commager, Henry Steele, ed. 1963. *Documents of American History*. Vol. 1. New York: Applton Century Crofts.

Corwin, Edward S. 1947. *Total War and the Constitution*. New York: Alfred A. Knopf, 1947.

Doenecke, Justus D. 1972. *The Literature of Isolationism: Guide to Non-interventionist Scholarship, 1930–1972*. Colorado Springs, Colo.: Ralph Myles.

———. 1976. Power, Markets, and Ideology: The Isolationist Response to Roosevelt Policy, 1940–1941. In *Watershed of Empire: Essays on New Deal Foreign Policy*, edited by Leonard P. Liggio and James J. Martin, 132–61. Colorado Springs, Colo.: Ralph Myles.

Duncan, George W. 1905. *John Archibald Campbell*. Alabama Historical Society Reprint no. 33. Montgomery: Alabama Historical Society.

Ekirch, Arthur A., Jr. 1966. *Ideas, Ideals, and American Diplomacy*. New York: Appleton Century Crofts.

———. 1969. *The Decline of American Liberalism*. New York: Atheneum.

———. 1972. *The Civilian and the Military: A History of the American Antimilitarist Tradition*. Colorado Springs, Colo.: Ralph Myles.

Engelbrecht, H. C., and F. C. Hanighen. 1934. *Merchants of Death*. New York: Dodd, Mead.

Fay, Sidney B. [1928] 1966. *The Origins of the World War*. 2 vols. New York: Free Press.

Flynn, John T. 1940. *Country Squire in the White House*. New York: Doubleday, Doran.

———. 1944. *The Truth about Pearl Harbor*. New York: J. T. Flynn.

————. [1944] 1973. *As We Go Marching*. New York: Free Life Editions.

Gaddis, John Lewis. 1982. *Strategies of Containment: A Critical Appraisal of Postwar American National Security Policy*. New York: Oxford University Press.

Gallagher, John, and Ronald Robinson. 1953. The Imperialism of Free Trade. *Economic History Review,* 2d ser., 6, no. 1: 1–15.

Gardner, Lloyd C. 1966. *A Different Frontier: Selected Readings in the Foundations of American Economic Expansion*. Chicago: Quadrangle.

Gillette, Howard, Jr. 1973. The Military Occupation of Cuba, 1899–1902: Workshop for American Progressivism. *American Quarterly* 25, no. 4 (October): 410–25.

Grattan, C. Hartley. 1929. *Why We Fought*. New York: Vanguard.

Griffith, Robert. 1982. Dwight D. Eisenhower and the Corporate Commonwealth. *American Historical Review* 87, no. 1 (February): 87–122.

Hatch, Nathan O. 1977. *The Sacred Cause of Liberty: Republican Thought and the Millennium in Revolutionary New England*. New Haven, Conn.: Yale University Press.

Hess, Karl, and Thomas Reeves. 1970. *The End of the Draft*. New York: Random House.

Higgs, Robert. 2005. "Not Merely Perfidious but Ungrateful": The U.S. Takeover of West Florida. *The Independent Review* 10 (fall): 303–10.

Horsman, Reginald. 1981. *Race and Manifest Destiny: The Origins of American Racial Anglo-Saxonism*. Cambridge, Mass.: Harvard University Press.

Jonas, Manfred. 1966. Isolationism in America, 1935–1941. Ithaca, N.Y.: Cornell University Press.

————. 1967. Pro-Axis Sentiment and American Isolationism. *The Historian* 29, no. 2 (February): 221–37.

Keynes, J. M. 1920. *Economic Consequences of the Peace*. New York: Macmillan.

Kolko, Gabriel. 1967. *The Triumph of Conservatism*. Chicago: Quadrangle.

————. 1970. *The Politics of War: The World and United States Foreign Policy, 1943–1945*. New York: Vintage Books.

LaFeber, Walter. 1963. *The New Empire: An Interpretation of American Expansion, 1860–1898*. Ithaca, N.Y.: Cornell University Press.

Lens, Sidney. 1964. *The Futile Crusade: Anti-Communism as American Credo*. Chicago: Quadrangle.

Liggio, Leonard P. 1966a. Americans: Redskins or Palefaces. *Left and Right* 2, no. 3 (autumn): 48–60.

————. 1966b. Isolationism, Old and New. *Left and Right* 2, no. 1 (winter): 19–35.

————. 1970. Massacres in Vietnam. *Libertarian Forum* 2, no. 3 (February 1): 3–4.

————. 1972. American Foreign Policy and National-Security Management. In *A New History of Leviathan: Essays on the Rise of the American Corporate State*, edited by Murray N. Rothbard and Ronald Radosh, 224–59. New York: E. P. Dutton.

Lotchin, Roger W. 1992. *Fortress California, 1910–1961: From Warfare to Welfare*. New York: Oxford University Press.

Lukacs, John A. 1966. *A New History of the Cold War*. Garden City, N.Y.: Anchor Books.

MacDonagh, Oliver. 1962. The Anti-Imperialism of Free Trade. *Economic History Review*, 2d ser., 14, no. 3: 489–501.

Marina, William F. 1968. *Opponents of Empire: An Interpretation of American Anti-imperialism, 1898–1921*. Ph.D. diss., University of Denver.

Martin, James J. 1964. *American Liberalism and World Politics, 1931–1941*. 2 vols. New York: Devin-Adair.

————. 1971. *Revisionist Viewpoints*. Colorado Springs, Colo.: Ralph Myles.

McCormick, Thomas J. 1967. *China Market: America's Quest for Informal Empire, 1893–1901*. Chicago: Quadrangle.

Menashe, Louis, and Ronald Radosh, eds. 1967. *Teach-Ins: U.S.A., Reports, Opinions, Documents*. New York: F. A. Praeger.

Miller, James. 1987. *"Democracy Is in the Streets": From Port Huron to the Siege of Chicago*. New York: Simon and Schuster.

Millis, Walter. 1935. *Road to War: America, 1914–1971*. Boston: Houghton Mifflin.

Mills, C. Wright. 1956. *The Power Elite*. New York: Oxford University Press.

———. 1958. *The Causes of World War Three*. New York: Simon and Schuster.

Miroff, Bruce. 1976. *Pragmatic Illusions: The Presidential Politics of John F. Kennedy*. New York: David McKay.

Monten, Jonathan. 2005. The Roots of the Bush Doctrine: Power, Nationalism, and Democracy Promotion in U.S. Strategy. *International Security* 29 (spring): 112–56.

Mueller, John. 1991. War: Natural, But Not Necessary. In *The Institution of War*, edited by Robert A. Hindle, 13–29. London: Macmillan.

Neumann, William L. 1945. *The Genesis of Pearl Harbor*. Philadelphia: Pacifist Research Bureau.

Nock, Albert Jay. 1922. *The Myth of a Guilty Nation*. New York: B. W. Huebsch.

Noer, Thomas J. 1978. *Boer, Briton, and Yankee: The United States and South Africa, 1870–1914*. Kent, Ohio: Kent State University Press.

Open Door Notes. [1899, 1900] 1966. In *Sources in American Diplomacy*, edited by Armin Rappaport, 139–142. New York: Macmillan.

Pérez, Louis A., Jr. 1985. Insurrection, Intervention, and the Transformation of Land Tenure Systems in Cuba, 1895–1902. *Hispanic American Historical Quarterly* 65, no. 2 (May): 229–54.

———. 1988. *Cuba: Between Reform and Revolution*. New York: Oxford University Press.

Pinckney, Orde S. 1960. William E. Borah: Critic of American Foreign Policy. *Studies on the Left* 1, no. 3: 48–61.

Porter, Bruce. 1994. *War and the Rise of the State*. New York: Free Press.

Radosh, Ronald. 1967. Democracy and the Formation of Foreign Policy: The Case of F.D.R. and America's Entrance into World War II. *Left and Right* 3, no. 3 (autumn): 31–38.

———. 1975. *Prophets on the Right: Profiles of Conservative Critics of American Globalism*. New York: Simon and Schuster.

Raico, Ralph. 1989. The Politics of Hunger: A Review. *Review of Austrian Economics* 3: 253–59.

———. 1999a. Rethinking Churchill. In *The Costs of War: America's Pyrrhic Victories*, edited by John V. Denson, 330–33. New Brunswick, N.J.: Transaction.

———. 1999b. World War I: The Turning Point. In *The Costs of War: America's Pyrrhic Victories*, edited by John V. Denson, 203–47. New Brunswick, N.J.: Transaction.

Rappaport, Armin, ed. 1966. *Sources in American Diplomacy*. New York: Macmillan.

Rothbard, Murray N. 1970. The Hoover Myth. In *For a New America: Essays in History and Politics from Studies on the Left, 1959–1967*, edited by James Weinstein and David W. Eakins, 162–79. New York: Random House.

———. [1973] 1978. *For a New Liberty*. New York: Collier Books.

———. [1982] 1998. *The Ethics of Liberty*. New York: New York University Press.

———. [1963] 2000a. *America's Great Depression*. Auburn, Ala.: Ludwig von Mises Institute.

———. [1963] 2000b. War, Peace, and the State. In *Egalitarianism as a Revolt Against Nature*, 115–32. Auburn, Ala.: Ludwig von Mises Institute.

———. 2002. *A History of Money and Banking in the United States*. Auburn, Ala.: Ludwig von Mises Institute.

Russett, Bruce M. 1972. *No Clear and Present Danger: A Skeptical View of the U.S. Entry into World War II*. New York: Harper Torchbooks.

Sale, Kirkpatrick. 1973. *SDS*. New York: Vintage Books.

SDS: The New Turn. 1967. *Left and Right* 3, no. 1 (winter): 9–17.

Semmel, Bernard. 1968. *Imperialism and Social Reform: English Social-Imperial Thought, 1895–1914*. Garden City, N.Y.: Anchor Books.

Simpson, Colin. 1972. *The Lusitania*. New York: Ballantine Books.

Smith, Goldwin. 1902. *Commonwealth or Empire: a Bystander's View of the Question*. London: Macmillan.

Smuckler, Ralph H. 1953. The Region of Isolationism. *American Political Science Review* 47, no. 2 (June): 386–401.

Stagg, J.C.A. 1981. James Madison and the Coercion of Great Britain: Canada, the West Indies, and the War of 1812. *William and Mary Quarterly*, 3rd ser., 38, no. 1 (January): 3–34.

Stenehjem, Michele Flynn. 1976. *An American First: John T. Flynn and the America First Committee*. New Rochelle, N.Y.: Arlington House.

Stromberg, Joseph R. 1976. Right-Wing Libertarians and the Cold War. *Libertarian Forum* 9, no. 1 (January): 4–7.

———. 1978. Felix Morley: An Old-Fashioned Republican Critic of Statism and Interventionism. *Journal of Libertarian Studies* 2, no. 3 (fall): 269–77.

———. 1999. The Spanish-American War as Trial Run, or Empire Its Own Justification. In *The Costs of War: America's Pyrrhic Victories*, edited by John V. Denson, 169–201. New Brunswick, N.J.: Transaction.

———. 2001. William McKinley: Architect of the American Empire. In *Reassessing the Presidency: The Rise of the Executive State and the Decline of Freedom*, edited by John V. Denson, 319–39. Auburn, Ala.: Ludwig von Mises Institute.

Sumner, William Graham. [1899] 1965. *The Conquest of the United States by Spain*. Chicago: Regnery.

Tansill, Charles C. 1938. *America Goes to War*. Boston: Little, Brown.

———. 1952. *Back Door to War*. Chicago: Henry Regnery.

Turner, Frederick Jackson. [1893] 1920. The Significance of the Frontier in American History. In *The Frontier in American History*, 1–38. New York: Henry Holt.

Tuveson, Ernest Lee. 1968. *Redeemer Nation: The Idea of America's Millennial Role*. Chicago: University of Chicago Press.

Vevier, Charles. 1960. American Continentalism: An Idea of Expansion, 1845–1910. *American Historical Review* 65, no. 2 (January): 323–35.

Walton, Richard J. 1973. *Cold War and Counterrevolution: The Foreign Policy of John F. Kennedy*. Baltimore: Penguin.

Weeks, William Earl. 1992. *John Quincy Adams and American Global Empire*. Louisville: University Press of Kentucky.

Weigley, Russell F. 1977. *The American Way of War: A History of United States Military Strategy and Policy*. Bloomington: Indiana University Press.

Weinberg, Albert K. [1935] 1963. *Manifest Destiny: A Study of Nationalist Expansion in American History*. Chicago: Quadrangle Books.

Weinstein, James. 1968. *The Corporate Ideal in the Liberal State, 1900–1981*. Boston: Beacon Press.

Wiarda, Howard J. 1997. *Corporatism and Comparative Politics: The Other Great "Ism."* London: M. E. Sharpe.

Williams, William Appleman. 1967. American Intervention in Russia: 1917–20. In *Containment and Revolution*, edited by David Horowitz, 26–75. Boston: Beacon Press.

———. 1969. *The Roots of the Modern American Empire*. New York: Random House.

———. [1962] 1972. *The Tragedy of American Diplomacy*. New York: Dell.

———. 1973. *The Contours of American History*. New York: New Viewpoints.

Wilson, Major L. 1974. *Space, Time, and Freedom: The Quest for Nationality and the Irrepressible Conflict, 1815–1861*. Westport, Conn.: Greenwood Press.

Wittner, Lawrence S. 1969. *Rebels Against War: The American Peace Movement, 1941–1960*. New York: Columbia University Press.

Acknowledgment: Reprinted from *The Independent Review*, 11, no. 1 (Summer 2006): 79–113. ISSN 1086-1653, Copyright © 2006.

2

New Deal Nemesis
The "Old Right" Jeffersonians

SHELDON RICHMAN

"Th[e] central question is not clarified, it is obscured, by our common political categories of left, right, and center."
—Carl Oglesby, *Containment and Change*

Modern ignorance about the Old Right was made stark by reactions to H. L. Mencken's diary, published in 1989. The diary received extraordinary attention, and reviewers puzzled over Mencken's opposition to the beloved Franklin Roosevelt, to the New Deal, and to U.S. entry into World War II.[1] Robert Ward's review (1989) was typical. Unable to fathom "Mencken's strange blindness regarding World War II" and his "near pathological hatred of…Roosevelt, whom he regarded as a mountebank," Ward wrote as though no one else in Mencken's America shared those views. He went on to say: "Mencken seemed actually to think that Roosevelt simply conned the United States into entering the war in order to make himself a hero…. Of course, this is shocking and untrue…." (3).

Even Charles A. Fecher, the editor of the diary and a Mencken scholar, could not believe what he read.

> His feelings about World War II are incredible in a man of his intelligence, knowledge, and perception….The whole obscene show is simply "Roosevelt's war."… And the war was far from being the only thing for which he blamed him. His hatred of Roosevelt was, indeed, maniacal—there is no other word to use…. It is hard to ascribe this hatred to ideology. [I]t may well be that he sensed Roosevelt was ushering in a new era of social history…and Mencken, deeply conservative, resentful of change, looking back upon the "happy days"

of a bygone time, wanted no part of the world that the New Deal promised to bring in.[2]

Thus Mencken's opposition to Roosevelt was dismissed—by a man who knew the writer's thought intimately—as the blind fear of change. In this introduction and in most of the commentary on the diary, Mencken was uniformly treated as a lone, idiosyncratic bigot, whose hatred of FDR and the war, if it was to be explained at all, could be the product only of racism and anti-Semitism. One would never glean from these reviewers' astonishment that something approaching a principled national political movement coalesced in opposition to Mencken's twin bugaboos, the New Deal and U.S. participation in the war, and to the man responsible for them, Franklin Roosevelt.[3]

But in fact, H. L. Mencken was not alone, however much he may have felt so. He was joined by a group of people from a variety of occupations—but primarily from politics and journalism—and political backgrounds. They, of course, didn't think of themselves as the "Old Right." That term would not have meaning until a "New Right" arose in the 1950s. Nevertheless, beginning roughly in the mid-1930s, a distinctly identifiable political coalition began to form, consisting of politicians and publicists alarmed by the growth of bureaucratic power in the hands of the national government's executive branch. A distinctive feature of the coalition was its willingness to apply this concern to foreign as well as domestic policy. This rising opposition foresaw danger for the Republic in both realms, and counseled a return to first principles: the U.S. Constitution, separation of powers, checks and balances, decentralization, limited popular rule, individual autonomy; in a word, republicanism. Thus the issue ultimately raised by the umbrella group now known as the Old Right was whether America would remain a land of limited government and individual freedom and initiative, or whether traditional American ideals would be subordinated to a government of unlimited executive power guided by collectivism at home and imperialism abroad—in short, republic versus empire.

The Old Right began as a group of people with disparate backgrounds but awakened by a common threat: Franklin Delano Roosevelt and his unprecedented accretion of executive power.[4] That the movement was placed on the right or called "conservative" has to be regarded a quirk of political semantics.[5] In a superficial sense it qualified as right-wing because it seemed to be defending the status quo from the state-sponsored egalitarian change of the New Deal. But in a deeper sense, the New Deal actually was a defense of the corporativist status quo threatened by the Great Depression. Thus the Old Right was not truly right-wing, and since that is so, it should not be bothersome that some palpable left-wingers, such as Norman Thomas and Robert La Follette, Jr., seemed at home in the Old Right.[6]

The Old Right includes several identifiable strands: "progressive" isolationists (such as Senator William Borah and John T. Flynn), Republican "conservative" isolationists (such as Robert Taft), libertarian and individualist iconoclasts regarded as leftist radicals in the 1920s (Mencken and Albert Jay Nock), conservative Democrats (such as Senator Bennett Champ Clark), World War I revisionists with a social democratic background (such as Harry Elmer Barnes), social democratic opponents of Roosevelt's foreign policy (such as Charles Beard), a trio of individualist women writers (Ayn Rand, Rose Wilder Lane, and Isabel Paterson), a group of free-market liberal economists and journalists (such as Frank Chodorov, Garet Garrett, Leonard Read, F. A. Harper, and no doubt others), and some individual members who defy classification.[7] The categories overlap, but they indicate the diversity.

Some Old Rightists opposed FDR from the start; others inclined toward him, and even supported him, during the election against Herbert Hoover in 1932 and during the first years of the New Deal. They had different rationales for their opposition to the domestic and foreign policies of the 1930s: some were nationalists and unilateralists, others pacifists and classical liberal internationalists in the Richard Cobden tradition.[8] But sooner or later they united in opposition to the actions and the tone of Roosevelt and his Brain Trust. As time went on, the group seemed to draw closer together temperamentally and even philosophically, perhaps in response to the government and the media's overwhelming opposition to it.

The dissimilitude of the strands making up this political braid illustrates that the term Old Right does not denote a precise political architectonic. Most of its members were not of a philosophical bent; rather, they were journalists and office-holders, reacting to events. They were serious thinkers, but for the most part not systematizers. Unsurprisingly, they had disagreements on particulars, especially those pertaining to affirmative ideas. But they knew what they didn't like.

Old Rightism was a frame of mind, a spirit rather than a rigorous philosophy. Its anima was an intransigent individualism in the face of a torrent of collectivism at home and outright dictatorship abroad. Even after the Republican Party establishment accommodated itself to the New Deal in the 1950s, the Old Right pressed the fight. In its particulars, this group held a deep respect for the founding ideals of the United States, namely, the principles of the Declaration of Independence, the Constitution, and a few other documents, such as Washington's Farewell Address. If the Old Rightists had a single hero it would have been Thomas Jefferson. They may not have agreed exactly on what he believed, but they would have endorsed Mencken's view that "Jefferson would have killed himself if he could have seen ahead to Roosevelt II" (1956b, 78).

Their common bogey was power. Concentrated power nullified the autonomous individual; unchecked bureaucracy was an octopus run amuck, its multiplying tentacles strangling what had made America vital. Most would have applauded Henry David Thoreau's observation made in "Civil Disobedience": "Yet this government never of itself furthered any enterprise, but by the alacrity with which it got out of the way" (Bedau 1969, 27), and for most, their aversion to power was especially pronounced in foreign affairs—so much so that this is emblematic of the Old Right.[9] Here all their principles intersected with a vengeance, resulting in a white-hot contempt for secret diplomacy, intrigue, foreign entanglements, imperialism, and their sine qua non, the independent, discretionary presidency—what has been called the Executive State.[10] To the Old Rightists, these practices were unconstitutional intrusions on the prerogatives of the people and of the people's representatives—intrusions worth fighting even when the Old Rightists themselves happened to agree with a particular objective. They also understood that private diplomacy was likely to lead to war, that great scourge of a free society. War, they believed, always resulted in all manner of government control: of the economy, of personal liberty, of the press—the things that must be left unmolested if the dignity and freedom of the individual are to be preserved. This was not high-flown theory for them, but the lessons of the past, most recently World War I, the great leap toward collectivism in America (Rothbard 1989).

Their opposition to war stemmed also from what it would likely do to the rest of the world.[11] Herbert Hoover and Robert A. Taft, during their food-relief efforts in Europe after World War I, understood that Bolshevism came to Russia only after the United States prevailed on the Provisional Government to stay in the war, despite the Russian people's abhorrence of that course. They concluded, according to the historian Leonard P. Liggio (1973), that "Bolshevism was the natural result of the dislocation of war, and they shared the fear that intrigues of the European Allies would sustain that dislocation and permit a wider appeal for Bolshevism" (4). Later they observed that the hardship imposed at Versailles had led to Nazi electoral victories.[12] Viewing the war, the vindictiveness of its participants, and the resulting famine, Hoover said, "Famine is the mother of anarchy," which in turn could only encourage the rise of Bolshevism (Patterson 1972, 76). He set up his famed Hoover Institution for the Study of War, Revolution and Peace precisely to study the connection between war and the rise of totalitarianism. Taft, Hoover, and others recalled this lesson as World War II approached, and when the war was over they felt grimly vindicated as the United States immediately embarked on the Cold War (Editorial 1981, 6; see also Doenecke 1982, 203).

In trying to define the Old Right, one historian emphasizes the negative:

The Old Right, which constituted the American Right-wing from approximately the mid-1930's to the mid-1950's, was, if nothing else, an Opposition movement. Hostility to the Establishment was its hallmark, its very life-blood. In fact, when, in the 1950's, the monthly newsletter *Right* attempted to convey to its readers news of the Right-wing, it was of course forced to define the movement it would be writing about—and it found that it could only define the Right-wing in negative terms: in its total opposition to what it conceived to be the ruling trends of American life. In brief, the Old Right was born and had its being as the opposition movement to the New Deal, and to everything, foreign and domestic, that the New Deal encompassed: at first, to burgeoning New Deal statism at home, and then, later in the '30's, to the drive for American global intervention abroad. Since the essence of the Old Right was a reaction against runaway Big Government at home and overseas, this meant that the Old Right was necessarily, even if not always consistently, libertarian rather than statist, "radical" rather than traditional conservative apologist for the existing order. (Rothbard n.d., 2–3)

As the Old Right passed from the scene in the mid-1950s (for reasons to be discussed later), it was supplanted by a New Right, a group of intellectuals associated with William F. Buckley, Jr., and *National Review* magazine (founded in 1955). This raises a question: Is one justified in speaking of an old and new right? And if there is a New Right, is it an essentially different movement or a new evolutionary stage of the old? Paul Gottfried and Thomas Fleming, in *The Conservative Movement* (1988), treat the right as essentially one continuous movement, and thus fail to recognize it as an amalgam of many conservative and libertarian elements.[13] They use the term old right only when they come to "the emergence of two new conservative forces": the neoconservatives and the "populist and religious New Right" (Gottfried and Fleming 1988, 59). An implication of their position is that the "Buckley Right" is merely the "Taft Right" after a postwar evolution.

One can get this impression because of Buckley's own ties to the Old Right.[14] But this cannot be satisfactory. To insist on this account is to ignore a virtual fire wall between the Taft right and the Buckley right. Many in the Old Right—including Taft, Nock, and Chodorov—rejected the label conservative, regarding it as a left-wing smear word (see Rothbard 1968a, 50; Crunden 1964, 174; and Liggio 1973). Taft's official biographer reports that "Mr. Republican" was uninterested in Russell Kirk's book *The Conservative Mind*. "Taft lacked many of the characteristics often assigned to the 'conservatives' with whom he was conveniently lumped" (Patterson 1972, 330). Although Patterson writes that Taft ultimately "was conservative in the practical sense ordinarily applied to mid twentieth-century American politicians," that is, Taft favored limited government, he ends by calling Taft's philosophy "libertarian" (332–33). On the eve of U.S. entry into World War II, Taft indicated who the real conservatives were: "The most conservative members of the party—the Wall Street bankers, the society group, nine-tenths of the plutocratic newspapers, and most of the party's financial contributors—are the ones who favor intervention in Europe."[15]

The Old Right was temperamentally different from the group associated with Buckley, many of whom were former Trotskyists and advocates of some variant of coercive communitarianism. What was new about this New Right? Clearly, it was the Cold War temperament and the shift in emphasis from individualism to government promotion of virtue. This can be summed up handily as the transmogrification of "Our Enemy, The State" (to use Albert Jay Nock's title) into "Statecraft as Soulcraft" (to use George Will's).

Where once the Right was fervently devoted to the freedoms propounded in the Bill of Rights, it now believes that civil liberties are the work of Russian agents. Where once it stood for the strict separation of Church and State, it now speaks of the obligation of the community to preserve a Christian America through a variety of Blue Laws and other schemes for integrating government and religion. Where once the Right was, above all, dedicated to peace and opposed to foreign entanglements, it now is concerned with preparing for war and giving all-out aid to any dictator, Socialist or otherwise, who proclaims his unbending "anti-Communism." Where once the Right wanted America to exert its moral effect upon the world by being a beacon-light of freedom, it now wants to turn America into an armed camp to crush Communism wherever it appears. (Hamowy 1961, 4–5)

The New Rightists' own words demonstrate the discontinuity between old and new. In a 1952 article, Buckley called for "extensive and productive tax laws…to support a vigorous anti-communist foreign policy." Because of the "thus far invincible aggressiveness of the Soviet Union," he stated, "we have to accept Big Government for the duration—for neither an offensive nor a defensive war can be waged…except through the instrument of a totalitarian bureaucracy within our shores."[16] He also wrote, "Where reconciliation of an individual's and the government's interests cannot be achieved, the interests of the government shall be given exclusive consideration" (quoted in Rothbard 1964, 230). One of his collaborators, James Burnham, lamented that Americans seemed reluctant "to accept the responsibilities of empire" and showed no "willingness to kill people, now and then, without collapsing into a paroxysm of guilt" (Burnham 1971, 749).

Compare such statements to this 1957 statement written by Old Rightist Felix Morley, a founding editor of *Human Events*:

We are trying to make a federal republic do an imperial job.…To make our policies conform to our institutions is to revert to isolationism. It would mean the termination of our alliances; withdrawal of all troops to our own shores; reduction of military expenditure to a truly defensive level; complete indifference to political developments abroad, regardless of whether these help or hinder the advance of Communism. (26)

Or this from Frank Chodorov:

> If we will, we can still save ourselves from the cost of empire building.
> We have only to square off against this propaganda, and to supple-
> ment rationality with a determination that, come what may, we will
> not lend ourselves, as individuals, to this new outrage against hu-
> man dignity....We will resist, by counterpropaganda, every attempt
> to lead us to madness. Above all, when the time comes, we will refuse
> to fight, choosing the self-respect of the prison camp to the ignominy
> of the battlefield. ([1947] 1980, 344)

There is no gainsaying that the Buckley right was indeed a New Right.[17]

The disagreement between Old and New Right over the Cold War is
more than a clash of empirical assessments of a Soviet threat. It runs deeper.
The remnant of the Old Right that remained to fight against the Cold War
was radically antiwar and antimilitarist in the conviction, as we shall see,
that waging the Cold War would bring to America precisely that which the
Cold Warriors claimed to oppose. Where some Old Rightists occasionally
sounded like Cold Warriors, the cause was their exasperation with the New
Deal and Fair Deal "liberals," whom they had reason to despise. When the
Old Right isolationists spoke out against entry into World War II, arguing
that participation would, among other things, aid the spread of Soviet communism, they were smeared as "Vichy Fascists," "Nazi fellow travellers,"
and anti-Semites; harassed by government agents; and in some cases even
prosecuted for sedition (Rothbard 1978, 87–89; see also Doenecke 1982,
212, and Steele, 1979). Later, to their horror, they witnessed Stalin's forces
rolling to the Elbe and cringed at Roosevelt's obeisance toward "Uncle Joe"
and the inevitable codification of Soviet gains at Yalta and Potsdam. They
also witnessed the communist exploitation of the upheaval the war caused
in China. All of this produced an understandable attitude of "we told you
so" toward the liberals. They missed few opportunities to throw the postwar communist gains in the liberals' faces. To be sure, a few Old Rightists slipped into unabashed boosterism for America's Third Crusade (Nash
1976, 126–27). Rothbard (1968b), in studying the issue, employs the useful distinction between broad and narrow revisionism. He writes:

> The narrow Revisionists, who form, unfortunately, the large major-
> ity, have reasoned somewhat as follows: The chief lesson of World
> War I is the injustice heaped upon Germany—first, in launching the

war against her, and then in coercing a confession of sole guilt in the brutal and disastrous Treaty of Versailles. The same focus on an injured Germany then blends into the analysis of World War II, caused essentially by continually repeated obstructions by the Allies of any peaceful revision of a *Versaillesdiktat* which they themselves admitted to be gravely unjust to Germany.

What lesson, then, does the narrow Revisionist draw for the postwar period? Since his concentration is narrowly upon the wrongs suffered by Germany, his conclusion then follows that these wrongs must be put right as quickly as possible; which, in the current context, becomes a compulsory unification of West and East (or for the Revisionist, Middle) Germany, on Western terms, and a return of the lands beyond the Oder-Neisse from Poland. In short, the narrow Revisionist ends, ironically, by yearning for the very sort of unilateral *diktat* and blind *revanche* which he so properly deplored when Germany suffered from their evils. Finally, in his current preoccupation with World War II and the German problem, the narrow Revisionist carries over the old anti-Comintern spirit, or what is now called "hard anti-Communism," into an entirely different era....The narrow Revisionist...has gotten himself enmeshed in a veritable tangle of contradictions. Beginning in dedication to peace, he has become a virtual advocate of total war (against the Soviet Union). (1968b, 316)

To the broad Revisionist, Rothbard continues,

peaceful revision and peaceful negotiation are not ideas solely applicable to Germany [but] are applicable to all times and places, and therefore to the postwar world as well....To the broad Revisionist the great lesson of the two World Wars is precisely to avoid as a very plague any further Great Crusade, and to maintain—if we value the lives and liberties of the American people—a steadfast policy of peaceful coexistence and abstinence from foreign meddling....[I]t is a conclusion in almost diametric opposition to the views of his old narrow-Revisionist colleague. (1968b, 318–19)

Inconsistencies by particular Old Rightists can be found, but they do not invalidate the distinction between old and new. A few Old Right figures, for example, at times inclined toward some aggressive anticommunist or anti-Soviet policies. But they did so with a sense of skepticism and misgiving, a position different from adopting wholeheartedly the New Right's Cold War temperament. This temperament denotes not merely an abhorrence of the doctrines of Marx and Lenin or distress for the victims of Soviet tyranny or concern about communists in the government, all of which the Old Right shared; it also means support for a commitment and readiness by the U.S. government to contain, wear down, and in many cases roll back Soviet forces. Its salient feature is its jihad character, the sense that it is the glorious destiny of the United States, leader of the Free World, to destroy Godless Communism.

Although the New Right was built predominantly by figures not associated with the Old Right, some Old Rightists broke ranks after World War II. The historian William Henry Chamberlin, who changed from communist sympathizer to right-wing war foe in 1940 to advocate of anti-Soviet activism and red-baiter of Old Rightists in 1945, and John Chamberlain, critic, editor, and economics writer, who followed a similar trajectory, both adopted the Buckley group's foreign policy.[18] Similarly, Senator Arthur Vandenberg, an opponent of U.S. participation in World War II, pirouetted into an establishment booster of the Cold War and bipartisan foreign policy.

Only by recognizing the distinctiveness of the Old Right, especially in its analysis of foreign policy, can one acquire an accurate picture of American political history and the rise of an overtly libertarian movement in the late twentieth century.

Professionally, the Old Right consisted of members of Congress, other politicians, writers, and businessmen. Many were veterans of the fight against Prohibition and in some cases members of the anti-Roosevelt American Liberty League.[19] What ultimately united these individuals was the determination to resist the swallowing up of American ideals, institutions, and traditions by the monster of collectivism, which in different forms they saw settled or settling in Moscow, Rome, and Berlin and threatening to settle in Washington. Key Old Right figures will be discussed in two groups: politicians and publicists.

THE POLITICIANS

Beginning in the mid-1930s a group of U.S. Senators and Representatives coalesced in opposition to the policies of Franklin Roosevelt. It was a diverse group, including some who were uneasy with Roosevelt from the start, even if they had voted with him, and some who, despairing over the Great Depression, at first had hopes that the New Deal would work. Those to be discussed were critical of Roosevelt in both foreign and domestic policy. Congressmen who opposed him in one realm only do not seem to qualify as Old Rightists. Several conservative Democrats, for example, including Senators Carter Glass of Virginia, Thomas P. Gore of Oklahoma, and Harry Byrd of Virginia, despised Roosevelt's domestic policies from the start, but supported his pro-war measures (see Patterson 1967, 19–31, 337). In contrast, the progressive Republican Senator Robert La Follette, Jr., of Wisconsin opposed the war measures while pushing for domestic policies even more interventionist than Roosevelt's.

The congressional foes of the domestic and foreign New Deal included a small number of conservative, or "Cleveland," Democrats, such as Bennett Champ Clark of Missouri, Patrick McCarran of Nevada, and David I. Walsh of Massachusetts (Patterson 1967, 337). The western and midwestern progressive-isolationist Republicans made up another group of congressional opponents of the New Deal, foreign and domestic. Some of them were politicians who won their first political medals in the 1920s and saw themselves as in the tradition of Theodore Roosevelt and Woodrow Wilson.[20] This bloc included William Borah of Idaho, Hiram Johnson of California, Gerald Nye of North Dakota, Henrik Shipstead of Minnesota, and several others. It is useful to consider with this group their ideological brother Senator Burton K. Wheeler of Montana, although he was a Democrat. These men began as sympathetic to the New Deal. The depression and what they regarded as Hoover's half-hearted response to it distressed the Republican progressives, and in the 1932 election they either supported Roosevelt (Hiram Johnson, for example) or were neutral (William Borah and Gerald Nye) because they could not bring themselves to bless Hoover (Feinman 1981, 20). (Roosevelt ran a campaign of contradictions, promising both to cut federal spending by 25 percent and to increase aid to the unemployed, that is, to reduce and increase federal power [Leuchtenburg 1963, 10–11].) In the famous first hundred days the progressive bloc was part of the "tractable Congress" (Patterson's term) that gave Roosevelt what he wanted. But the bloc was not firmly in his pocket. Its growing dislike of the New Deal "represented an older hostility to centralized power, be it corporate or governmental" (Patterson 1967, 116). The aversion to power sprang from its fundamental individualism (Graham 1967, 176).

The earliest fight with Roosevelt that has the markings of the inchoate Old Right's participation was, aptly, in foreign affairs, when the isolationists in 1935 defeated Roosevelt's proposal to have the United States join the World Court (Leuchtenburg 1963, 216–17). Other early conflicts with Roosevelt had to do with neutrality, as auguries of war arose in Europe. Here the essential constitutional issue emerged starkly. Throughout the neutrality fights of 1935, 1936, and 1937, the point of battle was executive discretion, with the isolationists trying to deprive Roosevelt of room to maneuver and the president trying to maximize his flexibility.

The event that arguably catalyzed the emergence of a full-fledged Old Right was Roosevelt's attempt to pack the Supreme Court. During the early New Deal, the U.S. Supreme Court was the one bulwark that kept Roosevelt from carrying out all his plans. In 1935 and 1936, respectively, the pillars of the New Deal—the National Industrial Recovery Act and the Agricultural Adjustment Act—dropped like trees giving way to the logger's blade.[21] It was a shocking blow to FDR and the zealous New Dealers. The progressives had been uneasy with these programs from the beginning. Although they tended to support Roosevelt's relief measures, they disliked the direction of the NIRA and AAA. In the fall of 1934, Borah wrote to a constituent:

> I feel very strongly that the situation in this country is critical in more ways than one. It is critical economically and governmentally....If I am not mistaken, the trend in some aspects is absolutely at war with the fundamental principles of American institutions, and will ultimately undermine many of the rights of the citizen. (Feinman 1981, 78)

Borah, Nye, Wheeler, and others distrusted programs such as the NIRA that handed extraordinary power to businessmen. They despised the government-enforced codes and price-fixing and the suspension of the antitrust laws. They equally abhorred the AAA's crop destruction and other controls. Some observers thought it odd that those veteran progressives objected to Roosevelt's first measures, but their objections to the programs were entirely consistent with their stated philosophy. As progressives, they distrusted the concentration of power, which is what they saw in the early New Deal.

> Their first and most frequent complaint was that the New Deal was unforgivably coercive, and far from entering upon that role with hesitation, apologies, and promises of early retrenchment, it gave all

signs of a permanent Federal paternalism. Without question it was NRA that most embodied this trend toward statism (with AAA corroborating evidence), but even after the death of NRA these progressives perceived signs enough that the New Deal could be summed up as a drive toward a permanent collectivism. (Graham 1967, 66–67)

They had been sympathetic to government activism earlier in the century, but things had changed.

The writings of the progressives are strewn with worried references to Mussolini and Hitler and Stalin, to the emergence of malignant totalitarian regimes. The progressive American, never entirely at home with the state because he was an American before he was a progressive, saw in Europe's conversion to totalitarianism a case of history teaching by negative example that those who proposed to grant further power to government in the cause of social reform were headed in the wrong direction. Reformers, apparently, had overestimated the amiability of government—that was the lesson of 1917 in Europe, and of 1922, and of 1933. (Graham 1967, 48)

If they had doubts about Roosevelt's direction before the Supreme Court acted, those doubts were reinforced with steel rods by his official response to the decisions. On February 5, 1937, Roosevelt asked Congress to restructure the court so that whenever a justice who had held his position for ten years or more waited longer than six months to retire after his seventieth birthday, the president could name an additional justice to the bench. Roosevelt justified this bill (not a constitutional amendment) on grounds that the court was overworked and inefficient because of the advanced age of many of the justices. Six of the nine members were over seventy, so under the proposed plan Roosevelt could name six additional justices.

The rationalization was transparent, as Roosevelt's adversaries hastened to point out, and the opposition quickly congealed (Leuchtenburg 1963, 233). The leader of the Senate opposition was the Democrat Burton K. Wheeler. He wrote to the socialist Norman Thomas, "It is an easy step from the control of a subservient Congress and the control of the Supreme Court to a modern democracy of a Hitler or a Mussolini" (Ekirch [1955] 1969, 199). And a future Republican senator who was yet to have his season also denounced the plan. "If the present attempt succeeds," said Robert A. Taft of Ohio, "it will practically mean an end of the Constitution and of judicial independence" (Cole 1983, 217). On July 22, 1937, the proposal was interred permanently in the Senate Judiciary Committee. Its demise elicited a "Glory be to God!" from Senator Johnson.[22]

Thwarted on the domestic front, Roosevelt turned to foreign affairs. On October 5, 1937, he went to Chicago to dedicate the Outer Link Bridge, which was funded by the Public Works Administration. With the Sino-Japanese war raging, he used the occasion to speak on foreign policy. He called for peace-loving states to cooperate against the war makers, using the analogy of the need to quarantine the contagiously ill (Cole 1983, 244–45).

Most of the isolationists in the Senate were livid; some threatened impeachment (Leuchtenburg 1963, 226). Borah predicted that if Japanese goods were boycotted, the United States would be "fooling with dynamite" (Cole 1983, 246). Shortly after Roosevelt's speech, Borah wrote:

> But this running around over the world trying to placate every situation and adjust every controversy is not the business of a democracy. A democracy must live at home or have no life. Totalitarian states which have absolute control over their subjects and may send them into any way that personal discretion or ambition suggests may engage in combat against aggressors, and so forth, but democracies cannot do so.[23]

Johnson syllogized, "The levying of sanctions means their enforcement and their enforcement means the Navy's activity. At once then you have war." He remarked that "the President with his delusions of grandeur sees himself the savior of mankind," and he went on to charge that Roosevelt was trying to take the public mind's off domestic woes (Cole 1983, 246–47). The fear that Roosevelt wished to intervene against Japan made the anti-interventionists suspicious of the naval appropriations bill that was before Congress.

The isolationists were so distrustful of Roosevelt that Johnson didn't want the Senate to adjourn for fear that the president would get involved in war. "We must be on guard…," Johnson said on the Senate floor, "every minute of the day and every minute of the night in the days to come, to see that we shall not participate in a war which is none of our concern" (Feinman 1981, 180).

When Germany invaded Poland in September 1939, the isolationists resisted against all odds Roosevelt's attempt to change the neutrality laws. Borah and Johnson were unalterably against ending the arms embargo. In his

last speech before his death in January 1940, Borah marshaled his legend-
ary oratorical skills to indict the "war hounds of Europe" and to condemn
the war as "nothing more than another chapter in the bloody volume of
European power politics." In a moving scene, the Senate gallery burst into
applause and fellow Senators congratulated him (Feinman 1981, 184).
Lend-Lease also attracted dispute: the fiery Johnson referred to it as "the
New Deal's triple 'A' foreign policy" and alleged that it would "plough under every fourth American boy."[24] The prospects of an alliance with the
Soviet Union upset Clark: "Once we have crawled into bed with 'Bloody
Joe' no restraints are possible on the spread of Communist propaganda in
this country" (*America First Bulletin* 1941, 1).

Senator Robert Taft, elected in 1938, zeroed in on Roosevelt's apparent
disregard of democracy:

> One day the President sends American troops to Iceland in the war
> zone. The next day he refuses to submit to Congress the question
> whether troops should be sent to foreign lands. That is not democ-
> racy. The occupation of Iceland indicates a deliberate policy to in-
> volve the United States in war without Congressional action....If the
> occupation of Iceland is defense, then any act the President cares to
> order is defense. (Stout 1942, 176)

Taft also feared that U.S. involvement in the war would lead to American
imperialism. The war advocates, he said, "seem to contemplate an Anglo-
American alliance perpetually ruling the world....Such imperialism is wholly foreign to our ideas of democracy and freedom" (Patterson 1972, 245).

But the moving oratory could not stop the Roosevelt juggernaut. Congress proceeded to enact what the president wanted: neutrality revision,
conscription, loans to Britain, extension of the draft, two lend-lease bills,
and other laws to facilitate American involvement in the war.

Still the isolationists did not give up. The Old Right members of Congress carried their activities beyond the Capitol. Some of them, for instance,
got involved in the America First Committee, which was formed in the
fall of 1940 after the destroyers-for-bases deal.[25] Senators who were either
members of or advisers to the committee included Nye, Wheeler, Johnson,
Shipstead, and Arthur Capper of Kansas (Feinman 1981, 190).

With the Japanese attack on Pearl Harbor and the U.S. declaration of
war, the fighting in Congress was essentially over. But within the Repub-

lican Party, the battle between isolationists and internationalists was just beginning. At a National Republican Committee meeting in April 1942, Taft opposed a resolution by Wendell Willkie that Taft thought sounded like a repudiation of the Republican congressional isolationists. He presciently feared they were "heading for a direct fight for control of the Party machinery" and that "it would be fatal to the future of the Party if Willkie, [Henry] Luce and Dorothy Thompson, together with the wealthy crowd in the east, succeed in their aim." He said Willkie was wrong to think that the Republican path to victory lay in "being more warlike than Roosevelt" (Cole 1983, 519).

At this point we must broaden the political inquiry to look beyond Congress. The two figures to be briefly discussed are Herbert Hoover and Charles A. Lindbergh, Jr.

Hoover, as Joan Hoff Wilson has dubbed him, is the "Forgotten Progressive," neither an advocate of laissez-faire nor a conservative in the New Right sense.[26] Despite inconsistencies after World War II, especially regarding Asia, he was a committed noninterventionist. His overriding conviction was that war leads to economic upheaval, which, in turn, leads to revolution and the self-styled savior who promises to right everything if he is given all power. The resulting totalitarian doctrines and social experiments doom the otherwise natural and peaceful evolution toward individual liberty. His view had a great influence on several Old Right publicists. In 1922 he wrote about the aftermath of the Great War:

> We have witnessed in the last eight years the spread of revolution over one-third of the world. The causes of these explosions lie at far greater depths than the failure of governments in war. The war itself in its last stages was a conflict of social philosophies—but beyond this the causes of social explosion lay in the great inequalities and injustices of centuries flogged beyond endurance by the conflict and freed from restraint by the destruction of war. (1)

Hoover came to oppose intervention because, as he had told Woodrow Wilson,

> we should probably be involved in years of police duty, and our first act would probably, in the nature of things, make us a party to establishing the reactionary classes in their economic domination over

the other classes. This is against our fundamental national spirit and I doubt whether our soldiers under these circumstances could resist infection with Bolshevik ideas. (Wilson 1975, 54–55)

He disliked Roosevelt's "quarantine" speech and approved the Munich settlement (Wilson 1975, 239). Although he later supported aid to England short of American troops, he opposed active U.S. participation in the war (against either Russia or Germany) and suspected that Roosevelt was intent on entry. He referred to FDR's "fireside chats" as "fire-provoking chats" (247). He also feared that the president's pressure on Japan was strengthening the regime there and that it would lead to war. When Germany attacked the Soviet Union, Hoover expected Hitler to defeat Stalin and make peace with England (247–48). When Japan attacked Pearl Harbor Hoover did not dissent in public, but privately he looked forward to an investigation. He wrote in several letters on December 8, 1941, "You and I know that this continuous putting pins in rattlesnakes finally got this country bitten."[27]

During the early stages of the Cold War, Hoover refused to appear before the House Un-American Activities Committee and to become chairman of President Truman's commission "to report on the question of infiltration of Communists in Government." According to Joan Hoff Wilson (1975), "Hoover's anticommunism was so nonmilitaristic that he was later called 'a tool of the Kremlin' by Cold Warriors during the Truman and Eisenhower administrations of the early 1950s" (237).

He generally opposed coercion both at home and abroad in the fight against communism. In a 1941 radio broadcast, he said "we cannot slay an idea or an ideology with machine guns. Ideas live until they have proved themselves right or wrong" (Wilson 1975, 238). He was critical of the Korean War, presuming that the "Reds just want to bleed us to death with these small-scale wars," though he had approved the Truman Doctrine and its aid to Greece and Turkey (Wilson 1975, 265). In the end he expressed a position that compromised: in place of the containment doctrine, strong air and naval protection of the Western Hemisphere and "watchful waiting before we take on any commitments." He predicted that the "evils of communism…will bring their own disintegration"—one of the Old Right's several correct predictions.[28]

Lindbergh was an American hero, a dashing aviator, an America First national-committee member and its most popular spokesman, and someone with as much charisma as Franklin Roosevelt (see Cole [1953] 1971,

1974). His work in rallying public opposition to entry into World War II was instrumental in keeping the pressure on the president and Congress for as long as it lasted. Smeared as a fascist and anti-Semite, he and his wife, Anne Morrow Lindbergh, persevered energetically only to see their efforts blown apart along with the ships at Pearl Harbor.

In his "A Letter to Americans" (1941) Lindbergh blamed the war on England and France's refusal "to take part in a European readjustment while there was still time to make it peacefully" (63–81). "Adjustments that should have been made in peace and moderation," he wrote, "were finally brought by war and resulted in immoderation" (Schoonmaker and Reid 1941, 63–64). Having failed to remove the seeds of future hostilities, England and France then became complacent and allowed Germany to surpass them in strength. By the time they were willing to fight, they were inferior militarily. The United States found itself in a similar situation. While the German-Russian alliance was still in force, Lindbergh wrote:

> We, in America, are being led to war by a group of interventionists, and foreign interests, against the will of a majority of our people. Every poll of public opinion has shown that from 80 to 95 per cent of Americans are opposed to entering this war. Both the Republican and Democratic parties were forced to incorporate antiwar planks in their platforms. Both presidential candidates were compelled to take a stand against our intervention. Yet, today, although no one has made an attempt to attack us, we already have one foot in the war. (Schoonmaker and Reid 1941, 69)

He forcefully rejected, as "entirely out of the question," the argument that Germany could invade the United States by air (78). Lindbergh closed the letter with a call to the American people to write their senators, representatives, and local newspapers:

> We should not be conscripting our youth for a foreign war they do not wish to fight....If our American ideals are to survive, it will not be through the narcotic of foreign war, but through a reawakening of the spirit that brought this nation into existence.[29]

With U.S. entry into the war a fait accompli, Taft took center stage for the Old Right. He did so more because of his station and prestige than because of the purity of his stand; for though many of his colleagues were

more consistent in battling U.S. globalism after World War II, Taft's emi-
nence made him the rallying point for the Opposition and for its hopes of
capturing the White House.

Despite his policy lapses, Taft earned his place as the leader of the Opposition because of his core belief in limited government and individual
liberty and his skepticism that America's proper role in the world was that of
policeman or proconsul. He had no illusions about an American mission to
bring democracy to the world at the point of a bayonet or in the radioactive
plume of a mushroom cloud. For him foreign policy had but one objective:
the security of the lives and property of the American people. As he prepared his bid for the Republican presidential nomination, he wrote in his
1951 book, *A Foreign Policy for Americans:*

> There are a good many Americans who talk about an American cen-
> tury in which America will dominate the world. They rightly point
> out that the United States is so powerful today that we should assume
> a moral leadership in the world to solve all the troubles of mankind.
> I agree that we need that moral leadership not only abroad but also
> at home. We can take the moral leadership in trying to improve the
> international organization for peace....
>
> If we confine our activities to the field of moral leadership we
> shall be successful if our philosophy is sound and appeals to the peo-
> ple of the world. The trouble with those who advocate this policy is
> that they really do not confine themselves to moral leadership. They
> are inspired with the same kind of New Deal planned-control ideas
> abroad as recent Administrations have desired to endorse at home.
> In their hearts they want to force on these foreign peoples through
> the use of American money and even, perhaps, American arms the
> policies which moral leadership is able to advance only through the
> sound strength of its principles and the force of its persuasion. I do
> not think this moral leadership ideal justifies our engaging in any
> preventive war, or going to the defense of one country against anoth-
> er, or getting ourselves into a vulnerable fiscal and economic position
> at home which may invite war. I do not believe any policy which has
> behind it the threat of military force is justified as part of the basic
> foreign policy of the United States except to defend the liberty of our
> own people. (17–18)

Perhaps Taft's greatest contribution was his attempt to force a public debate on postwar foreign policy. In the sliver of time between the close of the world war and the opening of the Cold War, the policymakers had put together a bipartisan coalition in support of American globalism. The dash toward bipartisan foreign policy might have squelched all debate had it not been for Taft's public dissent. He would have endorsed the remark of Felix Morley, a founding editor of *Human Events:* "Politics can stop at the water's edge only when policies stop at the water's edge. Policies no longer stop there" (1948, 4).

Early on, Taft expressed skepticism at President Truman's foreign policy and its official rationale. In 1947, when Truman promulgated his Truman Doctrine and asked for military aid to Greece and Turkey, Taft struck at the president's "policy to divide the world into zones of political influence, Communist and non-Communist" (quoted in Liggio [1965] 1978, 24). He feared that Truman had imperial aims and that the Russians would be provoked into war "just as we might go to war if Russia tried to force a communist government on Cuba" (quoted in Stromberg 1971a, 11; see also Berger 1967, 129). But Taft finally voted for the aid, after concluding that war would not ensue, because Truman had virtually made a commitment and "to repudiate it now would destroy his prestige in the negotiations with the Russian Government" (Berger 1967, 130). Taft's vote demonstrates Randolph Bourne's point that so-called democratic checks on executive war-making power are largely chimerical.[30]

In the same year, when Secretary of State Gen. George Marshall proposed the vast foreign-aid program for Europe, Taft was "absolutely opposed," arguing it would furnish anti-imperialist arguments for the communists. But, again, he ultimately voted with the administration, after unsuccessfully trying to amend the law, because of America's tradition of charity and because he believed the program would assist in the ideological battle against communism. However, he thought the premise of the program was that the Russians did not plan on war (Berger 1967, 132).

He did not regard the Soviet occupation of eastern Europe, accomplished during the rolling back of an invading force, a portent of aggression. The conflict with the Soviet Union, he said, was ideological, not military, and he maintained he had "not believed that Russia intends or desires conquest by force of arms of additional territory" (Liggio [1965] 1978, 29). When the administration tried to exploit the Czech coup in March 1948 for its own purposes, Taft responded:

> I do not quite understand the statements made yesterday by Secretary Marshall and President Truman. They do not imply that they believe that we do face a war question; and then they seem to use the concern which is aroused to urge the passage of this particular program [the Marshall Plan]. I do not believe that the two are connected.... I believe that the tone of the President's statement that his confidence in ultimate world peace has been shaken is unfortunate. Certainly it is no argument for the passage of the current bill....But let me say that I myself know of no particular indication of Russian intentions to undertake military aggression beyond the sphere of influence which was originally assigned to the Russians. The situation in Czechoslovakia is indeed a tragic one; but the Russian influence has been predominant in Czechoslovakia since the end of the war. The Communists are merely consolidating their position in Czechoslovakia; but there has been no military aggression, since the end of the war. (Liggio [1965] 1978, 30–31, quoting *Congressional Record*, 80th Cong., 2d sess., 2643–44)

The shiniest, fattest rhinestone in Truman's Cold War costume jewelry was the North Atlantic Treaty Organization, which he proposed after the Czech coup and the Berlin blockade. Taft led the opposition. "I cannot vote for a treaty which, in my opinion, will do far more to bring about a third world war than it will ever to maintain the peace of the world," he said (quoted in Liggio [1965] 1978, 33). Taft particularly objected to the obligation of the United States to arm western Europe, which he found provocative, and to the U.S. commitment to go to war if any of the members is attacked—even if the attack is justified or launched by another member. In other words, Taft did not like putting the United States, as he described it, "at the mercy of the foreign policies of 11 other nations" (Stromberg 1971a, 14). He also thought the treaty violated the purpose of the United Nations by dividing the world into "two armed camps" (16).

Taft's alternative was not "isolationism," but rather the extension of the Monroe Doctrine to western Europe. In other words, if the Soviet Union attacks western Europe, "it will be at war with us" (Stromberg 1971a, 14).

Taft's policy did not carry the day, and he voted against the North Atlantic Treaty. This vote stands out because in his ambivalence, either genuine or politically motivated, Taft cast other votes that contradicted the spirit of the Old Right. Despite his opposition to universal military training, for example, he voted for conscription three times, in 1948, 1950, and 1951. (He had opposed it in 1940 and 1941.)[31]

When Truman sent troops to Korea, Taft initially confined his objections to the constitutional: "If the president can intervene in Korea without congressional approval, he can go to war in Malaya or Indonesia or Iran or South America" (Stromberg 1971a, 18). Otherwise he supported vigorous prosecution of the war. He criticized the Truman administration for inviting the attack by announcing that Korea was not important to U.S. defense strategy. He said further that the difficult position the United States found itself in after Communist China entered the war resulted from the administration's decision to give Nationalist China on Formosa "one hundred per cent support." Departing from Hoover and Joseph P. Kennedy, however, he opposed withdrawal from Korea (Taft 1951, 107–9), and he supported air strikes on Manchuria and South China even at the risk of bringing Russia into the war (Berger 1967, 135).

Yet these actions do not fully convey Taft's position. He told reporters in 1951 that had he been president, he would not have sent troops to Korea. He also said he would "fall back to a defensible position in Japan and Formosa" (Patterson 1972, 485). Later he seemed willing to make a truce on the basis of the thirty-eighth parallel (489, 601). This position, along with that of Hoover and Kennedy, provoked *The New Republic* to denounce the Old Right as "the Stalinist caucus" (Liggio [1965] 1978, 39).

Despite Taft's tergiversation, he was seen as the best bet to challenge the Republican eastern establishment for the presidential nomination in 1952. Among other distinctions, he opposed Truman's seizure of the steel mills in April 1952 as an unconstitutional exercise of power. The establishment, uncomfortable with the man from Ohio who wished to cut foreign aid and have Europe pay more for its own defense, was able to win the nomination for political newcomer Dwight Eisenhower. Among the delegates voting against Taft were Richard Nixon and Barry Goldwater.

In his May 1953 final statement on foreign policy, Taft reiterated his strongest noninterventionist points, focusing especially on Indochina (Liggio [1965] 1978, 44). Taft died in July 1953, but his supporters in Eisenhower's cabinet apparently persuaded the president to resist calls for sending American soldiers, naval forces, and bombers to aid the French colonialists (45).

Other Old Right congressional figures possessed the resolve Taft at times seemed to lack. For example, George Bender of Ohio, a representative and later Taft's successor in the Senate, denounced the Truman doctrine as imperialistic:

> I believe that the White House program is a reaffirmation of the nineteenth century belief in power politics. It is a refinement of the policy first adopted after the Treaty of Versailles in 1919 designed to encircle Russia and establish a "Cordon Sanitaire" around the Soviet Union. It is a program which points to a new policy of interventionism in Europe as a corollary to our Monroe Doctrine in South America. (Liggio [1965] 1978, 24–25, quoting Cong. Rec., 80th Cong., 2d sess., 2831–32)

Perhaps the firmest of all congressional Old Rightists was Howard Buffett, representative from Nebraska (1947–53) and father of investment guru Warren Buffett, chairman of Berkshire Hathaway, Inc. Howard Buffett was Taft's midwest campaign manager in 1952 and a self-conscious member of the fledgling libertarian movement.[32] What he opposed most of all was imperialism and its chief requirement, conscription. In 1944, in a speech against U.S. government funding of an Arabian oil pipeline, Buffett blasted the project as a "gigantic long-distance venture into imperialism." He added, "to defend this far-away imperialistic economic venture a volunteer army large enough could not be raised" (Stromberg 1971b, 2).

Buffett was among the earliest of Cold War opponents and as a result was red-baited by a colleague. In battling the Truman Doctrine, he prophesied that "all over the world we would soon be answering alarms like an international fireman, maintaining garrisons, and pouring out our resources." He continued: "Even if it were desirable, America is not strong enough to police the world by military force. If that attempt is made, the blessings of liberty will be replaced by coercion and tyranny at home" (Stromberg 1971b, 5).

In 1948 he fought the selective-service bill, stating that "This measure would declare to the world that Hitler was right—that the threat of communism externally justified militarism and regimentation at home." He condemned the draft as embodying the "totalitarian concept that the state owns the individual" (Stromberg 1971b, 7). And when the Korean War came along, Buffett refused to be stampeded into support, as so many on the Left and Right were. Murray Rothbard (1968a) reported:

> Howard Buffett was convinced that the United States was largely responsible for the eruption of conflict in Korea; for the rest of his life he tried unsuccessfully to get the Senate Armed Services Committee to declassify the testimony of CIA head Admiral Hillenkoeter, which Buffett told me established American responsibility for the Korean outbreak. (49)

As the mid-1950s approached, the Old Right contingent in Congress dwindled as members died or retired. The last stand concerned the Bricker Amendment, which would have nullified any treaty provision that conflicted with standing law or with a provision of the Constitution. The liberals and the Eisenhower administration opposed it. In February 1954 it died, a metaphor for the Old Right itself.

THE PUBLICISTS

If the Old Right can be said to have had godfathers, they are H. L. Mencken and Albert Jay Nock. Mencken was born in 1880, Nock in 1870. Both were writers and editors; both were resolute individualists who saw the state as an imposition; both were branded left-wing radicals in the twenties and right-wing conservatives in the thirties. In truth, both were classical liberals, or libertarians. They were longtime good friends who agreed on virtually everything. When it was suggested in 1944 that they engage in correspondence about current issues in order to construct a book, Mencken turned down the project. "The truth is," he wrote in his diary, "that Nock and I are so close in our main ideas that it would be impossible to get up much interest in the correspondence between us. There would be no conflict whatsoever, but only an incessant ratification and acquiescence" (1989, 295). Mencken's taste in books of correspondence was indicated some time earlier, in 1910, when he and Robert Rives La Monte published a debate on socialism. In it Mencken expressed his abhorrence for any system that would interfere with the creative "superior" individual (see Mencken and La Monte 1910).

Throughout his long career as a newspaper man, literary critic, magazine editor, book author, social commentator, scholar, and philologist, the lifelong Baltimorean always ranked individual liberty at the top of his values. A man as widely read and discussed as Mencken was in the 1920s could hardly have failed to influence many people.[33]

Mencken, the self-styled "extreme libertarian," consistently set himself against those whom he saw as the enemies of liberty: William Jennings Bryan, Theodore Roosevelt, Woodrow Wilson, and A. Mitchell Palmer, to name a few. With unparalleled gusto, he battled Prohibition, censorship, and other manifestations of Puritanism.[34]

Mencken publicly fulminated against World War II until he suspended his relationship with the *Sun* papers of Baltimore in 1941. He wrote that the British were merely trying to squelch a rival power on the continent. "It is a rational reason," he wrote, "but it is as devoid of moral content as a theorem in algebra or a college yell" (quoted in Jonas 1966, 228). This article was reprinted in the 1941 book *Keeping U.S. Out of War* (edited by Porter Sargent). In 1939 he noted, "Wars are not made by common folk, scratching for livings in the heat of the day; but by demagogues infesting palaces" (quoted in Helfrich 1948, 4). Later, in his diary, he wrote, "War, in this country wipes out all the rules of fair play, even those prevailing among wild animals. Even the dissenters from the prevailing balderdash seek to escape the penalties of dissent by whooping up the official doctrine" (1989, 357).

Mencken of course also hated the domestic New Deal and everything else touched by "Roosevelt II," as he called FDR: "There is, in fact, only one intelligible idea in the whole More Abundant Life rumble-bumble, and that idea is the idea that whatever A earns really belongs to B. A is any honest and industrious man or woman; B is any drone or jackass" (Mencken 1956, 306). When Roosevelt devalued the dollar, Mencken displayed his impeccable libertarian instinct by crying, "robbery!" and threatened to go into court (Forgue [1961] 1981, xviii).

Albert Jay Nock, like Mencken, was a "tory anarchist," that is, an anti-egalitarian individualist advocate of minimal government. Influenced by Thomas Jefferson, Henry George, Herbert Spencer, and Franz Oppenheimer,[35] Nock combined a knowledge of history and sociology to construct a worldview antithetical to the ruling notions of his day. For Nock, as for Oppenheimer, there was an irreconcilable contest between social power, the network of consensual relations and transactions, and state power, the web of coercive impositions; when one gains, the other loses. In the twenties, when he edited *The Freeman* and published often in Mencken's *American Mercury*, he railed against plutocracy, tariffs, and conformity. As a regular *Mercury* columnist and book author in the 1930s, he attacked the same philosophy, though the targets had a new facade: egalitarian New Dealism.

What he disliked most about the state was that it impoverished the soul. In 1934 he wrote:

> The worst of this ever growing cancer of Statism is its moral effect. The country is rich enough to stand its frightful economic wastage for a long time yet, and still prosper, but it is already so poverty-stricken in its moral resources that the present drain will quickly run them out. I was talking tonight with an old acquaintance in the textile business who said his business had been in the red for eight years, but he had kept it going because he felt responsible for his people and did not like to turn them adrift. "I don't feel that way now," he said. "If the government proposes to tell me how I shall run my business, it can jolly well take the responsibility." That is the frame of mind that Statism inevitably breeds, and a nation that is in that frame of mind is simply no nation at all, as the experience of Rome in the second century shows. (Nock 1948, 11–12)

Although the Democrats won his immediate ire, the clear-eyed Nock had no illusions about the Republicans. He wrote in his journal in 1934:

> Silly talk about whether the New Deal is here to stay. Of course it is here to stay; the only real competition of political parties will be for the privilege and emoluments of administering it. Probably there will be superficial changes, but none essential; none, that is, which will at all redistribute actual power between the State and society. One may safely bet on that. (Nock 1948, 75)

In both eras, whether the punditi regarded him a radical or a conservative, he opposed war and American participation in it. He would not be stampeded into supporting the state as protector against the barbarians: "This matter of national defense would take on an entirely different aspect if people could be brought to understand that the only government they need to defend themselves against is their own government, and that the only way to defend themselves against it is by constant distrust and vigilance."[36] The recalcitrant fraction of society Nock sought to address—the

"Remnant"—was to be found among the Old Right publicists about to be discussed.

The Old Right publicists tended to cluster around a handful of publications. Their concerns included limited, constitutional government, individual liberty, the free market (in most cases), the bloated executive (including secret diplomacy), imperialism, colonialism, militarism, war, and in some cases McCarthyism. Before the crusade to get the United States into World War II, some Old Rightists were routinely published in such liberal journals as *The Nation* and *The New Republic*. Later they were barred from them. For example, the old classical liberal Oswald Garrison Villard, former editor and owner of *The Nation*, was forced out as a columnist because of his insistence on strict neutrality.[37] The liberal press also kept out Harry Elmer Barnes.

With venerable journals unavailable, the Old Rightists had little choice but to start new ones. In the 1930s, 1940s, and early 1950s such publications as *The Freeman* (published by the Henry George School, of which Frank Chodorov was director, and not to be confused with Albert Jay Nock's old 1920s magazine), analysis, *Human Events, Faith and Freedom,* and another magazine called the *Freeman*[38] were home to these writers. Among established publications, Colonel Robert McCormick's *Chicago Tribune* was still a bastion of anti–New Deal and isolationist thinking (see Edwards 1971). In these pages, the holdout opponents of foreign intervention, including the Cold War, made their case, even as the public and some former allies deserted them.

Concern with executive power colored much of what they wrote. In the first "sample" issue of *Human Events* in November 1943, Felix Morley criticized Secretary of State Cordell Hull for stating that the Declaration of Austria, an agreement among the Soviet Union, England, and the Roosevelt administration, had been "proclaimed in the name of 'the government of the United States.'" Morley reminded his readers that although the executives of the Soviet Union and England had virtually unlimited foreign-policy powers, the president of the United States did not. "As a former member of the Senate," wrote Morley, "which body must advise and consent by a two-thirds majority, in the ratification of any treaty, Secretary Hull might well have avoided this slip."[39]

From the first issue in March 1944, Morley and his colleagues set off an alarm against burgeoning government and permanent military alliances.

"True liberalism," they wrote in their statement of policy, "will survive neither subordination to a despotic bureaucracy at home, nor entanglement in any Balance of Power system directed from abroad by those over whom American public opinion has no control" (Hanighen and Morley 1944, x).

During the war they expressed fear that the United States had no plan for the aftermath and that the lofty words of the Atlantic Charter were mere ink ready to be washed away by a sea of big-power politics to the advantage of Stalin and Churchill. Morley and other *Human Events* authors (including the Socialist Party presidential candidate Norman Thomas) communicated their severe reservations about saturation bombing of Germany and Japan as well as about the United Nations with its big-power veto. They protested the dropping of atom bombs on Japan, the victor's justice of the Nuremberg Trials, and the general dehumanization of the German people. They repeatedly lamented the hypocritical disregard of self-determination as reflected in the Yalta agreement.[40]

Morley, in particular, seemed eager to demonstrate how the war was vindicating the earlier isolationists.

> Communism will develop throughout Europe, almost automatically, as an interminable war steadily undermines the economic stability without which representative government collapses and democracy becomes merely an empty word....Should the net result of our second major crusade in Europe be the communization of that Continent, many Americans will begin to ask whether such outcome is really worth the price we are paying for its accomplishment. (Morley 1944, 156–57)

Morley seemed to be speaking for most Old Rightists.

For years to follow, Morley pounded the rostrum on behalf of limited government. He refused to accept a compromise between the principles of a republic and those of a superpower. In 1957 he wrote,

> World leadership requires centralization of power in the capital of the nation that seeks dominance. It requires an aristocracy—an elite— that can be completely indifferent to the gusts of public opinion. It requires a socialized economy, a docile labor force, and a system of education that focuses on the training of the gifted....We must either change our Constitution—openly and honestly—to conform with

the imperial policies we seek to follow. Or we must modify those policies to conform to the Constitution as it now stands. The Federal system was not designed to promote world leadership by the United States. (31, 32)

The general subject of America's passage from republic to empire occupied much of the Old Rightists' time. Garet Garrett, the newspaper and magazine writer who since the thirties had warned of the New Deal's distortion of American institutions, in 1952 wrote an eloquent pamphlet on the fateful change. "We have crossed the boundary," he declared, "that lies between Republic and Empire." Roosevelt had brought the welfare state to America, but even he dared not enter a war without asking Congress for a declaration. "Nine years later a much weaker President did."[41]

With great rigor Garrett identified the requisites of empire: executive domination, subordination of domestic policy to foreign policy, "ascendancy of the military mind," a system of satellite nations, and a "complex of vaunting and fear." America had now fulfilled them all, along with a final one: the call of historical necessity.

It is not only our security we are thinking of—our security in a frame of collective security. Beyond that lies a greater thought.

It is our turn.

Our turn to do what?

Our turn to assume the responsibilities of moral leadership of the world.

Our turn to maintain the balance of power against the forces of evil everywhere...evil in this case being the Russian barbarian.

Our turn to keep the peace of the world.

Our turn to save civilization.

Our turn to serve mankind.

But this is the language of Empire. (Garrett [1953] 1964b,158–59)

Empire was also a preoccupation of Frank Chodorov, a pivotal figure in the Old Right.[42] Greatly influenced by Henry George and Albert Jay Nock, Chodorov was the ideal-type Old Rightist; that is, he was the consummate antistatist. He was heard to say more than once that the ideal government would be small enough to fit in his apartment kitchen. In 1947 Chodorov anticipated Garrett in his article "A Byzantine Empire of the West?," published as the Truman Doctrine was being debated (Chodorov 1980, 337–49). To the claim that the Russians had to be stopped from rolling over the rest of Europe, Chodorov replied,

> Suppose Russia imposes on the peoples of Europe the slavery conditions prevailing within her borders. Without arguing the point that these conditions have so reduced her own economy that the robbery of subject peoples has become a policy of necessity, we must admit as a matter of experience that slaves are poor producers, and we can predict the collapse of communism in Europe from lack of production. There is the added fact that, unlike the Russians, Western Europe did experience a measure of freedom, the memory of which will engender subversive activity, further slowing up the productive machinery. In short, the slave economy will bring about primitive conditions…, and the vulture state will die from lack of sustenance. It is poor prospect for the next generation of Europeans, to be sure, but is it any worse than another war? Something might survive a spell of communism, while the result of another war, no matter which side wins, will be annihilation. (Chodorov 1980, 346)

Chodorov also warned, on several occasions, that the negative effects of the Roosevelt–Truman foreign policy would not be confined to Europe. "If war comes—and when did imperialism not bring it?—the worst of what we call communism will come with it" (Chodorov 1980, 348).

John T. Flynn, the muckraking investigative journalist, began sounding such warnings before the end of World War II. Flynn, a former progressive and columnist at *The New Republic*, became an early critic of the corporativism of the New Deal (see Flynn 1933). Later he was chairman of the New York chapter of the America First Committee and highly influential on its policies (see Cole [1953] 1971, passim; Stenehjem 1976). At the height of the war, in 1944, he published *As We Go Marching*, in which he traced the rise of fascism in Germany and Italy and described disturbing similarities in the United States. He summed up the similarities in two words: corporativism and militarism. He saw the latter as the driving force of the former. How, he asked, could the federal government expand its power over the economy, and (in its view) avoid depression, without exciting the opposition of the conservative constituencies and the state and local authorities fearful of central encroachment?

> These two stubborn forces…will always force a government like ours to find a project for spending which meets these two conditions: It must be a strictly federal project and it must be one upon which the conservative and taxpaying elements will be willing to see money spent. The one great federal project which meets these requirements is the army and navy for national defense. And this, of course, is quite inadequate unless it is carried on upon a scale which gives it all the characteristics of militarism.…*Thus militarism is the only great glamorous public-works project upon which a variety of elements in the community can be brought into agreement.* (Flynn [1944] 1973, 207, emphasis added)

He saw the signs in the planning for universal military training, in the nascent alliance system, and in the inchoate imperialism.

> To sum it up…the germs of a vigorous imperialism are here among us—I mean the moral germs.…We have managed to run up a little history of imperial adventure upon a small scale of which we may well be ashamed.…We have managed to accumulate a pretty sizable empire of our own already—far-spreading territories detached from our continental borders.…We have now managed to acquire bases all over the world.…There is no part of the world where trouble can break out where we do not have bases of some sort in which, if we wish to use the pretension, we cannot claim our interests are menaced. Thus menaced, there must remain when the war is over a continuing argument in the hands of the imperialists for a vast naval establishment and a huge army ready to attack anywhere or to resist an attack from all the enemies we shall be obliged to have. Because always the most powerful argument for a huge army maintained for economic reasons is that we have enemies. We must have enemies. They will become an economic necessity for us.[43]

Flynn would not be stampeded by the Cold War into compromising his views. A free America, he declared, could wait out the communists; there will be no war unless the United States starts it. In 1950 radio commentaries he counseled, "the course of wisdom for the American people would be to sit tight and put their faith in the immutable laws of human nature." Thus the United States should "make an end of the cold war."[44]

The "need for an enemy" was a theme picked up by Morley later in books and articles. The economic planners, Morley wrote, were convinced that without massive government spending, the economy would collapse into its prewar state.

> Although economic and political considerations now make it dif-
> ficult for the Administration to curtail defense spending, it is equally
> impossible for anyone in authority to admit the fact. No official can
> openly suggest that the Kremlin may conceivably be sincere in seek-
> ing a relaxation of the now completely fantastic armaments race. One
> might as well expect the Secretary of the Treasury to say publicly
> that during an inflationary period Savings Bonds are a bad buy. And
> because it is in practice impossible for our officials to tell the whole
> truth they are gradually forced into overt deception. In spite of the
> cost-of-living indices the steadily depreciating "E" Bonds are adver-
> tised as "the safest investment in the world." In spite of the logical
> and good reasoning often found in Russian overtures it is consis-
> tently maintained that because communists are congenital liars, no
> conciliation of any kind is possible. (Morley 1959, 174–75)

Other Old Rightists also warned that the militaristic policies beginning with Roosevelt had permanently changed America for the worse (e.g., Beard 1948, esp. 573–98; Barnes 1980a, 1953).

Old Right thinkers did not confine their analysis to militarism's and socialism's poisoning of man's material circumstances. Harm to the spirit loomed just as large. In poignant essays Leonard Read and F. A. Harper emphasized people's deep need for freedom from coercion and the wither-ing effects of political power. A former Cornell University economics pro-fessor who eventually founded the Institute for Humane Studies, Harper discussed such issues in his 1951 essay "In Search of Peace":

> Charges of pacifism are likely to be hurled at anyone who in these
> troubled times raises any question about the race into war. If paci-
> fism means embracing the objective of peace, I am willing to accept
> the charge. If it means opposing all aggression against others, I am

willing to accept that charge also. It is now urgent in the interest of liberty that many persons become "peace-mongers." (Harper 1979a)

Harper proceeded to reject the stock rationalizations for state-sponsored collective security and the militarism it invariably brings. Then, confronting head-on the bedrock case for the Cold War as propounded by "conservatives," he wrote:

> Relinquish liberty for the purposes of defense in an emergency? Why? It would seem that in an emergency, of all times, one needs his greatest strength. So if liberty is strength and slavery is weakness, liberty is a necessity rather than a luxury, and we can ill afford to be without it—least of all during an emergency. (Harper 1979a, 2:386)

Read matched Harper's poignancy in *Conscience on the Battlefield*, a pamphlet published during the Korean War in 1951. In an exchange between a soldier dying of a war wound and the soldier's conscience, Read set forth a theory of personal responsibility that did not permit the excuse "I was only following the state's orders" (Read 1951, 8–9). Read's essay was not a mere lofty flight of philosophy, but a tough-minded analysis of foreign policy and world events. The soldier's "conscience" points out that the soldier would not have chosen to defend the South Koreans against the North Koreans.

> And for good reason. In many instances, you recognize your incompetence to assign causation even to your own acts. It is, therefore, next to impossible for you to determine the just from the unjust in cases that are remote to your experience, between peoples whose habits and thoughts and ways of life are foreign to you....You are as unaware of the forces at work in this Asiatic affair as you are of the causes of the quarrel between two headhunters. Am I wrong? If so, why have you been shooting Koreans and Chinese when the Russians are supposed to be the ones you fear? Are you expecting the North Koreans or the Chinese to invade the American shores? (Read 1951, 12–13)

In Chodorov, Read, and Harper we find representatives of the pure "libertarian," or laissez-faire, branch of the Old Right. This branch proclaimed a philosophy of private property, free trade, and free emigration—in short, pure capitalism.[45] Its members attacked wage and price controls, rent con-

trol, farm-price supports and crop controls, government education, inflation, and other interference with peaceful commerce.[46]

Meanwhile, three women writers—Ayn Rand, Isabel Paterson, and Rose
Wilder Lane—extolled capitalism on a more spiritual level. Rand, whose
novella *Anthem* was first published in the United States by Read, went on to
construct an entire philosophy of reason and individualism whose political
component justified natural rights, including property rights. The spirit of
individualism that infused this group can be seen in Paterson's 1943 book,
The God of the Machine. "The application of science to production," Paterson, a journalist, wrote, "requires assured possession of private property,
free labor, and time enough to return benefits for the effort and capital
expended....[A] man can think and work effectively only for himself" (Paterson 1943, 17).

Lane, a newspaper woman, novelist, and one time communist, published her "Credo" in the *Saturday Evening Post* in 1936.[47] She described
a trip to the Soviet Union and her crisis of faith as a communist. "I came
out of the Soviet Union no longer a communist, because I believed in personal freedom," she wrote. Freedom, the "anarchy of individualism," was
responsible for the creation of great wealth and an unprecedented standard
of living for more people than ever before. But this was in jeopardy from the
"planned" economy. She protested: "Free thought, free speech, free action,
and freehold property are the source of the modern world. It cannot exist
without them. Its existence depends upon abolishing these reactionary state
controls and destroying the socialist State" (Lane 1977).

The laissez-faire wing pushed its philosophy into areas where most "conservatives" preferred not to see it applied, for example, free trade and free
migration. V. Orval Watts, writing in Chodorov's *Freeman* in 1955, called
for legalization of trade with the Soviet Union. Rejecting both trade embargoes and government-subsidized trade, Watts, an author and educator
associated with the Foundation for Economic Education (FEE), argued
that free trade in goods would have an inevitable by-product, the export of
American ideas:

> An American, for example, cannot walk down a Moscow street with-
> out conveying to passersby certain truths about the outside world—
> through the quality of his shoes, the cut of his clothes, his unafraid
> bearing and peaceable manner. Everywhere he goes, and in every

contact, he does or says things which teach the meaning of freedom and expose the lies on which the Soviet rulers depend for inculcating fear and hatred of capitalism and of the peoples practicing it.[48]

Similarly, two other writers associated with Leonard Read, Oscar W. Cooley and Paul Poirot, called for a policy of free immigration. They regarded the freedom to come to America as merely an application of the founding ideals of the republic. Their pamphlet answered the stock objections to open immigration. For example, to the objection that newcomers might not assimilate, they responded,

> The assimilation of a foreign-born person is accomplished when the immigrant willingly comes to America, paying his own way not only to get here but also after he arrives, and peacefully submitting to the laws and customs of his newly adopted country. (1951, 14–15)

To the charge that the "wrong kind" of people will come, they said,

> The danger that "a poorer class" might come from Asia or Africa or Southern and Eastern Europe and contaminate our society, undoubtedly seems real to any person who thinks of himself as a member of a superior class or race. Such a person, like any good disciple of Marx, is assuming the existence of classes and is convinced that he is qualified to judge others and to sort them into these classes. (1951, 16)

They concluded:

> Our present policy toward immigrants is consistent with the rest of the controls over persons which inevitably go with national socialism. But the controlled human relationships within the "welfare state" are not consistent with freedom.[49]

Such positions shed light on how the Old Right used the word *isolationist*.

The issue of Joseph McCarthy seems to have presented a dilemma for some Old Rightists. They hated communism, yet they saw the threat—to economic and civil liberties—of an anticommunist crusade directed abroad or at home. For some Old Rightists, the McCarthy phenomenon had irresistible features: directed against some of the darlings of the liberals, the people who had pushed the United States into a wartime alliance with the Soviet Union and who used "McCarthyite" tactics against the isolationists, it was also a movement not under the control of the despised eastern establishment. But McCarthyism presented risks, including the glossing over of similarities between communism and any form of statism. In 1949 Flynn wrote,

> I insist that if every Communist in America were rounded up and liquidated, the great menace to our form of social organization would be still among us. I do not mean to underestimate the danger from the Communists....But they are not as dangerous to us as another wholly indigenous movement. The leaders of this movement now actually seek to outdo us in berating the Communists with whom they were marching together but two or three years ago. They are more dangerous because they are more numerous and more respectable and they are not tainted with the odium of treachery. (9)

The dangerous group he had in mind consisted of the British-style Fabians who sought to gradually fasten complete government control of the economy on the American people. Although Flynn supported McCarthy's efforts for a while, his reservations made him an atypical McCarthyite (Radosh [1975] 1978, 267ff.).

Felix Morley harbored another kind of objection to McCarthyism. His devotion to the rule of law made the McCarthy hearings troubling to him. Writing in *Barron's* in 1954, he recalled the origins and importance of the Fifth Amendment and how it had become a point of contention between McCarthy and his targets.

> This ancient Anglo-Saxon safeguard against confessions exacted by torture has ironically become the chief defense of people who would probably indorse "brain washing" if they were themselves in power. But to fight Communism with Communism, as Norman Thomas points out...is "losing to our enemy by imitating him."[50]

"Properly understood," Morley (1954) wrote, "the issue of McCarthyism is thus seen to be one of legislative encroachment on the judicial function, which students of American history will recognize as a problem that plagued this country long before Karl Marx was born or thought of" (9).

Chodorov made perhaps the most fundamental case against McCarthyism. He couldn't understand how it was determined who questioned whom in the "heresy trial."

What is it that perturbs the inquisitors? They do not ask the suspects: Do you believe in Power? Do you adhere to the idea that the individual exists only for the glory of the state? Ought not the TVA be extended to cover the whole country, so that by merely pulling a switch the State can control all production? Are you against taxes, or would you raise them until they absorbed the entire output of the country? Are you opposed to the principle of conscription? Do you favor more "social gains" under the aegis of the bureaucracy? Or would you advocate the dismantling of the public trough at which these bureaucrats feed? In short, do you deny Power?

Such questions might prove embarrassing to the investigators. The answers might bring out the similarity between their ideas and purposes and those of the suspected heretics. They too worship Power. Under the circumstances they limit themselves to one question: Are you or were you a member of the Communist Party? And this turns out to mean, have you aligned yourself with the Moscow branch of the church? (Chodorov 1962, 282; originally in analysis [September 1948])

Chodorov (1950) suggested a way to rid the government of reds: "Just abolish the jobs." He repeated this proposal in *Human Events* in his article "McCarthy's Mistake": "The only thing to do, if you want to rid the bureaucracy of Communists, is to abolish the bureaucracy." He urged Senator McCarthy to turn his attentions to government appropriations.[51]

In the midst of this radical analysis, the other "right wing" was gearing up for a fight. Signs of tension between the old and new had appeared in *Human Events*, in which William Henry Chamberlin endorsed NATO and McCarthy and admonished the "isolationists":

Whichever camp Americans may have belonged to before Pearl Harbor, present conditions dictate the following conclusions: The world has become too small for a big country like the United States to hide in. In the face of the undisguised Communist ambition to conquer the world by force, subversion, or a mixture of the two, there is no peace in appeasement, no safety in retreat, no security in cowardice. (Chamberlin 1958)

Chamberlin would become quite loose with such accusations. Reviewing the Old Rightist Louis Bromfield's 1954 antimilitarist book, *A New Pattern for a Tired World*, Chamberlin wrote that the author "finds himself in the company of Kremlin apologists." Later he red-baited Murray N. Rothbard and the businessman Ernest T. Weir for antimilitarist articles in Old Right journal *Faith and Freedom*. Writing in the virulently pro-Cold War, social democratic magazine *New Leader*, Chamberlin branded Rothbard and Weir "appeasers" and said that Rothbard laid "down a blueprint for American policy tailor-made to the specifications of the Kremlin" (quoted in Rothbard n.d., 139).

As early as 1949 Morley was headed for a break with his *Human Events* partner Frank Hanighen. According to Morley, Hanighen wanted to boost circulation by exploiting distrust of the Russians. Morley feared that would encourage militarization. The climax came with the triumph of the communists in China. "So, in the over-simplified jargon of the times, I became Isolationist, while Frank Hanighen moved to Interventionism" (1979, 436). In 1950, when Morley failed to buy out Hanighen and the other *Human Events* stockholder, the publisher Henry Regnery, and to take control of the newspaper, they bought him out.

> In retrospect I see this episode as symptomatic of that which has come to divide the conservative movement in the United States. Frank and Henry, in their separate ways, moved on to associate with the far Right in the Republican Party. My position remained essentially "Libertarian," though it is with great reluctance that I yield the old terminology of "liberal" to the socialists.…The vestment of power in HEW is demonstrably bad, but its concentration in the Pentagon and CIA is worse because the authority is often concealed and covertly exercised. (Morley 1979, 437)

The coming break was also previewed in 1954, when William F. Buckley, Jr., wrote "A Dilemma of Conservatives" in *The Freeman*. A one-time disciple of Nock and Chodorov, Buckley, using the terminology "containment conservatives" to describe the Old Right and "liberation conservatives" to describe the New, acknowledged the deep disagreement regarding the Soviet Union. He also acknowledged that the liberation conservatives' program would involve policies contrary to American tradition: "For to beat the Soviet Union we must, to an extent, imitate the Soviet Union." But, he argued, the liberationists maintain "there is in the long run less danger involved in mobilizing with the view to achieving a certain objective as fast as feasible than in adapting ourselves to a perpetual state of mobilization of the kind we would need to have if we were to aim at an uneasy modus vivendi." He finished the discussion with a prediction that the differences "ultimately...will separate us." Buckley did not specify who was advocating a "perpetual state of mobilization," but this was the very condition that the Old Right opponents of the Cold War were warning against. Presumably the only way to achieve "as fast as feasible" the objective of ending Soviet communism was to launch a war against Russia.[52]

The separation became more overt in the next issue of *The Freeman*. In his editorial "The Return of 1940?" Chodorov said the current debate over whether to postpone the struggle for freedom until the Russians are defeated reminded him of the debate in 1940 over whether the struggle should be postponed until Hitler was defeated (his answer was no). As an aid in the current debate, he wished to catalogue the results of the intervention of the 1940s to see if the isolationists had been right. The war, he wrote, brought a huge debt, high taxes, conscription, a growing bureaucracy, and a loss of personal independence. The isolationists had predicted these outcomes because they knew that "during war the State acquires power at the expense of freedom, and that because of its insatiable lust for power the State is incapable of giving up any of it." Chodorov predicted that another big war would bring the end of "our inalienable rights." "This is admitted by those who fear the Soviets at least as much as they love freedom, but, as did the 'interventionists' in 1940, they stress the immediate rather than the ultimate danger, and are willing to gamble with freedom. I am not" (1954a, 81).

In the November 1954 issue the debate broke open with an exchange between Chodorov and William S. Schlamm, an Austrian former communist, one time columnist for the *New Leader*, and adviser to Henry Luce.[53] In "But It Is Not 1940," Schlamm characterized Chodorov's position as "unmitigated frivolousness" and asserted that the communists were in deadly earnest about conquering the world (preferably without war), that they were not receptive to reason, and that an unarmed America would be at their mercy. While isolationism may have been a reasonable position in 1940, it was not in 1954.

The same issue carried Chodorov's reply, "The War to Communize America," in which he began by noting that the advocates of war with Russia acknowledge that conscription is needed, as it was necessary in World Wars I and II and in Korea.

> That raises a pertinent question: if Americans did not want these wars should they have been compelled to fight them? Perhaps the people were wrong in their lack of enthusiasm for these wars, but their right to be wrong cannot be questioned in what we call a democratic system. Those who presume to compel people to be "right," against their will, are taking unto themselves a mandate for which there is no warrant other than their own conceit. Did God select them to do the coercing? (1954, 172)

Chodorov said he couldn't escape seeing a pattern regarding the preparation for war. He looked at the pattern this way: The people are frightened into thinking that the enemy will invade and conquer. Yet after previous wars it was learned that the enemy contemplated no such action. Are things really different this time? "But I am not frightened," he continued, "because I am not convinced of the world-conquering potential of the Moscow gang, or of their ability to invade my country. If I were, or rather, if the youth of my country were, we could dispense with the 'selective service' buncombe" (1954b, 172).

The war advocate thinks he wins his case, Chodorov wrote, by asking whether one would prefer to give one's freedom up to an American or a Russian dictator. In reality, there is no choice. "The suggestion that the American dictatorship would be 'temporary' makes this whole argument suspect, for no dictatorship has ever set a limit on its term of office." He added as an aside that a foreign invader would be easier to overthrow than a homegrown ruler, and he maintained that to reduce the danger of war, the United States should withdraw its troops from Europe and Asia and "abandon…global military commitments." If Russia then moved into western Europe, it would mean one of two things: either the Europeans wanted communism, in which the United States would have no right to interfere, or they were unwilling victims, in which case they would resist. The very attempt to conquer Europe would weaken the Soviet Union and hasten its collapse without the United States having to fight a war. And while the Russians were overextending themselves, America would be strengthening itself by husbanding its defenses and resources. "Of course, it would be hard on the Europeans if they fell into Soviet hands," Chodorov continued, "but not any worse than if we precipitated a war in which their homes became the battlefield....The important thing for America now is not to let the fearmongers (or the imperialists) frighten us into a war which, no matter what the military outcome, is certain to communize our country" (1954b, 173–74). In response to those who warned Americans must fear the Russians, Chodorov declared, "I am more afraid of those who, like their forebears, would compel us against our will to fight the Russians. They have the dictator complex" (172).

Thus the debate was framed. In a letter to *The Freeman*, Buckley, who would soon start his own magazine, gave the decision to Schlamm. "I believe that we may indeed be facing both war and slavery," he wrote. "But we will have a fighting chance in a future war against the State, and I do not see that we will have a fighting chance to save ourselves from Soviet tyranny if we pursue Eisenhower's foreign policy—or Chodorov's. For that reason, I side with Willi Schlamm and number myself, dejectedly, among those who favor a carefully planned showdown, and who are prepared to go to war to frustrate the communist designs" (1955, 244). But Ralph Raico, future editor of the classical liberal *New Individualist Review*, had already issued a counterstatement: "William S. Schlamm made out the best case possible for war. After Frank Chodorov had finished his rebuttal, there wasn't much left on the opposition side."[54]

This debate was virtually replayed several months later, when Schlamm and Murray N. Rothbard, writing under the pen name "Aubrey Herbert," engaged in two exchanges in *Faith and Freedom* about whether the United States should go to war over Formosa.

By 1955, most of the Old Right stalwarts were gone. Taft died in 1953, McCormick in 1954. The Old Right publicists were getting old, and only a few younger ones had come along to take their place. In 1955, a key change occurred that doomed the Old Right and set back the movement for individual liberty for many years. Leonard Read and Frank Chodorov experienced various personal differences, and in order to force Chodorov out, Read decided to devote *The Freeman* to more abstract concerns, such as self-development, and to avoid ideological conflict; this move was a retreat from Chodorov's real-world analysis. When Chodorov left *The Freeman*, Buckley and his colleagues, former Trotskyists and Catholic theocrats, started *National Review;* the New Right now had a magazine under its own control.[55] The loss of *The Freeman* was disastrous for the Old Right, and the group's inability to survive the shift demonstrates the already frail condition of the movement (see Rothbard n.d., 144).

With neither *The Freeman* nor *National Review* open to the Old Right's dissection of the world, the remnant had virtually no place to go. This predicament was demonstrated in 1956 when Flynn submitted a manuscript to *National Review* carrying forth his theme, developed in *As We Go Marching*, that militarism was a "job-making boondoggle," a "racket—the oldest in history," and an excuse for the government to tax and borrow (Flynn n.d.). Buckley rejected the article on grounds that its thesis "is difficult to defend in the absence of any discussion whatever of the objective threat of the Soviet Union." "As you know," Buckley continued, "my own opinion, and that of the other anti-socialists on *National Review*, is that the Communists pose an immediate threat to the freedom of every one of us."[56] The intrepid old Flynn, having gone from darling to outcast of *The New Republic*, had now traversed the same route at *National Review*. Of course he could not have published the article in *The Freeman* either after Chodorov's departure.

Without a magazine, it was difficult for the aging Old Right to attract new blood. Meanwhile, the New Right ascended thanks to the polish and surface sophistication of *Buckley*, his slick magazine, and, in 1960, the Young Americans for Freedom. The cause for nonintervention and limited government looked bleak.

Chodorov, who had worked so hard for the movement, never lived to see it blossom. He had a debilitating stroke in 1961 and died in 1966. Without him at the helm, his beloved Intercollegiate Society of Individualists (ISI) was renamed the Intercollegiate Studies Institute because the conservatives, reacting to the rhetoric of Students for a Democratic Society in the early sixties, found the word *individualism* too left-wing and upsetting to businessmen.[57] Chodorov had seen the omens earlier and could not hide his exasperation. In a letter to *National Review* he wrote, "As for me, I will punch anyone who calls me a conservative in the nose. I am a radical" (Chodorov 1956).

Still, there were signs that his work would someday succeed. In 1961 a group of libertarian students at the University of Chicago started the quarterly *New Individualist Review* (*NIR*), under the auspices of ISI, with Ralph Raico as editor in chief. For the next seven years it published the top and emerging scholarly advocates of individual liberty: Ludwig von Mises, F. A. Hayek,[58] Milton Friedman (the last two were editorial advisers to

NIR), Murray N. Rothbard, Henry Hazlitt, Yale Brozen, Israel M. Kirzner, George Stigler, and others. It also published revisionist history by Harry Elmer Barnes. Traditionalist conservatives were not excluded, however; Russell Kirk contributed to the third issue. Indeed, the editors continued the Chodorovian tradition of exploring the rift between the libertarians and conservatives: Buckley and Ronald Hamowy, a later editor in chief, squared off in the November 1961 issue, and Raico went up against M. Stanton Evans on the relationship between classical liberalism and religion in the Winter 1966 issue.[59] (*National Review* had never practiced this tradition.)

Besides *NIR*, a network of classical liberal organizations with greater staying power was quietly forming. Led by Read's Foundation for Economic Education, founded in 1946, it was joined by the William Volker Fund;[60] its successor, the Institute for Humane Studies;[61] Robert LeFevre's Freedom School;[62] Liberty Fund; and other organizations. This fledgling and underfunded network nourished young scholars, supported the work of older ones, and planted the seeds of the classical liberal, or libertarian, movement that would begin to flourish in the mid-1970s.

NOTES

1. Nearly everyone, including Ronald Reagan and Newt Gingrich, feels obliged to pay tribute to Roosevelt.
2. Mencken 1989, xvi–xviii. Fecher's own book on Mencken is *Mencken: A Study of His Thought* (1978).
3. This is not all Fecher got wrong. He wrote that the anti-Semitic rabble-rouser Gerald L. K. Smith founded the America First Committee. Smith was not even a member, much less the founder. The league actually shunned Smith and other known anti-Semites. Fecher is confused: in 1943 Smith founded the America First Party; by then the America First Committee was defunct and had no direct connection with the party. See Cole 1971, 134, 188.
4. The latest study of the Old Right is Justin Raimondo's *Reclaiming the American Right: The Lost Legacy of the Conservative Movement* (1993).
5. As Jerome L. Himmelstein (1990) points out, the nineteenth-century conservatives were those who resisted "the major features of modern Western society—industrial capitalism, political democracy, and an individualist culture—in the name of an agrarian, aristocratic, communal social order. Liberal referred generally to support for those same changes" (26).
6. On America's corporativist history and the New Deal as a defense of corporativism, see Kolko (1963), Bernstein (1968, 263–88), Radosh (1972, 146–87), Rothbard (1972a), and Hughes (1977). See also Ekirch ([1955] 1967), Higgs (1987), and Vedder and Gallaway (1993).
7. The late Roy A. Childs, Jr., suggested the categories.
8. On the various motivations in foreign policy, see Carpenter (1980, 4–5).
9. See Rothbard 1978. Rothbard aptly emphasizes the Old Right's connection to the English

Manchester Schoolers Richard Cobden and John Bright and the leading American disciple of Herbert Spencer: William Graham Sumner (86). He also points out that confusion over the terms Left and Right came from the flip-flop of so many liberals and leftists on the war question in the late 1930s and the recrimination against liberals who stayed the noninterventionist course, such as Harry Elmer Barnes, John T. Flynn, and Oswald Garrison Villard (86–88). This change is painstakingly chronicled in Martin 1964. For a discussion of the regional rivalry between midwestern and eastern business interests, see Rothbard 1978, 88.

10. Compare this attitude with the occasional conservative posturing about the "imperial" Congress's "micromanaging" foreign policy at the expense of presidential prerogative.

11. Thus it is wrong to say that the Old Right cared only about what intervention would do to America, as the conservative syndicated columnist Patrick Buchanan has said on television talk shows.

12. See "Editorial" in *Literature of Liberty* 1981, 4. See in the same issue, Justus D. Doenecke's article "The Anti-interventionist Tradition: Leadership and Perceptions," 7–67. Also of interest by Doenecke are his article "American Isolationism" (1982) and his book *Not to the Swift: The Old Isolationists in the Cold War Era* (1979).

13. See also William Rusher's article "Who Ended the Cold War?" which appeared in the *Washington Times,* 15 December 1989. George H. Nash (1976) disagrees to an extent (123–30), though the title of his work, *The Conservative Intellectual Movement Since 1945,* implies there was essentially one continuous movement. For a similar view, see Himmelstein 1990, 28ff.

14. In earlier days, Buckley was a member of the America First Committee and a disciple of Nock and Chodorov.

15. Taft was commenting in *The Nation* (13 December 1941) on an article by Arthur Schlesinger, Jr., that had appeared in the magazine a week earlier, in which the historian claimed that American business favored appeasing Hitler. See J. Martin 1964, 1278.

16. Buckley 1952. Observe the difference between this and William Henry Chamberlin's version: "In any conflict between the individual and the state...my sympathies are always instinctively with the individual" (1940, 299). After World War II, Chamberlin apparently came around to Buckley's position.

17. For an expression of concern that the New Right's social policies were collectivist, see Frank Meyer (1955), in which Meyer, the "fusionist," accuses Russell Kirk of being "at the best equivocal" (559) on the relationship of the individual and society. He also argues that conservatism "carried with it, however, no built-in defense against the acceptance, grudging though it may be, of institutions which reason and prudence would otherwise reject, if only those institutions are sufficiently firmly established" (559).

18. See William Henry Chamberlin's *America's Second Crusade* (1950) for his views on the disaster of World War II. In 1940 he called himself an advocate of "mild anarchism," or "anarchy plus a police constable": "a state strong enough to maintain internal order, but not strong enough to carry on wars...and perform the other deviltries to which a strong state is prone" (1940, 300). See also John Chamberlain's *A Life with the Printed Word* (1982).

19. For a revisionist and critical look at the League, see my article "A Matter of Degree, Not Principle: The Founding of the American Liberty League" (1982).

20. Otis Graham counts sixty old progressives who opposed the New Deal. See his *An Encore for Reform: The Old Progressives and the New Deal* (1967); the list of names is on pages 192–93.

21. The court also struck down the Guffey Coal Conservation Act as unconstitutional and nullified New York State's minimum wage law.

22. Cole 1983, 219. Roosevelt had no more luck with his attempt to get authority to reorganize the executive branch. His initial proposal passed the Senate in modified form, but was buried in a House committee (221).

23. Feinman 1981, 170. Yet Borah was not totally against the president regarding the speech. See Maddox 1969, 232–33.

24. Cole 1983, 415. Roosevelt said his remark was "the rottenest thing that has ever been said in public life in my generation."

25. For the America First story and a collection of its documents, see Doenecke 1990.

26. See Hoover's own book *The Challenge to Liberty* [1934] (1971). See also the important revisionist work on Hoover as architect of the first New Deal by Rothbard: "Herbert Clark Hoover: A Reconsideration" (1966) and "Herbert Hoover and the Myth of Laissez Faire" (1972b, 111–45).

27. Wilson 1975, 248. For a statement by Hoover on entering the war, see "The Immediate Relation of the United States to this War" (1941, 3–12). See also Doenecke 1987.

28. Wilson 1975, 265–66. Hoover was joined in his opposition to the Korean War by Joseph P. Kennedy, former ambassador to Great Britain. An opponent of U.S. participation in World War II, Kennedy also wanted to keep America out of the Cold War. In late 1950 he called for U.S. withdrawal from Korea and West Germany. "What business is it of ours," he asked, "to support the French colonial policy in Indo-China or to achieve Mr. Syngman Rhee's concepts of democracy in Korea?" (*Vital Speeches* 1951, 170–73).

29. Schoonmaker and Reid 1941, 79, 81. Lindbergh was later accused of anti-Semitism when he named the Jews as one of three groups, along with the British and the Roosevelt administration, pushing for entry into the war. However, many people who knew Lindbergh, including a former president of B'nai B'rith, said Lindbergh was not an anti-Semite (Cole 1974, 171ff.)

30. See Randolph S. Bourne 1964, 83. Bourne writes: "The formality by which Parliaments and Congresses declare war is the merest technicality. Before such a declaration can take place, the country will have been brought to the very brink of war by the foreign policy of the Executive. A long series of steps on the downward path, each one more fatally committing the unsuspecting country to a warlike course of action will have been taken without either the people or its representatives being consulted or expressing its feeling. When the declaration of war is finally demanded by the Executive, the Parliament or Congress could not refuse it without reversing the course of history, without repudiating what has been representing itself in the eyes of the other States as the symbol and interpreter of the nation's will and animus."

31. Patterson 1972, 393. As a young man, in 1917, he had supported universal military training (70).

32. Buffett wrote articles for *Human Events*, *The Freeman*, and *New Individualist Review* on subjects ranging from conscription to inflation, and according to Murray N. Rothbard was influenced by F. A. Harper, founder of the Institute for Humane Studies (IHS). Buffett was a founding board member of IHS.

33. One person he influenced was Henry Hazlitt, who succeeded Mencken as editor of the *American Mercury*.

34. See Rothbard 1962. As the historian Ralph Raico has pointed out, Mencken inexplicably never credited Bryan for resigning as secretary of state after President Wilson took the nation into World War I.

35. See his *Jefferson* [1926] (New York: Hill and Wang, 1960) and his introduction to Spencer's [1892] *The Man versus the State* (Caldwell, Idaho: The Caxton Printers, 1969); see also Oppenheimer, *The State,* John Gitterman, trans. [1914] (New York: Free Life Editions, 1975).

36. Quoted in a letter to the editor from Ralph Raico (1954). Nock's definitive statement on politics was his 1935 book *Our Enemy, The State* (1977). That edition contains a highly important introduction on Nock by Walter Grinder. See also Nock's *The State of the Union: Essays on Social Criticism* (1991).

37. Villard was an early advocate of laissez-faire and an opponent of U.S. participation in World War I. Disillusioned with capitalism, he turned toward progressivism in 1919 and later embraced the New Deal and its welfare-state measures. Eventually he became alarmed with the resulting obese executive branch (he disliked the court-packing plan) and its potential for militarism, warning even that fascism loomed. See Wreszin 1965, 208ff. See also Radosh [1975] 1978, 67ff.

38. This Freeman was started in 1950 by Henry Hazlitt, John Chamberlain, and Suzanne LaFollette. In 1954 it was bought by Leonard E. Read, who in 1946 had set up the Foundation for Economic Education to promote the "freedom philosophy." When Read bought the magazine, Chodorov became the editor. Before this, Chodorov had edited his own broadsheet, analysis, which he merged with Human Events, when he became contributing editor.

39. Hanighen and Morley 1945, 3. Morley, with Frank C. Hanighen and William Henry Chamberlin, were the editors of *Human Events*. Morley was a Pulitzer Prize–winning editorial writer for the *Washington Post* in the 1930s and former president of Haverford College. See Morley (1949, 1951, 1959), and his memoir, *For the Record* (1979).

40. For an Old Right indictment of the Nuremberg Trials as an exercise in ex post facto law, see Taft 1964, 310–22.

41. Garrett [1953] 1964b, 117, 122. For the details of Garrett's life, see Ryant 1989.

42. For a biographical sketch, see Charles H. Hamilton's "Introduction" to *Chodorov's Fugitive Essays: Selected Writings of Frank Chodorov* (1980). Among Chodorov's other writings, see *One is a Crowd: Reflections of an Individualist (1952)* and *Out of Step: The Autobiography of an Individualist* (1962).

43. Flynn [1944] 1973, 223–25. Flynn was one of the first to foresee America's colonial war in Vietnam. See Radosh [1975] 1978, 253ff., and Doenecke 1979, 238ff.

44. Quoted in Radosh [1975] 1978, 251. Flynn was as unrelenting in his criticism of Franklin Roosevelt as anyone. See Flynn's *Country Squire in the White House (1940)* and *The Roosevelt Myth* (1948).

45. They were inspired by F. A. Hayek's vastly popular 1944 book *The Road to Serfdom,* which argued that government economic planning leads to totalitarianism. The works of Ludwig von Mises were also critical in shaping their views on economics.

46. On several occasions Chodorov called for tuition tax-credits for parents who send children to private schools. He also trenchantly attacked government debt, headlining the July 1948 issue of *analysis* "Don't Buy Bonds."

47. "Credo" was reproduced as *Give Me Liberty* (1977). Lane was the daughter of Laura Ingalls Wilder of *Little House on the Prairie* fame. See also her *The Discovery of Freedom: Man's Struggle Against Authority* ([1934] 1984).

48. Watts 1955, 295. The connection between peace and free trade has recurred throughout *The Freeman*'s long life and up to the present. See Bettina Bien Greaves's article on foreign policy and free trade in *The Freeman,* September 1979, and Frank Chodorov's "The Humanity of Trade," in July 1956, in which he wrote, "Perhaps the removal of trade restrictions throughout the world would do more for the cause of universal peace than can any political union of peoples separated by trade barriers." Both articles are reprinted in Joan Kennedy Taylor, ed. (1986).

49. Cooley and Poirot 1951, 33. Another FEE pamphlet worth noting is Dean Russell's *The Conscription Idea* (1953), which attacked the draft as "the abolition of liberty."

50. Morley 1954, 9. Morley was also unenthusiastic about the Alger Hiss case. See Morley 1979, 430.

51. Chodorov 1952a, 1. This should dispose of the claim, found in Gottfried and Fleming (1988, 6), that Chodorov was an enthusiastic McCarthyite.

52. Buckley 1954b. This was the second issue under Chodorov's editorial hand. In Chodorov's first issue, Buckley called for individualist education for discharged soldiers, who have been turned into collectivists by the military. See Buckley 1954a, 20–21.

53. Schlamm would later be a founder of *National Review.*

54. Raico 1954, 202. This clash of letters between Buckley and Raico presaged debates in New *Individualist Review* seven years later.

55. Buckley had tried to buy *The Freeman* in 1955, but he was turned down (John B. Judis, *William F. Buckley, Jr.: Patron Saint of the Conservatives* [New York: Simon and Schuster, 1988], 114). Chodorov was listed as a contributor of *The New Republic* because of his longtime friendship (he was the only Old Rightist on the masthead), but he apparently had no influence at the magazine and did not work in the office. Among the former Trotskyists and communists were Willmoore Kendall, Whittaker Chambers, James Burnham, William Schlamm, Max Eastman, Morrie Ryskind, Freda Utley, Ralph de Toledano, and Eugene Lyons.

56. Buckley 1956. Buckley had asked Flynn to review *A Republican Looks at His Party,* by Arthur Larson, an adviser to Eisenhower. Flynn used the assignment to attack the militarism of the administration's policy toward the Soviets, a policy *The New Republic* group thought was weak. See Judis 1988, 136.

57. Chodorov had begun ISI in 1952 as a way of keeping individualism alive for college students. He made Buckley its first president. See Rothbard n.d., 145.

58. Almost as though his intentions were to inspire the *NIR* students, in 1960 Hayek had written "Why I Am Not a Conservative" as a postscript to his treatise, *The Constitution of Liberty* (1960). Hayek wrote that "There is a danger in the confused condition which brings the defenders of liberty and the true conservatives together in common opposition to developments which threaten their different ideals equally" (397). For Hayek the "decisive objection" to conservatism was "that by its very nature it cannot offer an alternative to the direction in which we are moving. It may succeed by its resistance to current tendencies in slowing down undesirable developments, but, since it does not indicate another direction, it cannot prevent their continuance" (398). He criticized conservatives for being "inclined to use the powers of government to prevent change or to limit its rate to whatever appeals to the more timid mind. In looking forward, they lack the faith in the spontaneous forces of adjustment which makes the liberal accept changes without apprehension" (400). In sum, Hayek could not accept the "characteristic complacency of the conservative toward the action of established authority and his prime concern that this authority be not weakened rather than that its power be kept within bounds" (401). The *NIR* took this outlook to heart.

59. According to Ralph Raico, *NIR* at its height had a circulation of 1,500–2,000. The journal folded when the student-editors graduated and no replacements stepped in.

60. The Volker Fund, under Herbert Cornuelle, sponsored highly important conferences and meetings in the 1950s that featured such intellectuals as F. A. Hayek, Milton Friedman, James Buchanan, Bruno Leoni, George Stigler, and William Appleman Williams. Cornuelle also helped establish *Faith and Freedom,* an important late Old Right journal.

61. This institute was founded by F. A. Harper in 1961 in Menlo Park, California.

62. This organization was founded in 1956 by the former newspaperman.

REFERENCES

America First Bulletin. 1941. 28 June, 1. Quoted in Rex Stout, 1942. *The Illustrious Dunder-heads.* New York: Alfred A. Knopf, 156.

Barnes, Harry Elmer. 1980a. How "Nineteen Eighty-Four" Trends Threaten American Peace, Freedom, and Prosperity. In *Revisionism: A Key to Peace and Other Essays.* San Francisco: Cato Institute.

———. 1980b. Revisionism: *A Key to Peace and Other Essays.* San Francisco: Cato Institute, 1980.

———, ed. 1953. *Perpetual War for Perpetual Peace.* New York: Greenwood Press, Publishers.

Beard, Charles A. 1948. *President Roosevelt and the Coming of the War, 1941: A Study in Appearances and Realities.* New Haven: Yale University Press.

Bedau, Hugo Adam. 1969. *Civil Disobedience: Theory and Practice,* 78. New York: Pegasus. Quoting Henry David Thoreau, *Civil Disobedience* (1849).

Berger, Henry W. 1967. A Conservative Critique of Containment: Senator Taft on the Early Cold War Program. In *Containment and Revolution,* edited by D. Horowitz. Boston: Beacon Press.

Bernstein, Barton J. 1968. The New Deal: Conservative Achievements in Liberal Reform. In *Towards a New Past: Dissenting Essays in American History,* edited by B. J. Bernstein. New York: Pantheon Books.

Bode, Carl. 1969. *Mencken.* Carbondale: Southern Illinois University Press.

Bourne, Randolph S. 1964. The State. *In War and Intellectuals: Collected Essays, 1915–1919.* New York: Harper Torchbooks.

Bromfield, Louis. 1954. *A New Pattern for a Tired World.* New York: Harper & Brothers.

Buckley, William F., Jr. 1952. *Commonweal* (January). Quoted in Murray N. Rothbard, Confessions of a Right-Wing Liberal. *Ramparts* (Summer 1964): 50.

———. 1954a. Making a Man out of a Soldier. *Freeman* (July): 20–21.

———. 1954b. A Dilemma of Conservatives. *Freeman* (August).

———. 1955. Letter to the Editor. *Freeman* (January).

———. 1956. Letter to John T. Flynn. Flynn papers. 22 October.

Burnham, James. 1971. Joys and Sorrow of Empire. *National Review* (13 July): 749. Quoted in Joseph R. Stromberg, *The Cold War and the Transformation of the American Right: The Decline of Right-Wing Liberalism.* Master's thesis, Florida Atlantic University, 1971, 3.

Carpenter, Ted Galen. 1980. *The Dissenters: American Isolationists and Foreign Policy, 1945–1954.* Ph.D. diss., University of Texas, Austin.

Chamberlain, John. 1982. *A Life with the Printed Word.* Chicago: Regnery Gateway.

Chamberlin, William Henry. 1940. Personal Credo. In *The Confessions of an Individualist.* New York: Macmillan Company, 1940.

———. 1950. *America's Second Crusade.* Chicago: Henry Regnery Company.

———. 1958. Letter to an Isolationist. *Human Events* (29 December).

Chodorov, Frank. 1950. Trailing the Trend. *analysis* (April). Quoted in Charles H. Hamilton, ed. *Fugitive Essays: Selected Writings of Frank Chodorov* (Indianapolis: Liberty Press, 1980).

———. 1952a. McCarthy's Mistake. *Human Events* (12 November).

———. 1952b. *One Is a Crowd: Reflections of an Individualist.* New York: Devin-Adair Company.

———. 1954a. The Return of 1940? *Freeman* (September): 81.

———. 1954b. A War to Communize America. *Freeman* (November).

———. 1956. Letter. *New Republic* (6 October). Quoted in Charles H. Hamilton, ed., *Fugitive Essays: Selected Writings of Frank Chodorov.* (Indianapolis: Liberty Press, 1980), 29.

———. 1962. *Out of Step: The Autobiography of an Individualist.* New York: Devin-Adair Company.

———. 1980. A Byzantine Empire of the West? In *Fugitive Essays: Selected Writings of Frank Chodorov*, edited by C. H. Hamilton. Indianapolis: Liberty Press. First published in *Analysis* (April 1947).

Cole, Wayne S. [1953] 1971. *America First: The Battle Against Intervention, 1940–1941.* New York: Octagon Books.

———. 1974. *Charles A. Lindbergh and the Battle Against Intervention in World War II.* New York: Harcourt Brace Jovanovich.

———. 1983. *Roosevelt & the Isolationists, 1932–45.* Lincoln: University of Nebraska Press.

Cooley, Oscar W., and Paul Poirot. 1951. *The Freedom to Move.* Irvington-on-Hudson, N.Y.: Foundation for Economic Education.

Crunden, Robert M. 1964. *The Mind and Art of Albert Jay Nock.* Chicago: Henry Regnery Company.

Doenecke, Justus D. 1979. *Not to the Swift: The Old Isolationists in the Cold War Era.* Lewisburg, Pa.: Bucknell University Press.

———. 1981. The Anti-interventionist Tradition: Leadership and Perceptions. *Literature of Liberty* 4 (Summer).

———. 1982. American Isolationism. *Journal of Libertarian Studies* 6 (Summer/Fall): 201–16.

———. 1987. The Anti-interventionism of Herbert Hoover. *Journal of Libertarian Studies* 8 (Summer): 311–40.

———, ed. 1990. In *Danger Undaunted: The Anti-Interventionist Movement of 1940–1941 as Revealed in the Papers of the America First Committee.* Stanford, Calif.: Hoover Institution Press.

Editorial. 1981. *Literature of Liberty.* 4 (Summer).

Edwards, Jerome E. 1971. *The Foreign Policy of Col. McCormick's Tribune: 1929–1941.* Reno: University of Nevada Press.

Ekirch, Arthur A., Jr. [1955] 1967. *The Decline of American Liberalism.* New York: Atheneum.

———. 1969. *Ideologies and Utopias: The Impact of the New Deal on American Thought.* Chicago: Quadrangle Books.

———, ed. 1964. *Voices in Dissent.* New York: The Citadel Press.

Fecher, Charles A. 1978. *Mencken: A Study of His Thought.* New York: Knopf.

Feinman, Ronald L. 1981. *The Twilight of Progressivism: The Western Republican Senators and the New Deal.* Baltimore: Johns Hopkins University Press.

Flynn, John T. 1933. Inside the RFC. *Harper's Magazine* (January): 164–69.

———. 1940. *Country Squire in the White House.* New York: Doubleday, Doran & Co.

———. 1948. *The Roosevelt Myth.* New York: Devin–Adair Company.

———. 1949. *The Road Ahead: America's Creeping Revolution.* New York: Devin-Adair Company.

———. *As We Go Marching.* [1944] 1973. New York: Free Life Editions.

———. N.d. Manuscript. University of Oregon Library, the Flynn papers.

Forgue, Guy J. [1961] 1981. *Letters of H. L. Mencken.* Boston: Northeastern University Press.

Garrett, Garet. [1953] 1964a. *The People's Pottage.* Caldwell, Idaho: The Caxton Printers.

———. [1953] 1964b. The Rise of Empire. In *The People's Pottage.* Caldwell, Idaho: Caxton Printers.

Goddard, Arthur E., ed. 1968. *Harry Elmer Barnes: Learned Crusader.* Colorado Springs: Ralph Myles, Publisher.

Goldberg, Isaac. [1925] 1968. *The Man Mencken: A Biographical and Critical Survey.* New York: AMS Press.

Gottfried, Paul, and Thomas Fleming. 1988. *The Conservative Movement.* Boston: Twayne Publishers.

Graham, Otis L., Jr. 1967. *An Encore for Reform: The Old Progressives and the New Deal.* New York: Oxford University Press.

Hamilton, Charles H., ed. 1980. *Fugitive Essays: Selected Writings of Frank Chodorov.* Indianapolis: Liberty Press.

Hamowy, Ronald. 1961. "*New Republic*": Criticism and Reply. *New Individualist Review* 1 (November 1961): 3–7.

Hanighen, Frank C., and Felix Morley. 1944. A Statement of Policy. *Human Events* (1 March). Quoted in Frank C. Hanighen and Felix Morley, *A Year of Human Events,* vol. 1 (Chicago: *Human Events* Associates, 1945), x.

————. 1945. *A Year of Human Events,* vol. 1. Chicago: Human Events Associates.

Harper, F. A. 1979a. In Search of Peace. In *The Writings of F. A. Harper.* 2 vols. Menlo Park, Calif.: Institute for Humane Studies.

————. 1979b. *The Writings of F. A. Harper.* 2 vols. Menlo Park, Calif.: Institute for Humane Studies.

Hayek, F. A. 1944. *The Road to Serfdom.* Chicago: University of Chicago Press.

————. 1960. *The Constitution of Liberty.* Chicago: University of Chicago Press.

Helfrich, J. V. K. 1948. FDR's War. *Analysis* (July).

Higgs, Robert. 1987. *Crisis and Leviathan: Critical Episodes in the Growth of American Government.* New York: Oxford University Press.

Himmelstein, Jerome L. 1990. *To the Right: The Transformation of American Conservatism.* Berkeley: University of California Press.

Hoover, Herbert. 1922. *American Individualism.* Garden City, N.Y.: Doubleday, Page & Company.

————. *The Challenge to Liberty* [1934] 1971. Rockford, Ill.: Herbert Hoover Presidential Library Association.

————. 1941. The Immediate Relation of the United States to This War. In *We Testify,* edited by N. Schoonmaker and D. F. Reid. New York: Smith & Durrell.

Horowitz, David, ed. 1967. *Containment and Revolution.* Boston: Beacon Press.

Hughes, Jonathan R. T. 1977. *The Governmental Habit: Economic Controls from Colonial Times to the Present.* New York: Basic Books.

Jonas, Manfred. 1966. *Isolationism in America, 1935–1941.* Ithaca, N.Y.: Cornell University Press.

Judis, John B. 1988. *William F. Buckley, Jr.: Patron Saint of the Conservatives.* New York: Simon and Schuster.

Kolko, Gabriel. 1963. *The Triumph of Conservatism: A Reinterpretation of American History, 1900–1916.* New York: Free Press.

Lane, Rose Wilder. 1977. *Give Me Liberty.* Mansfield, Mo.: Laura Ingalls Wilder–Rose Wilder Lane Home Association. Originally published as "Credo."

————. [1934] 1984. *The Discovery of Freedom: Man's Struggle Against Authority.* New York: Laissez Faire Books.

Leuchtenburg, William E. 1963. *Franklin D. Roosevelt and the New Deal, 1932–1940.* New York: Harper Torchbooks.

Liggio, Leonard P. 1973. *A New Look at Robert Taft.* Paper presented to the American Historical Association, 28 December.

————. [1965] 1978. *Why the Futile Crusade?* New York: Center for Libertarian Studies.

Lindbergh, Charles A., Jr. 1941. A Letter to Americans. In *We Testify,* edited by Nancy Schoonmaker and Doris Fielding Reid (New York: Smith & Durrell). First published in *Collier's* (29 March 1941).

Maddox, Robert James. 1969. *William E. Borah and American Foreign Policy.* Baton Rouge: Louisiana State University Press.

Manchester, William. 1986. *Disturber of the Peace: The Life of H. L. Mencken.* 2d ed. Amherst.: The University of Massachusetts Press.

Martin, Edward A. 1984. *H. L. Mencken and the Debunkers*. Athens: University of Georgia Press.

Martin, James J. 1964. *American Liberalism and World Politics*. 2 vols. New York: Devin-Adair Company.

Mencken, H. L. 1956a. *A Carnival of Buncombe*, edited by Malcolm Moos. Baltimore: Johns Hopkins Press.

———. 1956b. *Minority Report: H. L. Mencken's Notebooks*. New York: Alfred A. Knopf.

———. 1975. *A Gang of Pecksniffs and Other Comments on Newspaper Publishers, Editors and Reporters*. Edited by T. Lippman, Jr. New Rochelle, N.Y.: Arlington House.

———. 1989. *The Diary of H. L. Mencken*. Edited by C. A. Fecher. New York: Knopf.

Mencken, H. L., and Robert Rives La Monte. 1910. *Men versus the Man, A Correspondence between Rives La Monte, Socialist, and H. L. Mencken, Individualist*. New York: Holt.

Meyer, Frank. 1955. Collectivism Rebaptized. *Freeman* (July): 559–62.

Morley, Felix. 1944. Portent in Greece. In *A Year in Human Events*, vol. 1, edited by F. C. Hanighen and F. Morley (Chicago: Human Events Associates, 1945). First published in *Human Events* (13 December).

———. 1948. Politics and Principles. *Human Events* 5 (27 October).

———. 1949. *The Power in the People*. New York: D. Van Nostrand Company.

———. 1951. *The Foreign Policy of the United States*. New York: Alfred A. Knopf.

———. 1954. *The Fifth Amendment*. Barron's (22 March).

———. 1957. American Republic or American Empire? *Modern Age* (Summer).

———. 1959. *Freedom and Federalism*. Chicago: Henry Regnery Company/Gateway Edition.

———. 1979. *For the Record*. South Bend. Ind.: Regnery/Gateway.

Nash, George H. 1976. *The Conservative Intellectual Movement Since 1945*. New York: Basic Books.

Nock, Albert Jay. 1948. *Journal of Forgotten Days, May 1934–October 1935*. Hinsdale, Ill.: Henry Regnery.

———. [1926] 1960. *Jefferson*. New York: Hill and Wang.

———. [1943] 1969. *The Memoirs of a Superfluous Man*. Chicago: Henry Regnery Company/Gateway Edition.

———. [1935] 1977. *Our Enemy, The State*. New York: Free Life Editions.

———. 1991. *The State of the Union: Essays in Social Criticism*. Edited by C.H. Hamilton. Indianapolis: Liberty Press.

Oppenheimer, Franz. [1914] 1975. *The State*. Translated by John Gitterman. New York: Free Life Editions.

Paterson, Isabel. 1943. *The God of the Machine*. New York: G. P. Putnam's Sons.

Patterson, James T. 1967. *Congressional Conservatism and the New Deal: The Growth of the Conservative Coalition in Congress, 1933–1939*. Lexington: University of Kentucky Press.

———. 1972. *Mr. Republican: A Biography of Robert A. Taft*. Boston: Houghton Mifflin Co.

Radosh, Ronald. 1972. The Myth of the New Deal. In *A New History of Leviathan*, edited by M. N. Rothbard and R. Radosh. New York: E. P. Dutton & Co.

———. [1975] 1978. *Prophets on the Right: Profiles of Conservative Critics of American Globalism*. New York: Free Life Editions.

Raico, Ralph. 1954. Letter to the Editor. *Freeman* (December).

Raimondo, Justin. 1993. *Reclaiming the American Right: The Lost Legacy of the Conservative Movement*. Burlingame, Calif.: Center for Libertarian Studies.

Rand, Ayn. 1946. *Anthem*. New York: Signet Books.

Read, Leonard E. 1951. *Conscience on the Battlefield*. Irvington-on-Hudson, N.Y.: Foundation for Economic Education.

Regnery, Henry. 1985. *Memoirs of a Dissident Publisher*. Chicago: Regnery Books.

Richman, Sheldon L. 1982. A Matter of Degree, Not Principle: The Founding of the American Liberty League. *Journal of Libertarian Studies* 6 (Spring): 145–63.

Rothbard, Murray N. 1962. H. L. Mencken: The Joyous Libertarian. *New Individualist Review* 2 (Summer): 15–27.

———. 1964. The Transformation of the American Right. *Continuum* 2 (Summer): 220–31.

———. 1966. Herbert Clark Hoover: A Reconsideration. *New Individualist Review* 4 (Winter): 3–12.

———. 1968a. Confessions of a Right-Wing Liberal. *Ramparts* (June): 48–52.

———. 1968b. Harry Elmer Barnes as Revisionist of the Cold War. In *Harry Elmer Barnes: Learned Crusader,* edited by A. E. Goddard. Colorado Springs: Ralph Myles, Publisher.

———. 1972a. *America's Great Depression.* Kansas City: Sheed and Ward.

———. 1972b. Herbert Hoover and the Myth of Laissez Faire. In *A New History of Leviathan,* edited by M. Rothbard and R. Radosh. New York: E. P. Dutton & Co.

———. 1978. The Foreign Policy of the Old Right. *Journal of Libertarian Studies* 2 (Winter): 85–96.

———. 1989. World War I as Fulfillment: Power and the Intellectuals. *Journal of Libertarian Studies* 9 (Winter): 81–125.

———. N.d. *The Betrayal of the American Right.* Unpublished manuscript.

Rothbard, Murray, and Ronald Radosh, eds. 1972. *A New History of Leviathan.* New York: E. P. Dutton & Co.

Ryant, Carl. 1989. *Profit's Prophet: Garet Garrett (1874–1954).* Selinsgrove, Pa.: Susquehanna University Press.

Schlamm, William S. 1954. But It Is Not 1940. *Freeman* (November).

Schlamm, William S., and Aubrey Herbert. 1955. Various Letters. *Faith and Freedom* (May–June).

Schoonmaker, Nancy, and Doris Fielding Reid, eds. 1941. *We Testify.* New York: Smith & Durrell.

Spencer, Herbert. [1892] 1969. *The Man versus the State.* Introduction by Albert Jay Nock. Caldwell, Idaho: Caxton Printers.

Steele, Richard W. 1979. Franklin D. Roosevelt and His Foreign Policy Critics. *Political Science Quarterly* 44 (Spring).

Stenehjem, Michele Flynn. 1976. *An American First: John T. Flynn and the America First Committee.* New Rochelle, N.Y.: Arlington House Publishers.

Stout, Rex. 1942. *The Illustrious Dunderheads,* 176. New York: Alfred A. Knopf. Quoting speech over NBC (15 July 1941).

Stromberg, Joseph R. 1971a. *The Cold War and the Transformation of the American Right: The Decline of Right-Wing Liberalism.* Master's thesis, Florida Atlantic University.

———. 1971b. Howard Buffett: Anti-Imperialist. Chap. 2 of *The Cold War and the Transformation of the American Right: The Decline of Right-Wing Liberalism.* Master's thesis, Florida Atlantic University.

Taft, Robert A. 1951. *A Foreign Policy for Americans.* Garden City, N.Y.: Doubleday & Company.

———. 1964. Equal Justice under Law. In *Voices in Dissent,* edited by A. A. Ekirch, Jr. New York: Citadel Press.

Taylor, Joan Kennedy, ed. 1986. *Free Trade: The Necessary Foundation for World Peace.* Irvington-on-Hudson, N.Y.: Foundation for Economic Education.

Vedder, Richard K., and Lowell E. Gallaway. 1993. *Out of Work: Unemployment and Government in Twentieth-Century America.* New York: Holmes & Meier for the Independent Institute.

Vital Speeches. 1951. 1 January, 170–73. Quoted in Justus D. Doenecke, The Anti-Interventionist Tradition: Leadership and Perceptions, *Literature of Liberty* 4 (Summer): 34.

Ward, Robert. 1989. Good Mencken, Bad Mencken. *New York Times Book Review* (24 December).

Watts, V. Orval. 1955. Should We Trade with Russia? *Freeman* (February): 295.

Wheeler, Burton K., with Paul F. Healy. 1962. *Yankee from the West.* Garden City, N.Y.: Doubleday & Company.

Williams, W. H. A. 1977. *H. L. Mencken.* Boston: Twayne Publishers.

Wilson, Joan Hoff. 1975. *Herbert Hoover: Forgotten Progressive.* Boston: Little, Brown.

Wreszin, Michael. 1965. *Oswald Garrison Villard: Pacifist at War.* Bloomington: Indiana University Press.

Acknowledgments: Reprinted from *The Independent Review*, 1, no. 2 (Fall 1996): 201–48. ISSN 1086-1653, Copyright © 1996.

I had immensely helpful discussions with the late Roy A. Childs, Jr., Justus Doenecke, Williamson Evers, Walter E. Grinder, Jeffrey Rogers Hummel, Ralph Raico, the late Murray N. Rothbard, and Jeffrey Tucker. For providing research material I thank Ted Galen Carpenter, Robert Kephart, and Brian Summers. The stock indemnity is of course extended. A special thanks to Leonard P. Liggio, friend and teacher. The Institute for Humane Studies' Harper Library was indispensable in writing this paper.

3

On the Brink of World War II

Justus Doenecke's Storm on the Horizon

RALPH RAICO

Justus Doenecke, professor of history at the University of South Florida, has made a distinguished career of researching the history of American "isolationism" before and after World War II. His latest book, *Storm on the Horizon: The Challenge to American Intervention, 1939–1941* (Lanham, Md.: Rowman and Littlefield, 2000), is marked by his unsurpassed familiarity with the relevant archives—reflected in the 170 pages of endnotes—and by his rare and refreshing objectivity. The work has already won the annual book award of the Herbert Hoover Presidential Library Association.

Doenecke begins with the inevitable terminological issue. He eschews referring to the protagonists of *Storm on the Horizon* as *isolationists*, the term preferred, then as now, by their interventionist adversaries. This rhetorically powerful argument by epithet has been deployed from 1898 to the present. Today, simply uttering the word itself is probably decisive on questions of foreign policy for most Americans. In its place, Doenecke rightly prefers the less-loaded terms *anti-interventionist* and *noninterventionist*.

As our author makes amply clear, there were "many mansions" in the antiwar movement, from Father Charles Coughlin and his magazine *Social Justice* to the Communist Party (until June 22, 1941, that is, when the CPUSA turned on a dime and became fanatically *pro-war*). Very sensibly, however, Doenecke pays the most attention to the pacifist and, above all, the liberal and conservative opponents of war, most of whom were associated in one way or another with the America First Committee (AFC), founded in September 1940.

During its brief existence and ever after, the AFC was and has been subjected to mindless smears. A recent example occurred in connection with Princeton University's unsealing of many of the papers of Charles

Lindbergh, the committee's most prominent speaker, and of his wife Anne Morrow Lindbergh. In a report for the Associated Press (March 30, 2001), Linda A. Johnson informs us that "Lindbergh gave numerous speeches at the time denouncing President Franklin D. Roosevelt and Jews as 'warmongers.'" As concerns the Jews, this statement is a lie or, more likely, the product of a slovenly scribbler who could not be bothered to ascertain the easily accessible truth (see Berg 1998, 425–27). Lindbergh gave only a single, famous (or notorious) speech mentioning the Jews, in Des Moines, in October 1941. There he identified them not as "warmongers" but as, along with the Roosevelt administration and the British government, one of the main forces pushing us into war with Germany.

It is noteworthy that among the hundreds of letters Princeton made public were expressions of support for Lindbergh's antiwar stance from well-known writers such as W. H. Auden and, rather lower down the literary line (although she won the Nobel Prize for Literature in 1938), Pearl Buck. Readers surprised by the appearance of these names in this context would likely profit from consulting Bill Kauffman's brilliant *America First! Its History, Culture, and Politics* (1995). As Kauffman shows, many of the celebrities of the American cultural scene—outside of Manhattan and Hollywood—strongly sympathized with the AFC: Sherwood Anderson, e. e. cummings, Theodore Dreiser, Edgar Lee Masters, Henry Miller, Sinclair Lewis, Kathleen Norris, Frank Lloyd Wright, Charles Beard, and H. L. Mencken, among others. The total membership of the AFC exceeded eight hundred thousand, and it had millions of fellow travelers. The young John F. Kennedy and Gore Vidal were junior members of America First at their respective prep schools.

Storm on the Horizon proceeds by examining in detail the various episodes of the war and the controversies they generated at home, beginning with the German invasion of Poland and the "phony war," and ending with the last, futile negotiations with the Japanese envoys and the attack on Pearl Harbor. Doenecke deals with every significant issue of American foreign or military policy in this period. Many of these issues were new to me—for instance, the debates over a possible loan to Finland after the Soviet attack in November 1939 and over the fortification of Guam. Also indicative of the richness of the book are the frequent fascinating tidbits Doenecke serves up; for example, American gunboats were still patrolling the Yangtze as late as 1940 (three years after the *Panay* incident, presumably still in the interest of Standard Oil). Also revealed is that the two principal antiwar papers, the *Chicago Tribune* and the *New York Daily News* supported Dewey against Taft for the Republican presidential nomination in 1940 (pp. 158–59).

The noninterventionists lost the battle for the Republican nomination, as they would lose all the battles in their short-lived campaign. The winner, Wendell Willkie, "a utilities lawyer and Wall Street magnate who had been a Democrat all but four years of his life…came into the convention with only a handful of delegates" (p. 159). However, he enjoyed the fervent support of Henry Luce's magazines, *Life*, *Time*, and *Fortune* (the *Chicago Tribune* once irreverently wondered why Luce didn't add *Infinity* to his stable), as well as, above all, the support of the *New York Herald-Tribune* and with it Wall Street and the rest of the eastern Republican establishment whose agent it was. Willkie won on the sixth ballot. He had already chided Roosevelt for tardiness in aiding the Allies and denounced other Republican leaders as "isolationists." With Willkie as the nominee, foreign policy, the crucial issue facing the nation, was taken off the table—as is customary in American elections—much to the delight of the British intelligence operatives working to embroil the United States in yet another world war (see Mahl 1998, 155–76).

A major landmark on the road to war was the transfer to Britain of some fifty naval destroyers in return for long-term leases on bases stretching from Newfoundland to British Guiana. The deal was effected by presidential decree and sharply criticized by most noninterventionists as contrary to U.S. and international law (whereas a few jingoists such as Colonel McCormick of the *Chicago Tribune* reveled in the expansion of American power). It contributed to the formation in September 1940 of the Tripartite Pact of Japan, Germany, and Italy. In turn, this agreement was misinterpreted in Washington as directed *aggressively* against the United States, rather than as intended *defensively* to forestall an American attack on any of the signatories (pp. 125–28). The pact permitted Roosevelt to claim, "the hostilities in Europe, in Africa, and in Asia are all parts of a single world conflict" (p. 310). Henceforth, this "fundamental proposition," specious as it was, would guide U.S. policy.

Emboldened by his reelection, Roosevelt proposed the Lend-Lease Bill (H.R. 1776), one of the greatest extensions of presidential power in American history, which became law in March 1941. Although the AFC opposed Lend-Lease, it was faced with a quandary, as some anti-interventionists pointed out at the time: by supporting aid to Britain "short of war," it had opened the door to the incremental steps toward war that Roosevelt was taking and representing as his indefatigable struggle for peace.

Today Roosevelt's record of continual deception of the American people is unambiguous. In that sense, the old revisionists such as Charles Beard have been completely vindicated. Pro-Roosevelt historians—at least those who do not praise him outright for his noble lies—have had to resort to euphemism. Thus, Doenecke cites Warren F. Kimball, who is shocked— *shocked*—by FDR's "lack of candor" in leading the nation to war. Doenecke is much more straightforward. He notes, for example, the true role of the "neutrality patrol" that the president established in the western Atlantic in May 1941: "By flashing locations of German U-boats, the patrol would alert British merchantmen to veer away while inviting British cruisers and destroyers to attack" (p. 178). "From later March through May 1941, the president told such intimates as Harold Ickes and Henry Morgenthau that he hoped an incident on the high seas might result in providing convoys or possibly even a state of war with Germany" (p. 181). Still, some confirmed revisionists may conclude that Doenecke does not give due weight to FDR's colossal duplicity. Thus, although he mentions Roosevelt's meeting with George VI in Hyde Park in June 1939 (p. 125), he is silent on the president's promise to the British monarch—before the war even began—of full U.S. support in any military conflict with Germany (Wheeler-Bennett 1958, 390–92).

The German invasion of Russia in June 1941 appeared to strengthen the anti-interventionist case, in two ways. On the one hand, it pulled the rug out from under those who had argued (as some still argue) for the infinite moral superiority of the anti-Hitler coalition. Even the tabloid *New York Daily News* was able to perceive a truth that has somehow escaped practically all current commentators: "The Soviets' Christian victims have far outnumbered the Nazis' Jewish victims" (p. 212). On the other hand, with the first German reverses in December, doubt was cast on the notion that U.S. participation in the war was required to foil a Nazi victory. As Doenecke observes, "The tide of battle, however, had swung in the Soviets' favor long before American aid had arrived in quantity" (p. 225). Taft and others had remarked that if Hitler could not conquer Britain, how was he supposed to be able to attack the United States (p. 115)? Now that the Wehrmacht was confronting the Red Army, noninterventionists could reasonably question the fantasy that Hitler was on the verge of conquering the world.

Still, hysterical scenarios from Washington and the pro-war press continued to highlight the "invasion routes" that the Germans and occasionally the Japanese might take to the conquest of the United States, via the Caribbean, the Aleutians, and Alaska, or from West Africa to Brazil and thence, somehow, to New Orleans and Miami. This last scenario was the most frequently bruited about. Anti-administration spokesmen pointed out that even if a German Expeditionary Force were somehow able to occupy West Africa and pass over the Atlantic to Brazil, it would still be as far from the United States as it had been in Europe. And how was a modern mechanized army to traverse the jungles and mountains of South and Central America to invade the United States (p. 135)? Roosevelt fed the hysteria by claiming that he possessed a "secret map" showing Nazi plans to conquer South and Central America, as well as secret documents proving that Hitler planned to supplant all existing religions with a Nazi Church (p. 266). Needless to say, these statements were further falsehoods.

Another landmark on the road to war was the Atlantic Charter meeting between FDR and Churchill off the Newfoundland coast in August 1941. Churchill reported to his cabinet: the president had confided that "he would wage war, but not declare it, and that he would become more and more provocative....Everything was to be done to force an 'incident'" (p. 239–40). A month later, FDR did provoke the "incident" involving the U.S. destroyer *Greer*, which he used as a pretext for his order to "shoot on sight" any German and Italian vessels in the three-quarters of the North Atlantic that, as Doenecke states, now comprised our "defensive waters." The AFC accused FDR of initiating "an undeclared war, in plain violation of the Constitution." The public did not care very much, and the president not at all. A few days later, American ships and planes began escorting convoys carrying munitions of war to Britain (pp. 259–61). Attacks on U.S. warships multiplied as Congress voted to arm U.S. merchant ships, depriving them of any immunity as neutrals, and to permit U.S. naval vessels to enter the previously off-limits "combat zones." What prevented a war from breaking out was Hitler's resolve to keep the United States at bay until he was ready for the American onslaught.

By this time, Herbert Hoover was privately warning that FDR and his people were "doing everything they can to get us into war through the Japanese back door" (p. 317). In response to Japanese advances in Indochina, Roosevelt, together with Churchill, froze all Japanese assets, effectively imposing an embargo on oil shipments and starting the clock on the final stranding of the Imperial Japanese Navy. Edwin M. Borchard, Yale Law professor and authority on international law, commented: "While threatening Japan with dire consequences if she touches the Netherlands East Indies, our embargoes force her to look in that direction" (p. 306). Glimpsing the future that America's rulers had in store for the republic, Borchard noted, "Apparently we are getting to the point where no change can be made in the world's political control without offense to the United States" (p. 308).

One of the many merits of *Storm on the Horizon* is that it exhibits the contrast between the Old Right and the later conservative movement that took shape in the mid-1950s as a global anticommunist crusade. (On the earlier movement, see the excellent study by Sheldon Richman [1996].) One important difference concerns the conservatives' attitudes toward western imperialism, particularly in East Asia. William Henry Chamberlin criticized Roosevelt's evident intention to sacrifice American lives in order to keep the Dutch in the East Indies and the British in Singapore (p. 290). John T. Flynn ridiculed the notion of going to war against Japan over the Philippines because such a conflict would, in reality, be in the service of only a few dozen U.S. corporations (p. 299). Unlike later conservatives, who were ready to portray any anticommunist despot (for example, Syngman Rhee) as practically a Jeffersonian democrat, the noninterventionists tended to see Chiang Kai-shek for what he was, an autocrat and a gangster (p. 287).

The anti-interventionists were a courageous bunch, and they paid a price for their scruples. Harry Elmer Barnes was purged from the *New York World-Telegram*, Oswald Garrison Villard from *The Nation*, and Flynn from *The New Republic*. *The Baltimore Sun* even had the nerve to fire H. L. Mencken, that paper's sole claim to fame in its 164-year history. Universities banned antiwar speakers from their campuses, and local officials tried to prevent the AFC from holding rallies (p. 275). In and out of the administration, interventionists smeared their opponents as mouthpieces of the Nazis, cogs in the Nazi propaganda machine, or, at best, "unwitting" tools of fascism. Roosevelt's secretary of the interior, Harold Ickes—a notable bottom feeder—called Oswald Garrison Villard and Norman Thomas allies of Hitler (p. 271). The influential Friends of Democracy, before and during the war, slandered noninterventionists such as Robert Taft for being "very closely" tied to the Axis line. This organization won the gushing plaudits of Eleanor Roosevelt (Ribuffo 1983, 189). Egged on by Roosevelt, the FBI "began to tap the telephones and open the mail of vocal opponents of FDR's foreign policy and to monitor anti-intervention rallies." It "instituted surveillance of several of the president's prominent congressional critics," including Senator Burton K. Wheeler and Senator Gerald Nye. "The White House and the Justice Department also leaked to antifascist journalists information from FBI files that was embarrassing to anti-interventionists" (Haynes 1996, 28–29).

Left-liberal intellectuals, academic and otherwise, never cease bemoaning a time of terror in America known as the Age of McCarthyism. In so doing, they lack what might be termed the dialectical approach. For many conservatives who supported Senator McCarthy in the early 1950s, it was essentially payback time for the torrent of slanders they had endured before and during World War II (at a press conference in December 1942, FDR presented John O'Donnell, the Washington correspondent of the *Daily News*, with an Iron Cross for meritorious service to the Reich [White 1979, 44–45]). Postwar conservatives took deep satisfaction in pointing out the communist leanings and connections of those who had libeled them as mouthpieces for Hitler. Unlike the antiwar leaders, who were never "Nazis," the targets of McCarthyism had often been abject apologists for Stalin, and some of them actual Soviet agents.

Once or twice, Doenecke himself inadvertently and somewhat oddly comes close to echoing these interventionist charges. In June 1940, congressional interventionists passed a resolution allegedly reaffirming the Monroe Doctrine: it proclaimed the nonadmissibility of any transfer of sovereignty within the Western Hemisphere from one nation to another—for example, of the Dutch West Indies to Germany. The German diplomatic response denied any wish to occupy such territories, but observed in passing that the Monroe Doctrine could claim validity only under the condition that the United States refrain from interference in European affairs. Doenecke states that "several anti-interventionists adopted Foreign Minister Joachim von Ribbentrop's logic of two separate spheres" (p. 121). What the anti-interventionists adopted, however, was not Ribbentrop's logic, but the clear meaning of the Monroe Doctrine itself.

If *Storm on the Horizon* has any serious fault, it would mainly concern Doenecke's technique of proceeding from one event to the next, canvassing a few anti-interventionist voices involved in each in its turn. Though he insists on the importance of the underlying ideologies of the noninterventionists, some may find that his procedure militates against the presentation of a coherent account. Moreover, it is arguable that he might have paid more sustained attention to the views of Senator Taft, John T. Flynn, Felix Morley, Father James Gillis (editor of *The Catholic World*), and the international law experts Edwin M. Borchard and John Bassett Moore, and less to those of Hugh Johnson, Lawrence Dennis, William Randolph Hearst, and *Social Justice*.

Nonetheless, *Storm on the Horizon* is a work of outstanding scholarship. Students of the greatest antiwar movement in American history, revisionists and nonrevisionists alike, are permanently in Justus Doenecke's debt.

REFERENCES

Berg, A. Scott. 1998. *Lindbergh*. New York: G. P. Putnam's Sons.
Haynes, John E. 1996. *Red Scare or Red Menace: American Communism and Anticommunism in the Cold War Era*. Chicago: Ivan R. Dee.
Kauffman, Bill. 1995. *America First! Its History, Culture, and Politics*. Amherst, N.Y.: Prometheus.
Mahl, Thomas E. 1998. *Desperate Deception: British Covert Operations in the United States, 1939–44*. Washington, D.C.: Brassey's.
Ribuffo, Leo P. 1983. *The Old Christian Right: The Protestant Far Right from the Great Depression to the Cold War*. Philadelphia: Temple University Press.
Richman, Sheldon. 1996. New Deal Nemesis: The "Old Right" Jeffersonians. *The Independent Review* 1 (Fall): 201–48.
Wheeler-Bennett, John W. 1958. *King George VI: His Life and Reign*. New York: St. Martin's.
White, Graham J. 1979. *FDR and the Press*. Chicago: University of Chicago Press.

Acknowledgments: Reprinted from *The Independent Review*, 6, no. 4 (Spring 2002): 607–13. ISSN 1086-1653, Copyright © 2002.

4

The Republican Road Not Taken

The Foreign-Policy Vision of Robert A. Taft

MICHAEL T. HAYES

First elected to the Senate in 1938, Robert A. Taft represented Ohio from 1939 until his death in 1953. Although Taft was defeated for the Republican presidential nomination three times, in 1940, 1948, and 1952, he was universally acknowledged as the leader of the Republican Party's congressional wing. Taft offered both a positive vision of international organization following World War II and a prescient critique of the internationalist policies developed by Presidents Roosevelt and Truman. Dwight Eisenhower embraced and continued these internationalist Democratic policies during his two terms in office (1953–61), so his victory over Taft at the Republican convention in 1952 represented a decisive rejection of the alternative foreign policy advocated by Taft and other isolationist Republicans of that period. The significance of Taft's defeat—and the thesis of this article—was well articulated by journalist Nicholas von Hoffman, writing in the midst of the Vietnam War almost two decades later. Observing that Taft's critique of internationalism had been vindicated subsequently on almost every point, von Hoffman characterized Taft's foreign-policy vision as "a way to defend the country without destroying it, a way to be part of the world without running it" (qtd. in Radosh 1975, 147).

Many of Taft's contemporaries dismissed him as an "isolationist" in foreign policy (for good examples, see Schlesinger 1952 and Van Dyke and Davis 1952). Although subsequent scholarship has suggested that this characterization was highly misleading (Berger 1967, 1971, 1975; West 1952), Taft was isolationist if isolationism is defined, following careful scholarship, as "an attitude of opposition to binding commitments by the United States government that would create new, or expand existing, obligations to foreign nations" (Rieselbach 1966, 7). Like many Americans of his era, Taft did not welcome the intrusion of foreign policy and gladly would have "let the rest of the world go its own way if it would only go without bothering the United States" (Osgood 1953, 433). For much of his career, Taft advocated what he called "the policy of the free hand," whereby the United States would avoid entangling alliances and interference in foreign disputes. This policy permitted government leaders the freedom of action to decide in particular cases whether a sufficiently vital U.S. interest warranted involvement (Taft 1951, 12).[1]

The real problem with the term isolationism is not that it misrepresented Taft's general orientation, but rather that it permitted defenders of various Roosevelt and Truman policies to discredit Taft without having to engage his arguments seriously. Labeling opponents of administration policies as "isolationists" implied that they were naïve, like ostriches with their heads buried in the sand, nostalgic for an earlier era in which the United States could hide behind the safety of two oceans and avoid involvement in international affairs (Doenecke 1979, 11–12; Graebner 1968).[2] In reality, however, none of the members of the isolationist wing of the Republican Party ever believed it possible for the United States to isolate itself from the rest of the world, and so all of them accordingly rejected that label.

Taft's foreign-policy views were neither naive nor nostalgic. To the contrary, his critique of internationalism deserved to be taken seriously and was vindicated subsequently on many points. Taft criticized the Roosevelt/ Truman approach to postwar international organization, correctly pointing to features of the United Nations that would prevent its serving as a real force for peace and equality under the law. He also challenged the Truman administration's assessment of the Soviet military threat against western Europe, a threat that now appears to have been overstated consciously and deliberately to secure congressional support for the Marshall Plan, universal military training, and an expanded air force (Berger 1967; Kofsky 1993). He anticipated correctly that a steady rise in defense outlays could lead to a "garrison state" and the erosion of civil liberties (Higgs 1987). Finally, Taft was prescient in warning that even well-meaning internationalism would necessarily degenerate over time into a form of imperialism that would breed resentment against the United States around the globe, eventually endangering U.S. national security.

Taft was no backward-looking conservative.[3] On domestic issues, he sought to maximize individual liberty while minimizing relationships based on power and control. In the terminology of political philosophers, he saw the United States as a civil association operating under the rule of law. Although he recognized the need to accommodate change in order to preserve the institutions and practices he valued as truly precious, he regarded many New Deal measures as radical rather than reformist and fought against the New Deal wherever he found it to be a threat to the basic form of the American polity as a civil association operating under the rule of law. His foreign-policy views were an extension of this same political philosophy to international affairs; he proposed that postwar international organization be centered around an international tribunal founded on the rule of law, establishing within international affairs the same regime he espoused in the domestic realm.

In this chapter, I lay out Taft's political philosophy, then show how Taft's foreign-policy vision grew out of this same libertarian vision and contrast that vision with Eisenhower's to make clear just what was lost when the Republicans nominated Eisenhower instead of Taft in 1952. Finally, drawing on the work of A. James Reichley (2000), I distinguish between altruistic and national-interest isolationism with respect to Taft specifically. Although Taft exhibited both types of isolationism at different times, he was consistently isolationist throughout his career, and his underlying libertarian philosophy gave an overall coherence to his foreign policy even as he moved from one type to the other.

TAFT'S POLITICAL PHILOSOPHY

Throughout his political career, Taft sought to preserve what he regarded as an "American way of life" in which the liberty of individual Americans would be circumscribed only by the rule of law. (For an especially clear and concise statement of this philosophy, see Taft 1949.) Although he recognized the need to reform institutions and practices in order to preserve the core elements of the system he cherished, he consistently fought against New Deal policies that he believed would change the fundamental character of the system. (For the best statement of Taft's distinction between necessary reforms and radical New Deal innovations, see Taft [1935] 1997).[4]

Taft viewed the United States as a civil association, not a purposive association (Oakeshott 1991, 438–61). Within a purposive association, citizens are related to one another by virtue of their pursuit of some shared purpose, and they derive their identity as citizens from this common enterprise. The first purposive associations were religious, with the state assuming the role of guardian and promoter of orthodox beliefs; some nostalgic conservatives still view the state in this way (Hayes 2002). Religion is not the only basis for purposive associations, however; a society becomes a purposive association any time it defines itself in terms of some common enterprise, whether that enterprise be the promotion of economic efficiency, the spread of democracy throughout the world, or the pursuit of some vision of social justice (Oakeshott 1991, 450–53). Taft rejected all such visions because individuals can never really be free within a purposive system inasmuch as their actions must always be instrumental to the achievement of the common purpose.

By contrast, within civil associations no common purpose unites people into a shared enterprise. Rather, people are free to pursue their own individual purposes as long as they do not interfere with the rights of others to do likewise. The social order is spontaneous rather than planned or directed (Hayek 1973; Horwitz 2001). The bases for association here are territorial boundaries and a commonly accepted set of rules governing people as they pursue happiness in their own individual ways (Oakeshott 1991, 454–57). By this reasoning, we are Americans not because we have particular values or common goals, but rather because we live within the territorial boundaries of the United States and pursue our own individual strategies for attaining happiness subject to the Constitution and laws of the United States. Taft certainly viewed the United States as a civil association rather than a purposive association.

To Taft, a free economy was the natural corollary of a free society, and his desire to preserve economic freedom led him to oppose a variety of domestic and foreign policies promulgated by the Roosevelt and Truman administrations, including the steady growth of federal spending, increased power to federal agencies, and increased defense outlays that might lead to what he called a "garrison state." A free economy, however, was desirable primarily because it was founded on liberty. The normative case for the free market ultimately rests less on its potential efficiency in allocating resources than on the way it orders relationships among citizens. Within a free-market economy, transactions are purely voluntary, and relationships among individuals are based on mutual consent rather than on power (Knight 1982). That free economies outperform socialist economies was important to Taft, but it was nonetheless a subsidiary benefit. Taft saw that increases in the general standard of living empowered individual Americans in a variety of ways, thus adding to their effective liberty (Kirk and McClellan 1967, 132–39; Smith and Taft 1939, 13–21).

The role of government within a civil association is necessarily limited, in distinct contrast to its role in a purposive association. Within a civil association, "governing is recognized as a specific and limited activity; not the management of an enterprise, but the rule of those engaged in a great diversity of self-chosen enterprises" (Oakeshott 1991, 429). Because individuals pursuing their own ends inevitably impinge on others doing likewise, absolute liberty is undesirable, and some restrictions on individual freedom of action may actually increase effective liberty (Kirk and McClellan 1967, 67–68). Taft articulated this vision of the role of government in a debate with U.S. Representative T. V. Smith in 1939: "Government has been generally conceived to be a keeper of the peace, a referee of controversies, and an adjuster of abuses, not a regulator of the people, or their way of life, or their business and personal activities" (Smith and Taft 1939, 15).

Equally important, in Taft's view, within a properly functioning civil association the state's power over its citizens must be circumscribed by the rule of law (Hayek 1973; Oakeshott 1991, 425–34). Under the rule of law, all laws exhibit two qualities (Hayek 1960, 1973; Hayes 2001, 174–75). First, all rules governing the behavior of citizens and government officials are as clear and specific as possible. Where rules are unambiguous, citizens can understand easily what the rules are and know the consequences of violating them. They can take such rules into account as they pursue their own individual purposes and activities. Moreover, clear and specific rules minimize the arbitrary exercise of power by limiting the discretion available to government officials as they enforce the laws; hence, we have in the classic phrase a "government of laws, not of men." Throughout his career, Taft consistently opposed grants of broad discretionary power to administrative agencies, and he viewed the growth of the federal government under the New Deal and Fair Deal as giving rise to a new system of policymaking by pressure groups that elevated the pursuit of self-interest at the expense of the public interest, thus reducing the role of "political principle as a force in the determination of Government policy" (Taft 1950, 155; for a more recent critique of interest-group liberalism along the same lines, see Lowi 1979).

Second, under the rule of law, all laws are impersonal, applying equally

to everyone. Legislation should never discriminate by singling out identifiable groups for privileges or punishments. This evenhandedness is the
principle of equality under the law. Adherence to this principle of equal
treatment of all individuals, regardless of their wealth or power, is the only
reliable defense the weak can have against the strong (Hayes 2001, 181–89;
Lowi 1979, 298).

Taft's commitment to equality under the law is exemplified by his primary legacy in domestic policy, the Taft-Hartley Act of 1947. In contrast
to many Republicans, Taft accepted labor unions as essential features of
modern capitalism. He insisted on the right to strike, and he sought to
minimize government intervention in union–management relations. At the
same time, he believed that the government had to act to assure equal justice under law. The National Labor Relations Act had specified unfair management practices without providing any corresponding list of unfair union
practices, and the National Labor Relations Board had favored unions over
management. A new law was needed, in Taft's judgment, both to restore the
balance between unions and management and to protect the rights of individual workers against union leaders (Kirk and McClellan 1967, 109–31;
Patterson 1972, 352–66).

TAFT'S LIBERTARIAN FOREIGN-POLICY VISION

Because of his leadership role within the Republican Party (which was no
less real during those periods in which he did not occupy a formal leadership position within the party), Taft felt compelled to master a broad
range of issues outside his normal interests and committee responsibilities.
In particular, although his primary interests lay in domestic policy, he felt
an obligation to take a leadership role on foreign policy as well, given the
importance of such issues as U.S. involvement in World War II, the shape
of the postwar order, and the Korean War. As Taft said in a speech to the
U.S. Chamber of Commerce in 1951, "People have accused me of moving
into foreign policy. The fact is that foreign policy moved in on me" (qtd. in
Patterson 1972, 474).

When forced by events to deal with international problems, Taft brought
with him the deeply held and carefully formulated political philosophy re-
viewed in the preceding discussion. He believed that the primary purpose
of U.S. foreign policy, in light of which all specific policies must be con-

sidered, must always be "to protect the liberty of the people of the United States" (Taft 1951, 11). For example, he opposed new military outlays or international commitments when he believed they would increase the overall level of government expenditures enough to threaten the viability of the free economy.

The secondary purpose of foreign policy, subordinate for Taft only to the defense of liberty, was the maintenance of peace (Taft 1951, 11–12). He abhorred war and consistently sought to avoid U.S. involvement in war if possible. He also questioned policies (such as the Truman Doctrine and the development of the North Atlantic Treaty Organization [NATO]) that he believed might provoke a war with the Soviet Union that otherwise might be avoided. Taft doubted that wars accomplished much in the end, noting that the two world wars fought in the twentieth century had produced millions of casualties while leaving in their wake dictatorships and totalitarian governments. He believed that the degree of economic mobilization and centralized planning that wars require is antithetical to a free economy and thus to liberty (Taft 1951, 11–12). Throughout his career, he regarded proposals for increased military outlays as threatening the development of a "garrison state" at home and as potentially provoking war or arms races abroad (Berger 1967, 133).

Although Taft accepted the need to go to war whenever the liberty of the American people was directly threatened, he believed war should never be undertaken to advance any other purpose. He especially opposed resort to war to advance moral crusades of any sort—for example, Roosevelt's depiction of World War II as a crusade to establish the "four freedoms" around the world:

> Nor do I believe we can justify war by our natural desire to bring freedom to others throughout the world, although it is perfectly proper to encourage and promote freedom. In 1941 President Roosevelt announced that we were going to establish a moral order throughout the world: freedom of speech and expression, "everywhere in the world"; freedom to worship God "everywhere in the world"; freedom from want, and freedom from fear "everywhere in the world." I pointed out then that the forcing of any special brand of freedom and democracy on a people, whether they want it or not, by the brute force of war will be a denial of those very democratic principles which we are striving to advance. (1951, 16)[5]

Although Taft was unwilling to use force to impose democracy on other nations, he did view liberty as desirable for all people everywhere, and he believed a workable international organization must be founded on the sovereign equality of free and independent states. As early as 1944 he suspected that Roosevelt, Churchill, and Stalin would carve up the postwar world into spheres of influence that denied any voice to the peoples of Poland, Finland, Estonia, Latvia, and Lithuania in direct violation of the language of the Atlantic Charter, in which the three powers had committed to respecting the rights of all peoples to choose their form of government and to restoring sovereign rights and self-government to nations that had been deprived of them forcibly. The real question, as Taft recognized, was not whether the great powers should force freedom on unwilling nations but rather whether the great powers would permit self-determination for previously occupied nations. In his view, a United Nations created by powers this cynical and prevented by the veto power from defending weak states against the designs of the strong could never establish an international order founded on "the freedom and equality of treatment for every nation" (Taft [1944] 2001, 555–56). Although Taft voted for membership in the United Nations, he eventually came to believe that the United States should "develop our own military policy and our own policy of alliances, without substantial regard to the non-existent power of the United Nations to prevent aggression" (Taft 1951, 44).

Taft's vision for a peaceful and just postwar world differed sharply from that advanced by Presidents Roosevelt and Truman precisely because it represented an international application of the same libertarian philosophy that shaped his domestic-policy views. Taft proposed a system in which all nations would "agree on a definite law to govern their relations with each other and also agree that, without any veto power, they will submit their disputes to adjudication and abide by the decision of an impartial tribunal" (Taft 1951, 40). Decisions of the international court would be enforced by an international police force, to which the United States would contribute troops. All nations would be treated equally under this international rule of law, thus providing real protection for the rights of the weak against the strong. Taft objected to the United Nations because it was not based on any underlying foundation of law and because Security Council members' ability to veto resolutions effectively precluded the development of any truly universal law, "for surely nothing can be law if the five largest nations can exempt themselves from its application" (Taft 1951, 39–40).

At the same time, Taft explicitly rejected the idea of a world government that would reproduce the U.S. constitutional structure on a global level—with a supreme legislature, executive, and court—and that would initiate a system of international federalism in which laws made at the world level superseded decisions made at the nation-state level. Taft believed that a world government of this sort inevitably would infringe on the liberties of all member states and their citizens. In particular, he believed that such a plan would "subject the American people to the government of a majority who do not understand what American principles are and have little sympathy with them," bringing "an end to that liberty which has produced in this country the greatest happiness, the greatest production, the highest standard of living the world has ever seen" (Taft 1951, 44–45).

In Taft's vision, by contrast, international law would govern only the relationships *among* states; the international tribunal would have no authority whatever to regulate the internal affairs of sovereign states. Rather, the international order would constitute a spontaneous global social order, or civil association, in which the freedom of action of individual states and their citizens would be circumscribed only by the rule of law, which would apply only to their interactions with one another:

> [F]orce should not be called for against any nation because of any internal domestic policy, except rearmament in excess of a quota imposed or agreed to. Interference in domestic policies, even such vital matters as tariffs or the treatment of minorities, would be more likely to make war than to prevent it. The test is: is the subject one on which the people of the United States would be willing to have other nations interfere with our internal actions? If not, we should not attempt to impose such interference on others. (Taft 1951, 38)

Until all nations, including the United States, are willing to enter into such an agreement, however, the weak can have no real protection against the strong, and "international progress toward peace is bound to fail" (Taft 1951, 41).

Taft placed two preconditions on U.S. participation in the international organization he envisioned after World War II: fair boundaries had to be negotiated, providing for full self-determination for previously occupied nations; and fair economic arrangements had to be established in which every nation would have access on equal terms to the raw materials of the world (Taft [1944] 2001, 555–56). His contemporary scholarly critics saw these conditions as permitting him to pay lip service to the idea of international organization while providing a basis for ultimate opposition to the kind of institution that realistically would be acceptable to the great powers. When viewed in light of the foreign-policy vision identified here, however, these two conditions can be recognized properly as reflecting Taft's lifelong commitment to the principles of self-determination and equality under the law.

THE REPUBLICAN ROAD NOT TAKEN

Whatever its merits, Taft's vision of an international tribunal built on a foundation of international law almost surely could not have been achieved in the immediate postwar period because the Soviet Union would not have accepted any body of international law that codified the status quo:

> If, as it would appear, laws tend to stabilize power relationships and to establish moral values, then anyone who suggests that it is possible to agree upon the content of international law assumes that the most powerful states, at least, are satisfied with the present power distribution, and that they are in substantial agreement on moral values. But implicit in his [Taft's] approach to the Soviet threat is the recognition that the Soviet Union does not want to stabilize the distribution of power in its present form any more than it wants to accept American standards of morality. (Armstrong 1955, 214)

However, a foreign policy based on Taft's libertarian principles would have taken the United States down a very different road even if his vision of international organization based on the rule of law proved unattainable. Taft and Eisenhower started from entirely different first principles. As we have seen, Taft ranked liberty above all other values. Although he was unwilling to embark on moral crusades to extend liberty to other nations, he nevertheless valued liberty for all people, and he consistently championed the principle of self-determination. If he perceived limits on what the United States could accomplish elsewhere in the world, he also appreciated the distinct limits of American virtue: the United States was no less vulnerable to the temptations of empire than any other nation placed in the same position.

By contrast, Eisenhower based his foreign policy first and foremost on the need to secure access to raw materials, as he made clear in 1951:

> From my viewpoint, foreign policy is, or should be, based primarily upon one consideration. That consideration is the need for the U.S. to obtain certain raw materials to sustain its economy and, when possible, to preserve profitable foreign markets for our surpluses. Out of this need grows the necessity for making certain that those areas of the world in which essential raw materials are produced are not only accessible to us, but their populations and governments are willing to trade with us on a friendly basis. (qtd. in Cook 1984, 112–13)

Thus, although Eisenhower was clearly more willing than Taft to commit the United States to membership in the United Nations and in collective security arrangements such as NATO, this difference was not their only significant one. A second, equally important difference centered around Eisenhower's support for tax incentives, subsidies, relaxation of antitrust laws, and other government policies designed to encourage and protect American corporations' direct investment in Third World countries. (For more on this point, see Cook 1984, 293–346.)

Eisenhower and his successors never fully realized (or at least never acknowledged publicly) that aggressive U.S. involvement in the Third World as advocated by the "forward-looking" internationalists would eventually necessitate tight control of political and economic developments in those nations. Fostering foreign investment through changes in the tax code or the relaxation of antitrust laws would not be enough. Sooner or later, *protecting* those foreign investments from political instability, communist guerrilla movements, or reformist regimes interested in nationalization would also be necessary. Political change in developing countries would have to be subordinated to U.S. economic and political interests. When U.S. corporate interests were threatened, as in Iran or Guatemala, regimes would be toppled. (On Iran, see Kinzer 2003 and Roosevelt 1979; on Guatemala, see Cook 1984, 217–92.) More often, however, U.S. interests would be furthered by regime stability, and state terrorism—including detention, torture, death squads, and "disappearances"—would be employed to prevent the formation of labor unions or political parties that might challenge incumbent regimes (Cook 1984, 328–32; Herman 1982). U.S. support for right-wing military governments thus would make it impossible for the subject nations to deal with internal problems through the development of social movements or the peaceful transfer of power (LaFeber 1984, 15–16).

A study of U.S. national-security policy toward Latin America illustrates the logic of this process very well (Schoultz 1987). The primary goal of U.S. foreign policy toward Central and South America throughout the postwar period was to maintain regime stability. Human rights was, at best, a residual concern that came into play only in the absence of a perceived security problem in the region—which was almost never during the Cold War period. Although all policymakers with a responsibility for Latin America shared this emphasis on regime stability, they divided into two groups in their explanation of the causes of instability, one group stressing the role of communist subversion in fostering instability, and the other identifying the underlying causes as extreme poverty and growing income inequality. Unfortunately for the Latin Americans, no one had a sophisticated theory of how instability might be managed once it had become a problem, and the group that viewed instability as caused by poverty rather than by communist subversion nevertheless saw a real danger in the potential for communists to exploit instability to overthrow regimes friendly to the United States. In such circumstances, most of the time both groups perceived policies that fostered human rights as potentially destabilizing, and the United States found itself trapped into supporting regimes that frequently employed rape, torture, and murder to maintain themselves in power. This same pattern holds for U.S. involvement in the Middle East (see Zunes 2003, 6–34).

Taft's record in the Senate on foreign-policy issues suggests strongly that he would have pursued a different foreign policy toward developing nations. In distinct contrast to Eisenhower, Taft did not base his vision of foreign policy on the need to secure stable access to raw materials and foreign markets. To the contrary, his foreign policy rested on the twin goals of maintaining the liberty of the American people and preserving peace. This difference in fundamental values led him to question the importance of expanded foreign investment to the U.S. economy and to warn that such investment eventually might lead to resentments that would make Third World countries vulnerable to communist propaganda, thus threatening the peace and liberty of the United States:

It is said that foreign investment will make for peace. I don't think history shows anything of the kind. Ordinarily after an investment is obtained, the people of a country are likely to regard its owners as absentee landlords only concerned with draining away the assets of the country. Foreign investors are likely to be regarded as exploiters of natural resources and cheap labor. In the past they often have been such. Their activities are likely to build up hostility to the United States. This is even more true today with the growth of Socialist and Communist Parties in many countries. Witness the agitation against American sugar investments even in Puerto Rico and Cuba. (Taft 1945, 637)[6]

Moreover, in distinct contrast to Eisenhower, Taft perceived significant potential dangers stemming from the provision of military assistance to foreign governments. In 1946, he successfully opposed a Truman administration bill that would have authorized the president to send military advisers to nations requesting them, arguing, "we should not send military missions all over the world to be teaching how to fight the American way" (qtd. in Berger 1971, 176). Taft viewed such assistance as undercutting the United Nations and as provoking the Soviet Union by supplying and training nations that potentially might serve as our allies in an aggressive war.

Although Taft agreed with Eisenhower on the need to provide developing countries with economic assistance to help restore their economies in the aftermath of war and "to relieve human misery, which may lead to war," he was much more pessimistic about what such aid could achieve, and he believed it should be limited in amount and scope. In his view, conditions attached to this aid in order to promote the achievement of American goals might easily elicit resentment by recipient nations over time. In such circumstances, it would be tempting "to slip into an attitude of imperialism and to entertain the idea that we know what is good for other people better than they know themselves. From there it is an easy step to the point where war becomes an instrument of public policy rather than the last resort to maintain our own liberty" (Taft 1949, 119).

Thus, the choice of Eisenhower over Taft was not a triumph of forward-looking leadership over backward-looking leadership, but rather a fateful decision to continue along a path that eventually would lead to "an informal empire, an empire based on the projection of force over every corner of the world and on the use of American capital and markets to force global integration on our terms at whatever costs to others" (Johnson 2000, 7). The American public did not and still do not fully understand the ultimate consequences of this critically important decision because the isolationist critique was dismissed without ever being engaged and debated seriously. Taft's vision of foreign policy—the Republican road not taken—would have produced a substantially different postwar global order whether or not his distinctive vision of international organization was ever implemented successfully.

ALTRUISTIC AND NATIONAL-INTEREST ISOLATIONISM

Taft's foreign-policy vision represented a blend of idealism and realism. Taft understood fully both the role of national interest and the pursuit of power in foreign policy, and he always gave primacy to U.S. national interests. Although his proposal for an international tribunal might be characterized as utopian, given the postwar balance of power, he advanced it because he believed such an institution could contribute to the preservation of peace and to the liberty of Americans. Taft's political contemporaries resolved this seeming contradiction by dismissing his proposal for an international tribunal as insincere, a political expedient necessitated by the overwhelming postwar support (at both elite and mass levels) for some kind of international organization, and many scholars support this assessment. As we have seen, however, Taft's vision of international organization was not merely a political expedient; to the contrary, it was a natural extension of his core political philosophy to the international realm. An accurate understanding of Taft must include both these elements, however contradictory they may seem.

Taft's foreign-policy views cannot be captured adequately by making a simple, dichotomous distinction between isolationism and internationalism. To the contrary, as political scientist A. James Reichley (2000) has shown, at least four distinct foreign-policy orientations may be identified. Reichley derives his four-cell typology from the cross-tabulation of two underlying dimensions. The first dimension differentiates policymakers who are prepared to intervene economically, politically, or militarily in foreign affairs from those (such as Taft) who are extremely reluctant to intervene (193). Although this first dimension clearly captures the conventional dis-

Figure 1
Four Distinct Foreign-Policy Orientations

	Internationalist: Willing to intervene in foreign affairs	*Isolationist: Reluctant to intervene in foreign affairs*
Emphasis on the national interest as primary value in foreign policy	National-interest interventionism	National-interest isolationism
Significant emphasis on altruism in foreign policy	Altruistic interventionism	Altruistic isolationism

Source: Reichley 2000.

tinction between isolationists and internationalists, Reichley argues that we need to consider a second dimension as well. This second dimension distinguishes between policymakers who focus primarily on "America's national interest as almost the sole value to be pursued in the conduct of foreign policy" and those who emphasize "more altruistic concerns, such as spreading democracy or achieving a fairer distribution of the world's goods" (193). Acknowledging that few, if any, pure cases exist and that almost all policymakers attach at least some value to both dimensions, Reichley nevertheless identifies four distinct foreign-policy orientations, as shown in figure 1.[7]

Reichley identifies two distinctive types of internationalists. National-interest interventionists are essentially foreign-policy "realists." Following Morgenthau's (1962) ideas, they define international politics as primarily a struggle for power among nations pursuing their national interests. Altruistic interventionists, by contrast, tend to be foreign-policy "idealists" who seek to inject moral considerations into foreign policy, typically by moving away from power politics and toward a system of international law and international organization.

Reichley likewise identifies two distinctive forms of isolationism. National-interest isolationists are reluctant to intervene in world politics because they regard international commitments as limiting U.S. freedom of action, making war more likely and entangling the United States in foreign disputes (or burdens) that really do not concern it. Altruistic isolationists, by contrast, are motivated primarily by an opposition to imperialism. Their altruism is not manifested through positive efforts to promote democracy or to redistribute wealth among nations; rather, they are isolationist because they eschew the pursuit of national power, with its inevitable goal of conquest or domination of other nations. To the contrary, they seek a world in which power relations among states are minimized, and, accordingly, they reject any attempt to impose the will of one nation on other nations.

Although Taft was clearly an isolationist within Reichley's framework, his foreign-policy vision is not captured adequately by either of the two isolationist categories.[8] Taft's positive vision—his support for an international regime based on the equality of nations under the rule of law—clearly reflected an altruistic form of isolationism. So did his consistent rejection of imperialism in any form. At the same time, his opposition to specific Truman policies, as described earlier, forced him most of the time into a posture of national-interest isolationism.

The common thread that gave overall coherence to Taft's foreign policy was a consistent libertarianism. His devotion to liberty extended to other nations as well as to the United States. His ideal for the international system was a spontaneous social order governed by the rule of law, and he clearly saw the principle of self-determination as foundational to such a system. Although the world's failure to adopt such a system eventually led him to reject the United Nations as a constraint on American freedom of action, that failure did not diminish his fundamental libertarianism. He was prescient in warning that foreign investment would lead to exploitation and imperialism, creating resentments that eventually might threaten U.S. national security. And where Eisenhower and his successors shored up ruthless dictators to ensure regime stability, Taft viewed the world as "big enough to contain all kinds of different ways of life" without threat to U.S. interests (Patterson 1972, 243). Although he would neither lead a crusade to liberate foreign nations nor commit U.S. troops to foreign conflicts in which American liberty was not threatened directly, he almost surely would have been appalled to find U.S. foreign policies linked in any way to the development of state terrorism and to the widespread denial of legal due process and fundamental political rights in developing nations.

With the collapse of the Soviet Union, the United States is now the world's only remaining superpower, making it much easier to implement Taft's vision than it would have been in the 1950s. Although few nations would acquiesce willingly in the development of a body of international law ratifying a U.S. empire, almost surely there would be much less resistance to statutes establishing equality under the law as a matter of principle. Although progress toward such a system necessarily would be difficult and incremental at best, discrete foreign-policy actions might be evaluated in the near term with regard to their tendency to move us closer to or farther away from the kind of regime Taft advocated.

At present, we clearly are moving in the opposite direction, pursuing homeland security through the acquisition of overwhelming military capability and a reliance on preventive war. Both homeland security and international stability are more likely to be attained, however, by the patient, incremental pursuit of the kind of regime Taft envisioned—one founded on the rule of law and equality of nations under the law. Although such a system would be more consistent with the ideals for which we claim to stand as a nation, it remains an open question whether the United States, as the world's richest country and its dominant military power, will prove willing to forgo empire for a different kind of system in which equality under the law at least begins to supersede power as the basis for international relations.

NOTES

1. By 1951, if not earlier, Taft had come to believe that various developments had combined to render the policy of the free hand obsolete. The development of atomic weapons and improvements in the speed and range of aircraft had effectively eliminated the geographical isolation that previously had made the country safe from foreign attack. In addition, Taft regarded the threat of communism as unprecedentedly serious—more of a threat than national socialism, for example—because of its ideological component (Taft 1951, 18–19).
2. This article focuses on Taft's foreign-policy views, but Taft was only the most articulate and best-known member of a larger group characterized as isolationist. For more on this larger movement, see Radosh 1975; Rothbard 1964, 1978; and Stromberg 2000, 2001.
3. Elsewhere I have developed a typology of four distinct worldviews in which I distinguish between *adaptive* and *nostalgic conservatives* (Hayes 2001, 2002). Nostalgic conservatives are genuinely and unapologetically reactionary, desiring a return to the practices or institutional forms of an earlier age in which they believe society was organized around some revealed truth that subsequently has been eroded by modernity. Whatever the (sometimes substantial) merits of their arguments, such conservatives can be characterized legitimately as "backward looking." By contrast, adaptive conservatives acknowledge the need for institutional reform in response to changing circumstances if they are to preserve what they regard as truly precious. Viewed in these terms, Taft clearly was an adaptive conservative.
4. On many domestic issues, Taft was much more liberal than Eisenhower, as Eisenhower himself conceded. For example, Taft was an early advocate of federal aid to education and

a cosponsor of the ambitious Wagner-Ellender-Taft public-housing bill, enacted in 1949 (Davies 1964; Kirk and McClellan 1967, 139–56).

5. Taft's opposition to Roosevelt on this point illustrates at least three of his core principles. Basing the case for war on the need to establish the four freedoms throughout the world not only would deny other nations the freedom to determine for themselves what form of government they preferred, as emphasized in the quotation, but also would justify war on some basis other than the defense of Americans' liberty, therefore transforming the United States from a civil association into a purposive association, in which the liberties of Americans would be sacrificed to the pursuit of a shared crusade to create a new moral order.

6. Taft strenuously opposed any government programs to guarantee foreign investments by American corporations. As Berger observes, "So while Taft was unenthusiastic about either private or public economic expansion abroad, when confronted with a choice he preferred private enterprise. He also emphasized that any government-sponsored programs should be under American control" (1971, 175).

7. Reichley developed this typology to help interpret the foreign-policy divisions of the first part of the twentieth century. Accordingly, he characterizes Teddy Roosevelt as a national-interest interventionist, Woodrow Wilson as an altruistic interventionist, Henry Cabot Lodge as a national-interest isolationist, and Robert LaFollette as an altruistic isolationist.

8. Reichley notes correctly that few if any pure types exist. Although Eisenhower and Truman each combined elements of both forms of interventionism, Eisenhower wanted to shift the balance more toward the national interest and away from international altruism (Cook 1984, 92).

REFERENCES

Armstrong, John P. 1955. The Enigma of Senator Taft and American Foreign Policy. *Review of Politics* 17 (April): 206–31.

Berger, Henry. 1967. A Conservative Critique of Containment: Senator Taft and the Early Cold War Program. *In Containment and Revolution*, edited by David Horowitz, 125–39. Boston: Beacon.

———. 1971. Senator Taft Dissents from Military Escalation. In *Cold War Critics: Alternatives to American Foreign Policy in the Truman Years*, edited by Thomas G. Paterson, 167–204. Chicago: Quadrangle.

———. 1975. Bipartisanship, Senator Taft, and the Truman Administration. *Political Science Quarterly* 90 (summer): 221–37.

Cook, Blanche Wiesen. 1984. *The Declassified Eisenhower: A Divided Legacy.* Garden City, N.Y.: Doubleday.

Davies, Richard O. 1964. "Mr. Republican" Turns "Socialist": Robert A. Taft and Public Housing. *Ohio History* 73 (summer): 135–43.

Doenecke, Justus D. 1979. *Not to the Swift: The Old Isolationists in the Cold War Era.* Lewisburg, Pa.: Bucknell University Press.

Graebner, Norman A. 1968. Isolationism. *Encyclopedia of Social Sciences*, edited by David Sills, 217–21. New York: Macmillan, the Free Press.

Hayek, Friedrich A. 1960. *The Constitution of Liberty.* Chicago: University of Chicago Press.

———. 1973. *Law, Legislation, and Liberty.* Vol. 1, *Rules and Order.* Chicago: University of Chicago Press.

Hayes, Michael T. 2001. *The Limits of Policy Change: Incrementalism, Worldview, and the Rule of Law.* Washington, D.C.: Georgetown University Press.

————. 2002. James Madison on Religion and Politics: Conservative, Anti-rationalist, Libertarian. In *James Madison and the Future of Limited Government*, edited by John Samples, 147–63. Washington, D.C.: Cato Institute.

Herman, Edward S. 1982. *The Real Terror Network: Terrorism in Fact and Propaganda*. Boston: South End.

Higgs, Robert. 1987. *Crisis and Leviathan: Critical Episodes in the Growth of American Government*. New York: Oxford University Press.

Horwitz, Steven. 2001. From Smith to Menger to Hayek: Liberalism in the Spontaneous-Order Tradition. *The Independent Review* 6 (Summer): 81–97.

Johnson, Chalmers. 2000. *Blowback: The Costs and Consequences of American Empire*. New York: Henry Holt, Owl Books.

Kinzer, Stephen. 2003. *All the Shah's Men: An American Coup and the Roots of Middle East Terror*. New York: John Wiley and Sons.

Kirk, Russell, and James McClellan. 1967. *The Political Principles of Robert A. Taft*. New York: Fleet.

Knight, Frank H. 1982. Ethics and Economic Reform. In *Freedom and Reform: Essays in Economics and Social Philosophy*, 55–153. Indianapolis: Liberty Fund. [Originally published in 1947 by Harper and Brothers.]

Kofsky, Frank. 1993. *Truman and the War Scare of 1948: A Successful Campaign to Deceive The Nation*. New York: St. Martin's.

LaFeber, Walter. 1984. *Inevitable Revolutions: The United States in Central America*. New York: W. W. Norton.

Lowi, Theodore J. 1979. *The End of Liberalism: The Second Republic of the United States*, 2d ed. New York: W. W. Norton.

Morgenthau, Hans J. 1962. *Politics among Nations: The Struggle for Power and Peace*, 3d ed. New York: Knopf.

Oakeshott, Michael. 1991. *Rationalism in Politics and Other Essays*. Indianapolis: Liberty Fund.

Osgood, Robert Endicott. 1953. *Ideals and Self-Interest in America's Foreign Relations: The Great Transformation of the Twentieth Century*. Chicago: University of Chicago Press.

Patterson, James T. 1972. *Mr. Republican: A Biography of Robert A. Taft*. Boston: Houghton Mifflin.

Radosh, Ronald. 1975. *Prophets on the Right: Profiles of Conservative Critics of American Globalism*. New York: Simon and Schuster.

Reichley, A. James. 2000. *The Life of the Parties: A History of American Political Parties*, 2d ed. Lanham, Md.: Rowman and Littlefield.

Rieselbach, Leroy N. 1966. *The Roots of Isolationism: Congressional Voting and Presidential Leadership in Foreign Policy*. Indianapolis: Bobbs-Merrill.

Roosevelt, Kermit. 1979. *Countercoup: The Struggle for the Control of Iran*. New York: Mc-Graw-Hill.

Rothbard, Murray N. 1964. The Transformation of the American Right. *Continuum* (summer): 220–31.

————. 1978. The Foreign Policy of the Old Right. *Journal of Libertarian Studies* 2 (spring): 85–96.

Schlesinger, Arthur. 1952. The New Isolationism. *Atlantic* 189 (May): 34–38.

Schoultz, Lars. 1987. *National Security and United States Policy Toward Latin America*. Princeton, N.J.: Princeton University Press.

Smith, T. V., and Robert A. Taft. 1939. *Foundations of Democracy: A Series of Debates*. New York: Knopf.

Stromberg, Joseph R. 2000. Mere "Isolationism": The Foreign Policy of the Old Right. *The Freeman* 50 (February). Available at: www.independent.org/newsroom/article.asp?id=122

———. 2001. An American Original. *The Old Cause* (online). Available at: www.antiwar.com/stromberg/pf/p-s042401.html.

Taft, Robert A. 1945. Government Guarantee of Private Investments Abroad. *Vital Speeches* 11 (August 1): 634–38.

———. 1949. The Republican Party. *Fortune* 39 (April): 108–18.

———. 1950. The Dangerous Decline of Political Morality. *The Reader's Digest* 57 (November): 153–56.

———. 1951. *A Foreign Policy for Americans.* Garden City, N.Y.: Doubleday.

———. [1935] 1997. The New Deal: Recovery, Reform, and Revolution. In *The Papers of Robert A. Taft*, vol. 1: 1889–1939, edited by Clarence E. Wunderlin Jr., 480–90. Kent, Ohio: Kent State University Press.

———. [1944] 2001. What Foreign Policy Will Promote Peace? In *The Papers of Robert A. Taft*, vol. 2: *1939–1944*, edited by Clarence E. Wunderlin Jr., 552–62. Kent, Ohio: Kent State University Press.

Van Dyke, Vernon, and Edward Lane Davis. 1952. Senator Taft and American Foreign Policy. *Journal of Politics* 14 (May): 177–202.

West, W. Reed. 1952. Senator Taft's Foreign Policy. *Atlantic Monthly* 189 (June): 50–52.

Wunderlin, Clarence E., Jr. 1997. *The Papers of Robert A. Taft.* vol. 1, *1889–1939.* Kent, Ohio: Kent State University Press.

———. 2001. *The Papers of Robert A. Taft.* vol. 2, *1939–1944.* Kent, Ohio: Kent State University Press.

Zunes, Stephen. 2003. *Tinderbox: U.S. Middle East Policy and the Roots of Terrorism.* Monroe, Me.: Common Courage.

Acknowledgments: Reprinted from *The Independent Review,* 8, no. 4 (Spring 2004): 509–25. ISSN 1086-1653, Copyright © 2004. The author gratefully acknowledges the insightful comments of John Vasquez and two anonymous reviewers.

PART II
The Case Against Nation Building

5

The Prospects for Democracy in High-Violence Societies

JAMES L. PAYNE

What does it take to implant democracy in a foreign land? For more than a century now, the United States has been sending troops into troubled countries, holding elections, and hoping democracy will take root. The results, overall, have been disappointing.

The results of one of the first efforts, the 1898 intervention in Cuba, are typical. Following the Spanish-American War, the United States administered Cuba for four years, turning power over to an elected Cuban president in 1902. A violent revolution forced him from office, and U.S. troops came back in 1906. After more reforms and new elections, the United States again turned power over to the Cubans in 1909. More instability ensued, including another violent revolt. The U.S. Marines came back yet a third time in 1917, restored order, held elections again, then withdrew in 1922. Since that time, Cuba has endured a succession of unstable and autocratic regimes, most recently Fidel Castro's totalitarian dictatorship.

Recent nation-building efforts—in Haiti, Afghanistan, and Iraq—seem to indicate that our understanding has not progressed since the days of the Cuban intervention. The problem is not that we have the wrong theory about nation building. A bad theory can be corrected and improved. The problem is that U.S. policymakers do not have any theory. They dogmatically assume that wherever U.S. troops end up as a result of this or that foreign-policy initiative, democracy can be made to flourish.

Undersecretary of State Paula Dobriansky expresses this mindset: "One should not make the mistake of believing that there is anything inherent in Islam, or *any other faith or culture,* that will prevent the emergence of democracy" (2004, 76, emphasis added).

Perhaps Dobriansky is correct in saying that Islam does not preclude democracy, but her sweeping insistence that there can be no possible cultural barriers to democracy—anywhere, anytime—flies in the face of the U.S. experience. Common sense suggests that there are bound to be countries in which democracy cannot be made to succeed, at least not within any reasonable time. We might save ourselves frustration and guide policy more intelligently if we began to understand what the limits to democracy are.

DEMOCRACY'S MINIMUM REQUIREMENT

Although the nation builders have casually assumed that democracy can be established anywhere, the scholars have gone to the opposite extreme. For them, democracy is a delicate flower that requires a host of social and institutional prerequisites. Over the years, they have compiled a long list of requirements. One scholar suggests that democracy requires a populace endowed with nine psychological traits, among which are tolerance, realism, flexibility, and objectivity, and, further, that the country must have economic well-being, economic equality, and an educated citizenry (Cohen 1971). Another political scientist names seven conditions necessary for democracy, including "a strong concern for the mass of people" and "high social mobility" (De Grazia 1952, 546–47). Two other scholars claim that democracy rests on seven basic beliefs, including "respect for individual personality," "belief in rationality," and "equality of opportunity" (Corry and Abraham 1958, 29, 33, 35).

Such comprehensive lists overshoot the mark greatly, however. They represent an effort to describe the perfect context for democracy—or, indeed, the perfect context for the perfect democracy. They are thus largely irrelevant to the task of understanding real-world democracy, which is always compromised and flawed. Instead of pointing to all the desirable features, we need to focus on the bare minimum needed for even an imperfect democracy to exist.

What is that minimum? I would put it this way: *a restraint in the use of violence in domestic political affairs.* In a functioning democracy, we tend to take this condition for granted. We assume that opposition leaders do not routinely take up arms to try to shoot their way into power. We assume that presidents do not routinely jail and murder their critics and opponents. In many foreign lands, however, this assumption about peaceful participants is not satisfied. Many people are disposed to resort to violence in political disputes. They are willing to kill—and to risk being killed—to counter a perceived wrong or to implement what they believe to be right or just to get themselves into power. These places are "high-violence" societies, and in them democracy cannot thrive.

A good picture of a high-violence society is this description of the Haiti of the early part of the twentieth century, before the United States occupied the country in 1915: "No man in those times ventured on the public roads for fear of being drafted in a revolutionary or, perhaps worse, a governmental army. They stayed in their hills, and all marketing to the towns was done by the women. Numbers were killed in each revolution, towns looted and sections burned, and no life was safe and no justice existed once the government in power marked a man as its enemy and could lay hands upon him" (Davis 1929, 266).

Haiti is another example of failed U.S. nation building, by the way. After spending eighteen years fighting local terrorists and trying to administer the country, U.S. forces left in 1934. Since that time, the country has suffered the dictatorship of the Duvaliers, father and son, and more waves of political violence, prompting another U.S. intervention from 1994 to 2000 and yet another in 2004.

To say that a high-violence society cannot support democracy does not mean that a democracy requires perfect domestic peace. It can survive violence if the violence is independent of the political elite. There is an enormous difference, which observers usually ignore, between an assassination carried out by a lone killer and one planned by political leaders and condoned by a large segment of the public. The former has no more political significance than a fatal automobile accident. The latter—which I call a "political murder"—sets the stage for a civil war or a dictatorial crackdown.[1] It is not the assassination, riot, or terrorism that identifies a high-violence society. Rather, the distinguishing mark is some leaders' deliberate use of these acts of violence as tools in their struggle against others.[2] Leaders who employ such acts are not repudiated; their followers excuse their bloody deeds as necessary, understandable tactics.

DEMOCRATS REFUSE TO FIGHT FOR DEMOCRACY

The idea that nations differ in the disposition to resort to political violence takes some getting used to. For one thing, it seems politically incorrect these days to suggest that one group of people may differ significantly from another. However, we are not speaking of a biological or genetic difference. The inclination to resort to violence is a cultural orientation. It is transmitted from one generation to another, and, as the historical record shows, it can be unlearned.

We resist the notion that some cultures are more politically violent than others for another reason, too: we assume that motives completely explain violence. At least since the time of John Locke, we have been taught to interpret violence as the understandable response to an "intolerable" situation. The American Revolution is a classic example. The cause of this violence is supposed to have been the colonists' justified anger at King George's "long train of abuses and usurpations." Using the same logic, we say that if people are revolting in this or that foreign land, they have a strong reason to do so: they are hungry, or they are a disparaged minority, or they are fanatics who want to impose their religion or ideology.

Of course, motives, ideals, and ideologies do play a role in political violence. No one takes up the sword for no reason. Possible motives for violence always exist in every country. People everywhere resent certain injustices and abuses, and some always embrace extreme worldviews and ideologies. What we overlook, however, is that in some cultures, participants readily respond violently to their grievances, whereas in more peaceful cultures the same grievances do not produce a violent reaction.

For example, a common complaint of those who start civil wars is that they have been the victims of an unfair electoral process, that they were "cheated" out of their rightful victory. At first glance, this grievance seems an adequate motive for a revolt. A closer look reveals, however, that elections in democracies frequently involve serious errors and ambiguities, irregularities that the losers believe robbed them of victory. Yet they do not turn to violence. George W. Bush's election in 2000 is an example. Besides giving rise to claims of ballot irregularities in Florida, this election violated a core principle of democracy: the candidate who obtained the most popular votes nationwide was denied victory (by the Electoral College arrangement). Many Democratic Party leaders were—and still are—angry about that election, but they did not resort to force to retaliate.

The point is profoundly paradoxical: in an established democracy, participants do not take up arms to protest even a transgression of democratic principles, such as (real or imagined) electoral fraud. The hallmark of these societies is a relatively low disposition to resort to political violence *for any reason.* In a high-violence society, in contrast, all sorts of complaints, even apparently trivial ones, seem to provoke a violent reaction.

GOOD GUYS AND BAD GUYS

Also impeding our ability to recognize a high-violence society is our inclination to take sides in foreign political disputes: one political group is the gang of thugs, and almost everyone else is peaceful. Unfortunately, we tend to perceive all politics everywhere in these terms. We see a dictator using force to repress and persecute his opponents, so we naturally condemn him, but then, as part of the psychological mechanism of taking sides, we further assume that his opponents are blameless. Although this assumed condition may be the case, our impulse to look for "good guys" in many Third World situations leads us to overlook the fact that many or most of the other participants in those situations are also violent and thuggish by democratic standards.

Iraq affords a good illustration of this process of distortion. Saddam Hussein was certainly a nasty dictator who engaged in every sort of violence, from murdering rivals and massacring minority groups to invading neighboring countries. In the process of taking sides against him, however, many observers supposed that he alone was responsible for the violence in Iraq. Thus, they saw all the other participants—Shiites, Kurds, and so forth—as blameless and peaceful. From this perspective, simply removing Saddam would result in a stable, peaceful regime. Unfortunately, this assumption was, and is, wrong. Iraq is a high-violence society, a place where many people are disposed to act in thuggish ways, and their violence makes a democracy untenable.

It is understandable that we should condemn a foreign dictator's violence, but our disapproval should not lead us to assume that the ruler is the only one in that society disposed to use force.

THE EVOLUTION AWAY FROM FORCE

How does a high-violence society get to be that way? Although this question is a natural one to ask, it betrays a misunderstanding. It suggests that a violent politics is a variable condition, like an illness that can be contracted, got over, and then contracted again. If we study the political history of different cultures, however, we will not see such an up-and-down pattern. Instead, we will find that all countries seem to begin as high-violence societies and then evolve away from this pattern. Many years ago countries such as England, France, Italy, and Norway were characterized by an extremely violent politics. For example, the regime of Henry VIII in England (1509–47) was as violent and as vicious as any modern dictatorship. Henry murdered not just inconvenient wives, but scores of noblemen as well as loyal aides, advisors, and even children. Nor was he the only one who lived by the sword in those days. He faced revolts in Lincolnshire, Scotland, Ireland, and Yorkshire. The Yorkshire revolt was put down with the aid of a promise of amnesty, which Henry subsequently betrayed, ordering his henchmen to perform "dreadful execution" on "the inhabitants of every town, village, and hamlet that have offended" (Henry's edict qtd. in Durant 1957, 566–67). Today we call this kind of action genocide; in the old days, it was politics as usual.

Hence, a high-violence society does not get that way because of any particular cause or condition. It is better understood as a society mired in the past, a society that has failed to make the transition away from primitive, counterproductive modes of interaction. With regard to political violence, Iraq in the early twenty-first century is almost exactly what England was in the mid–fifteenth century. The question we need to ask, then, is not "What went wrong with Iraq?" Instead, it is "What went right with England—and the other areas that evolved away from the violent politics of an earlier time?"

The latter question is not a simple one to answer. Both historians and political scientists have all but ignored the topic of political violence, and as a result we have little knowledge about how and why a society evolves away from a violent politics. The best I can do at this point is to offer some preliminary observations.

ELEMENTS INVOLVED IN EVOLVING AWAY FROM VIOLENCE

1. *The evolution away from violence appears to take a long time.* It may seem, from our modern perspective, that because political violence is wrongheaded and inefficient, we will have no great difficulty in instructing people to stop it. Unfortunately, the impulse to violence is embedded in and reinforced by a broad cultural mindset that encompasses a host of attitudes, including extreme self-centeredness, intolerance, naïveté, hubris, paranoia, and emotionalism. It may not take centuries—as it did in England, for example—to overcome this profoundly immature outlook, but it cannot be talked away in a week, a year, or even a decade.

2. *Because the evolution away from violence is mainly a cultural change, institutional measures have little effect on it.* The adoption of a certain kind of constitution, for example, will not make much difference. In the nineteenth century, countries all over Latin America copied the U.S. Constitution on the theory that this paper document was the cause of U.S. political stability. These attempts to imitate U.S. institutions failed to check the furious pace of revolution. England proves the converse of the point: it evolved to a peaceful politics without the benefit of any written constitution.

3. *Growing wealthier probably plays an underlying role in assisting the evolution away from force.*[3] As people become wealthier, they live better, and their lives become more pleasant. Hence, they begin to place a greater value on their lives and, by extension, on others' lives. This effect of prosperity is not entirely a mechanical, rational process. A man who becomes rich and comfortable does not suddenly abandon his violence-prone outlook. Instead, the effect of prosperity percolates through the culture, gradually changing underlying perspectives related to violence, such as the value placed on human life and the sensitivity to suffering.

4. *Communication is another factor that probably promotes the movement away from violence by enabling observers to see the folly and waste of violence in conflicts that do not involve them directly.* Again, this effect is not a direct or mechanical one. Noticing that a war is foolish, for example, is not enough. This perception must gradually enter thought processes and culture, weakening the attractions of war, lowering the status of professions related to war, and so on.

5. *The movement away from violence probably begins with the elites because they are the first to experience prosperity and its life-enhancing effects.* They are also the first to benefit from communication (universities, books) and therefore are likely to be the first to question the traditional emphasis on violence. The lower classes, for whom life is more difficult and therefore less valued, probably remain more disposed toward violence in the early stages of the society's evolution toward a peaceful politics.

This difference in perspectives can mean that a society that has made some progress toward a nonviolent politics can retrogress, for a time, when the lower classes become politically active. In eighteenth-century France, for example, politics within the established elites was relatively nonviolent.

Political murder had been abandoned for more than a century. However, the lower classes were still strongly oriented toward violence. They carried out bloody riots and, finally, the Revolution of 1789, and they endorsed and sustained the bloody leaders who came to the fore at that time.

6. *In a society that has made a nearly complete transition to low-violence politics, it is still possible for a relatively small criminal subgroup to gain control of the government.* Once in control, this subgroup may establish an extremely violent dictatorship and thereby give a misleading picture of society's overall attachment to violence—this situation is the "gang of thugs" possibility mentioned earlier. The violent leaders' takeover is facilitated by two circumstances: (1) a naive, vigorous ideology that justifies extreme measures, including violence, and (2) a body of lower-class followers who accept, or at least excuse, political violence.

When a dictatorship has originated in this way, if the thugs are removed and their ideology discredited by events, then the country will revert once again to democracy. I believe that this pattern prevailed in Germany, Italy, and Japan, the three cases that nation builders often cite as examples of the successful imposition of a democratic regime.

Germany, prior to Hitler's dictatorship, had a long tradition of liberal institutions. Elections had been held at least since the 1850s, and considerable freedom of expression prevailed from then until 1933. The country did have an emperor (before 1918), many administrations had autocratic tendencies, and plenty of popular disturbances occurred, but politics among political elites was not violent. Writing of German life in the 1920s, American reporter William L. Shirer observed that "Most Germans one met—politicians, writers, editors, artists, professors, students, businessmen, labor leaders—struck you as being democratic, liberal, even pacifist" (1960, 118).

Hitler was a deviant from this elite culture, a leader who combined demagogy and violence in a lethal brew. He organized gangs of thugs, the storm troopers, to intimidate other participants, and a secret death squad to eliminate opponents. Although Hitler's stands on nationalism, against capitalism, and in defense of workers made Nazism appealing to large numbers of Germans, the key to his success was "the systematic, step-by-step slaughter of [his] most capable political opponents, murdered by his party of political criminals" (Rosenbaum 1998, 45).

The pattern was similar in Italy, where, again, a thug—Mussolini—used a simplistic ideology and violent lower-class followers to gain control of a basically peaceful country. Italy had been more or less a democracy since its unification in 1861, with frequent elections and general respect for freedoms of press, organization, and assembly. The country did have a long tradition of street fighting, however, and Mussolini took advantage of it to form gangs *(squadristi)* that intimidated and assaulted local officials and leaders of other parties, killing an estimated six hundred people in local actions (Schneider 1928, 44–54; Salvemini 1967, 85). Like Hitler, Mussolini hid the violent nature of his deviant, criminal group behind oratory about the need for national rebirth and so forth. Therefore, when he was called upon to form a government in 1922, most Italians did not realize they were turning government over to a committed thug.

Japan did not have a fascist party with a single leader. The violence that overshadowed the parliamentary regime (elections had been held since 1890) came from younger military officers who were in the grip of a primitive nationalistic ideology. They had the idea that by murdering top political leaders—happily sacrificing their own lives in the process—some kind of national rebirth would occur. These groups included the Black River Society, the Imperial Way, and a broad "network of clandestine study groups and associations linking military officers and civilian ideologues" (Gordon 2003, 188). In the 1930s, these radicals began a widespread campaign of assassination, starting with the murder of the prime minister in 1930 and spreading to the slaying of other political and business leaders. Young military officers attempted a coup in 1931, and a group of young naval officers murdered the prime minister in 1932. In 1936, a force of fifteen hundred troops loyal to the Imperial Way took over central Tokyo and sent squads to murder most of the cabinet members and other opponents. This revolt was repressed, and the perpetrators punished, but it further terrified civilian leaders and pushed control of the government more fully into military hands. Thus, the campaign of violence from this one subgroup eclipsed a functioning democracy and turned Japan into a "government by assassination" (Byas 1942).

In all three countries, Germany, Italy, and Japan, a highly deviant, violent minority extinguished democracy, and in all three cases the democracy had been long established. All that was needed to have a democracy again, therefore, was the removal of the violent leadership cadre and the discrediting of its ideology. The drafting of a constitution and the implementation of reforms, though they may have been beneficial in themselves, were not necessary to allow a peaceful, democratic politics to reemerge.

LONGER THAN YOU THINK

The foregoing observations suggest, then, that if one is going to invade a country and overthrow a dictatorship in the hope of creating democracy there in short order, one should be sure it does not have a high-violence society. One needs to gauge the extent to which participants outside the dictatorship group are peaceful. If democracy was already functioning to some extent prior to the dictatorship, as evinced by competitive elections and relative freedom of expression, that background condition indicates that most participants in the country are fairly peaceful and that democracy can succeed once the dictator is removed.

If, however, the country has nothing but violent traditions—dictatorship, repression, political murder, revolt, and massacre—then one is naive to expect that democracy can be established there quickly. An occupying country such as the United States may pay lip service to (and expend human lives for) the idea of establishing democracy in such high-violence societies, but in the short term that goal has no well-founded chance to succeed. In practice, the occupier will end up following a policy of stability, which involves the following elements: (1) violent repression of the most visible violent opposition forces; (2) truces with gangs and warlords willing to keep a lower profile; and (3) creation of a puppet government that eventually becomes or gives way to a dictatorship. It is only after many decades of autocratic rule that the society may achieve the transition away from violence, thus making the emergence of democracy possible.

A good example of this pattern is the Philippines, which the United States occupied following the 1898 Spanish-American War. For the first fourteen years, the U.S. administration busily suppressed revolts (in which some two hundred thousand locals were slain). Following independence in 1946, democratic politics began to emerge, with competitive elections and some freedom of expression. Violence, however, was not far away, first in the form of the Hukbalahap rebellion, defeated in 1953, and later in riots and revolts that led to the autocracy of the Marcos regime. This relatively mild dictatorship was chased from office by public demonstrations in 1986, a date that may perhaps be said to mark the country's coming of age as a full democracy.

It would not be correct to say, then, that a high-violence society such as Iraq cannot become a democracy. It probably will become one in the long run. One doubts, however, that those who urged the invasion of Iraq in order to establish democracy there had any inkling that the process will most likely require the greater part of a century.

NOTES

1. For a discussion of political murder and its role in a high-violence society, see Payne 2004, chap. 7.
2. G. Bingham Powell Jr. makes the same point: "Party involvement in violence is particularly dangerous to the survival of the democratic regime" (1982, 168).
3. Cross-national studies seem to indicate a positive correlation between democracy and wealth; see, for example, Cutright 1963 and Diamond 1992.

REFERENCES

Byas, Hugh. 1942. *Government by Assassination.* New York: Knopf.

Cohen, Carl. 1971. *Democracy.* Athens: University of Georgia Press.

Corry, J. A., and Henry J. Abraham. 1958. *Elements of Democratic Government.* New York: Oxford University Press.

Cutright, Philips. 1963. National Political Development: Measurement and Analysis. *American Sociological Review* 28: 253–64.

Davis, H. P. 1929. *Black Democracy: The Story of Haiti.* New York: Lincoln MacVeagh.

De Grazia, Alfred. 1952. *The Elements of Political Science.* New York: Alfred A. Knopf.

Diamond, Larry. 1992. Economic Development and Democracy Reconsidered. In *Reexamining Democracy: Essays in Honor of Seymour Martin Lipset,* edited by Gary Marks and Larry Diamond, 261–84. Newbury Park, Calif.: Sage.

Dobriansky, Paula J. 2004. Advancing Democracy. *National Interest* 77: 71–78.

Durant, Will. 1957. *The Reformation: A History of European Civilization from Wyclif to Calvin: 1300–1564.* New York: Simon and Schuster.

Gordon, Andrew. 2003. *A Modern History of Japan from Tokugawa Times to the Present.* New York: Oxford University Press.

Payne, James L. 2004. *A History of Force.* Sandpoint, Idaho.: Lytton.

Powell, G. Bingham, Jr. 1982. *Contemporary Democracies: Participation, Stability, and Violence.* Cambridge, Mass.: Harvard University Press.

Rosenbaum, Ron. 1998. *Explaining Hitler: The Search for the Origins of His Evil.* New York: Random House.

Salvemini, Gaetano. 1967. *The Fascist Dictatorship in Italy.* New York: Howard Fertig.

Schneider, Herbert W. 1928. *Making the Fascist State.* New York: Oxford University Press.

Shirer, William L. 1960. *Rise and Fall of the Third Reich.* New York: Simon and Schuster.

Acknowledgment: Reprinted from *The Independent Review,* 9, no. 4 (Spring 2005): 563–72. ISSN 1086-1653, Copyright © 2005.

6

Does Nation Building Work?

JAMES L. PAYNE

In plunging into war, hope generally triumphs over experience. The past—the quiet statistical tabulation of what happened when such plunges were taken before—tends to be ignored in the heat of angry oratory and the thump of military boots. At the outset, it is easy to believe that force will be successful in upholding virtue and that history has no relevance.

Lately, this confidence in the force of arms has centered on nation building—that is, on invading and occupying a land afflicted by dictatorship or civil war and turning it into a democracy. This objective has been a major theme of the U.S. government's recent actions in Iraq and Afghanistan, but the policy is not likely to be limited to those countries. The U.S. government now enjoys a military preeminence in the world, and the temptation to deploy its armed forces to repair or transform other regimes is likely to prove attractive again in the future.

Moreover, the idea of invading countries to "fix" them has recently gained considerable support in the academic and foreign-policy community. Among the first to advocate the assertive use of U.S. military forces around the world were William Kristol and Robert Kagan. In a 1996 article in *Foreign Affairs,* they urged the United States to adopt a posture of "benevolent global hegemony." This means "actively promoting American principles of governance abroad—democracy, free markets, respect for liberty" (27). To John Quincy Adams's advice that America should not go "abroad in search of monsters to destroy," they mockingly replied, "But why not?" (31). In their endorsement for foreign-policy activism, Kagan and Kristol have been joined by a number of policy wonks, journalists, and academics, a group that has come to be known as "neoconservatives."

In their enthusiasm for nation building by force of arms, neither the theorists nor the practitioners have examined the historical experience with this kind of policy. They are aware that a historical record exists, but they do not take it seriously. In a speech two weeks before the invasion of Iraq, President George W. Bush pointed to other interventions that had been successful:

> America has made and kept this kind of commitment before—in the peace that followed a world war. After defeating enemies, we did not leave behind occupying armies, we left constitutions and parliaments. We established an atmosphere of safety, in which responsible, reform-minded local leaders could build lasting institutions of freedom. In societies that once bred fascism and militarism, liberty found a permanent home. There was a time when many said that the cultures of Japan and Germany were incapable of sustaining democratic values. Well, they were wrong. (Bush 2003)

Although this reference to Germany and Japan demonstrates an interest in the past, it is disappointingly selective. Yes, Germany and Japan would seem to be success stories for the idea that a U.S. army of occupation can leave behind an enduring democracy. But these cases are not the only pertinent ones. U.S. military forces have gone into troubled countries dozens of times through the years, but without the same results. They went into Cuba three times and tried to set up a democracy—in 1898, again in 1906, and again in 1917. Each time, after the troops left, civil war and dictatorship followed, and what has apparently found a "permanent home" in Cuba is not liberty but Fidel Castro's dictatorship.

Kristol and Kagan are equally selective in their use of the historical record. In the *Foreign Affairs* article in which they advocate a muscular foreign policy, they approvingly cite the case of Haiti, where, they observe, "the United States completed the withdrawal of 15,000 soldiers after restoring a semblance of democratic government" (1996, 21). Again, the method of historical comparison is used carelessly. If Kristol and Kagan wish to claim that the U.S. military invasions succeed in establishing democracy, they are obliged to review all the cases of intervention. A disinterested analyst does not point to one case that appears to support the policy and ignore the cases that do not support it. In fact, even the Haiti case contradicts their thesis. Haiti appeared to represent a success story only during the brief period in

1996, when Kristol and Kagan were writing their article. Shortly afterward, it sank back into violent anarchy, the condition in which it remains today.

In pondering the policy of nation building, then, we need an overall picture of how such efforts turn out. Before government leaders roll the dice of war, invading a country in the hope of establishing a democracy, they ought to know what their odds are.

The first step is to compile a list of cases. I focus here on the strongest, military version of nation building, illustrated by the case of Iraq: the use of ground troops to support a deliberate effort to establish a democracy. I leave aside many cases of lesser military involvements, such as episodes in which the United States sent only military aid or military advisors, funded rebel movements, or used only air power or sea power. If these lesser interventions fail, one can always say that the democratic power did not make a serious effort. The insertion of ground troops, however, manifests a high level of seriousness. It generally gives the occupier sweeping powers, including the ability to replace government officials, to establish political bodies such as legislatures, and to hold elections. My definition of nation building also requires that the invading country make "a deliberate effort to establish a democracy." Thus, I leave aside purely peacekeeping missions, punitive missions, and countries with U.S. military bases, but with no significant U.S. role in local politics.[1]

WHO ARE THE NATION BUILDERS?

Most discussions about spreading democracy focus on the United States as the nation builder, but other countries have also attempted this kind of project. Generations ago, many European nations, both as colonial powers and as the managers of trusteeships, were deeply involved in invading and administering foreign lands. Can the record of their accomplishments or failures be included in assessing the validity of the nation-building policy?

The problem is that colonialism, for most of the European nations, did not involve an effort to promote democracy. Countries such as Spain, Portugal, France, and Belgium were not themselves especially democratic, and in any case they were not self-consciously proud of being democracies. They were not interested in promoting self-government, and they viewed colonies as lands to be ruled and exploited, perhaps eventually annexed.

Great Britain, however, was an exception. By the latter part of the nineteenth century, the British had embraced the idea of spreading democracy (or "self-government," as they usually put it) to the territories under their control. Furthermore, the British had a self-conscious pride in their political institutions. Like Americans, they saw their government as a wonderful and wisely evolved system, worth spreading to less-fortunate lands. Several generations ago the British, not the Americans, were considered the leaders in nation building. Their far-flung empire was presumed to have given them a wealth of experience in democratic tutelage. When the League of Nations was establishing trusteeships in the 1920s, Britain seemed the natural authority to guide places such as Palestine, Jordan, and Iraq to self-government.

My selection of cases of attempted nation building, then, includes both British and American efforts. My time frame embraces interventions and colonies begun after 1850. Study of this 150-year period enables us to include most of the former British colonies, except the very oldest (such as the United States, Canada, Australia, India, Pakistan, and a number of small Caribbean political entities established in the eighteenth century). In order for a country to qualify here as a complete case of nation building, troops must have left it (or be uninvolved locally, if based in the country) so that we may determine whether in the absence of military support a stable democracy continued to exist. For this reason, we cannot use ongoing involvements such as Bosnia, Kosovo, Afghanistan, and Iraq. The case of South Vietnam cannot be used because the U.S. troop withdrawal coincided with the North Vietnamese conquest of the country; hence, there was no opportunity to find out whether the South Vietnamese democracy would have thrived on its own.

The application of my definition identifies fifty-one instances of attempted nation building by Britain and the United States over the past 150 years. In each episode, the democratic power placed land forces in the area, made a conscious effort to affect local politics in the direction of promoting democracy, and then left. The question is, How often did it succeed?

Success involves more than holding an election and setting up a government. Nation building implies *building*—that is, constructing a lasting edifice. The nation builders concur in this notion of durability. Their idea is not just to hold elections, get out, and have the country revert to anarchy or dictatorship. As President Bush said, the aim in Iraq is to create "lasting" institutions of freedom. To call the nation-building effort a success,

Table 1

Nation-Building Military Occupations by the United States and Great Britain, 1850–2000

U. S. Occupations		British Occupations	
Austria 1945–55	success	Botswana 1886–1966	success
Cuba 1898–1902	failure	Brunei 1888–1984	failure
Cuba 1906–1909	failure	Burma (Myanmar)	
Cuba 1917–22	failure	1885–1948	failure
Dominican Republic		Cyprus 1914–60	failure
1911–24	failure	Egypt 1882–1922	failure
Dominican Republic		Fiji 1874–1970	success
1965–67	success	Ghana 1886–1957	failure
Grenada 1983–85	success	Iraq 1917–32	failure
Haiti 1915–34	failure	Iraq 1941–47	failure
Haiti 1994–96	failure	Jordan 1921–56	failure
Honduras 1924	failure	Kenya 1894–1963	failure
Italy 1943–45	success	Lesotho 1884–1966	failure
Japan 1945–52	success	Malawi (Nyasaland)	
Lebanon 1958	failure	1891–1964	failure
Lebanon 1982–84	failure	Malaysia 1909–57	success
Mexico 1914–17	failure	Maldives 1887–1976	success
Nicaragua 1909–10	failure	Nigeria 1861–1960	failure
Nicaragua 1912–25	failure	Palestine 1917–48	failure
Nicaragua 1926–33	failure	Sierra Leone 1885–1961	failure
Panama 1903–33	failure	Solomon Islands	
Panama 1989–95	success	1893–1978	success
Philippines 1898–1946	success	South Yemen (Aden)	
Somalia 1992–94	failure	1934–67	failure
South Korea 1945–61	failure	Sudan 1899–1956	failure
West Germany 1945–52	success	Swaziland 1903–1968	failure
		Tanzania 1920–63	failure
		Tonga 1900–1970	success
		Uganda 1894–1962	failure
		Zambia (N. Rhodesia)	
		1891–1964	failure
		Zimbabwe (S. Rhodesia)	
		1888–1980	failure

therefore, we need to confirm that the military occupation of the target country resulted in the establishment of a democracy that lasted at least several decades.

To identify results in these terms, I inspected the political history of each country after the troop withdrawal. I looked for events betokening the collapse of democratic rule, including the suppression of opposition leaders or parties; major infringements of freedoms of speech, press, and assembly; violent transfers of power; murder of political leaders by other leaders; or significant civil war. I required large and multiple failures along these lines as evidence of democratic failure. A few arrests of opposition leaders, a few assassinations of ambiguous meaning, a simple military coup, the resignation of an executive in the face of massive street demonstrations—none of these by itself was enough to disqualify the country as a democracy. If numerous free and fair elections were held, this outcome was taken as strong evidence that democracy survived. Elections that were one-sided and to some degree rigged by the incumbents were taken as a negative sign, but they did not, in themselves, disqualify the country as democratic.

The results of applying these classification principles to the political outcomes in the fifty-one cases of intervention are shown in table 1. Overall, the results indicate that the military intervention left behind a democracy in fourteen cases, or 27 percent of the time. Our first conclusion, then, is that nation building by force is generally unsuccessful. A president who went around the world invading countries in order to make them democratic would probably fail most of the time.

THE WORLDWIDE TREND AGAINST THE USE OF FORCE

In assessing the effectiveness of nation-building efforts, we need to be careful not to confuse conjunction with cause. That some military interventions have been *followed by* democracy does not mean that the interventions caused the democracy. As I have explained elsewhere (Payne 2004), there is a worldwide movement against the use of force, and this trend promotes democratic development. Rulers are becoming less disposed to use violence to repress oppositions, and government critics are less inclined to resort to armed force against rulers. The result of this broad, historical trend is that countries are becoming democracies on their own, without any outside help. After all, most of the democracies in the world have come about in this way, by internal evolution. No one invaded Britain or Holland or Finland or Costa Rica to turn them into democracies, and the same holds for many other countries. This trend has to be kept in mind in evaluating the "success" of a nation-building effort.

For example, we might be tempted to praise the British occupation of Malaysia for "bringing" democracy to that country. In the same period, however, Thailand, which had not been occupied, also joined the camp of democratic nations. In fact, in the Freedom House survey of political rights and civil liberties, Thailand ranks ahead of Malaysia (Karatnycky 2002, 730). It is quite possible, then, that Malaysia would have become as democratic as it is today without British intervention.

South Korea presents an interesting lesson in the effectiveness of democratic tutelage. Beginning in 1945, when the U.S. troops landed after World War II, the United States was heavily involved in guiding political decisions in South Korea. This political involvement essentially ceased after 1961, and the South Koreans were allowed to go their own way politically. That way proved to be a military dictatorship under General Park Chung-Hee, which lasted until his murder by other officials in 1979. Thereafter followed two coups, a violent uprising in Kwangju, and many bloody street demonstrations. By 1985, however, the suppression of civil liberties had been greatly relaxed, and competitive elections were held. Since that time, South Korea can be called a democracy (albeit a noisy one with plenty of corruption). So here is a case in which sixteen years of tutelage under the Americans brought failure with regard to the establishment of democracy, but the country evolved to democracy on its own twenty-five years after U.S. involvement in local politics ceased.

In deciding whether nation-building efforts work, therefore, it is not enough to show that some occupations are followed by democracy. The key question is: Does democracy emerge more frequently in the occupied countries than in nations evolving on their own? Because of the difficulty of defining a proper control group, this question cannot be given a definitive answer. It is clear, however, that once autonomous democratic development is taken into account, the apparent nation-building successes, meager as they are to begin with, are themselves probably only spurious proof of the nation builders' claims.

For example, at first glance, it might seem that the U.S. intervention in the Dominican Republic in 1965 brought democracy to that country.

But consider the larger trend in Latin America. Almost all the countries in this region were not democracies at the start of the twentieth century, but almost all have evolved to a democratic politics now. It is quite possible, then, that the Dominican Republic would have become a democracy on its own. Indeed, some observers believe that this change was already under way in 1965 (Wiarda 1989, 436). Moreover, they believe the U.S. intervention aborted a middle-class democratic revolution that was on the verge of succeeding (U.S. officials feared—on perhaps flimsy evidence—that it would be taken over by Castro Communists). Thus, one can with justice say that the United States did not "bring" democracy to the Dominican Republic in 1965. It was already coming, and the U.S. action merely delayed its arrival by a year or two.

IS THERE EXPERTISE IN NATION BUILDING?

Another way to assess the effectiveness of nation building is to examine the time dimension. If nation building were an effective therapy, then it should follow that the longer it is applied, the more certain its success will be. To use the medical analogy, the nation-building "doctors" will be more likely to cure the patient if they can apply their vital therapy over a longer period of time. The idea that longer military occupations are more effective in creating democracy is widely believed. Among those who take this position is Richard Haass, the president of the Council on Foreign Relations and formerly the director of policy planning for the State Department during the invasion of Iraq. Haass asserts that "[i]t is one thing to oust a regime, quite another to put something better in its place. Prolonged occupation of the sort the United States carried out in Japan and West Germany after World War II is the only surefire way to build democratic institutions and instill democratic culture" (2005).

Are "prolonged" occupations really more effective? The facts contradict this claim. The United States has been involved in many occupations much longer than the seven years in West Germany, but it has failed in most cases. The United States occupied and administered Haiti from 1915 to 1934. Those nineteen years of control proved not to be a "surefire" route to democracy, but merely an interlude in a violent and chaotic politics that continues to this day. Other cases of long U.S. interventions that failed to establish democracy include Nicaragua (1912), thirteen years; Nicaragua

(1926), seven years; the Dominican Republic (1911), thirteen years; and Panama (1903), thirty years.

The British experience confirms the point. Numerous former British colonies had sixty, seventy, and more years of occupation and administration, yet failed to sustain democracy after the British left. For example, Zimbabwe, much in the news today because of dictator Robert Mugabe's extreme actions, experienced ninety-two years of British administration. Other long-occupied countries that failed to sustain democracy after the British left include Nigeria (ninety-nine years), Sierra Leone (seventy-six years), Ghana (seventy-one years), and Burma (sixty-three years).

That long occupations so often fail to establish stable democracies indicates that something is seriously wrong with the medical model of nation building. The "doctors" apparently do not have an effective therapy. Indeed, a close look reveals that they have no therapy at all. The dirty little secret of nation building is that *no one knows how to do it.* Huge amounts of government and foundation money have been poured into this question, and, in response to the dollars, the scholars and bureaucrats have produced only reams of verbose commentary. Even after all these efforts, no concrete, usable body of knowledge exists, no methodology of how "to build democratic institutions and instill democratic culture," as Haass puts it.

There are no experts on nation building. The people who end up doing the so-called nation building are simply ordinary government employees who wind up at the scene of the military occupation. Many times they are military officers with no background in politics, sociology, or social psychology (not that it would help them, in any case). For the most part, these government employees see their mission as that of trying to get themselves and the U.S. forces out of the country without too much egg on their faces. They have no clearer idea of how to "instill democratic culture" than does the proverbial man on the street.

PURSUING AN "UNDEFINED GOAL"

A look at some specific examples of nation building illustrates the intellectual vacuum. The U.S. invasion of Panama in 1989 is credited as a nation-building success. Was this positive outcome the result of the expert application of political science? One of the nation builders, Lieutenant Colonel John T. Fishel, has written a book on the Panama experience that paints quite a different picture. Fishel was chief of policy and strategy for U.S. forces in Panama, and his job was to figure out how to implement the mission statement. The orders looked simple on paper: "Conduct nation building operations to ensure democracy." Fishel quickly discovered, however, that the instruction was meaningless because democracy was an "undefined goal." It seemed to him that it was not the job of military officers to figure out how to implement this undefined objective, but, as he observes with a touch of irritation, "there are no U.S. civilian strategists clearly articulating strategies to achieve democracy." Worse, "[t]he fact that there was no clear definition of the conditions that constitute democracy meant that the Military Support Group and the other U.S. government agencies that were attempting to assist the Endara government had only the vaguest concept of what actions and programs would lead the country toward democracy" (1997, 84). In practice, the goal of "ensuring democracy" boiled down to installing Guillermo Endara, the winner of a previous election, as president, supporting him as he became increasingly high-handed and unpopular, and then stepping away after his opponent was elected in 1994. Not exactly rocket science.

One sign of how ill-prepared military invaders are to carry out the complex tasks that "building democracy" might entail (if anyone knew what those tasks were) is their inability to carry out the simpler tasks of effecting an occupation in a rational and orderly way. For example, in the Panama invasion, the U.S deployed troops on the outskirts of Panama City and failed to move any units into the center. As a result, looters and thugs took over downtown Panama City, a "predictable" chaos, says Fishel. "The critical question," he asks, "is how the intelligent and experienced senior U.S. military leadership failed to see the obvious and take action" (1997, 58). Were the military planners trying to tell us something when they gave the invasion and nation building in Panama the code name BLIND LOGIC?

JOSEPH STALIN: NATION BUILDER?

Austria presents an instructive example of what nation building has actually amounted to on the ground. In my tabulation (table 1), Austria is classified as a case of successful nation building: U.S. troops occupied the country from 1945 to 1955, and a democracy was established. A closer look reveals, however, that the U.S. political role was minimal and rather unhelpful at that.

At the end of the war, Austria was occupied jointly by the Soviet Union and the Western powers. The Soviets brought Karl Renner, the elderly and respected Austrian socialist leader, to Vienna to head a provisional government. Renner's provisional government declared the establishment of the Democratic Austrian Republic on April 27, 1945. The United States refused to recognize this government, fearing that the Soviets were up to no good in having fostered it. Finally, six months later, when it became obvious that the provisional government was popular and functioning, the United States recognized it.

Austria thus presents an ironic lesson in how "nation building" unfolds. The United States—the democratic power—stood in the way of local leaders who were attempting to establish a democratic regime, and the Soviet Union—the world's leading dictatorship—unintentionally acted as midwife for it. Obviously, in Austria no democracy needed to be "built." The democratic leaders there were strong enough to establish a democracy on their own, and they did so in spite of the occupying "nation builders."

The pattern was similar in Italy. Local Italian leaders overthrew Mussolini in 1943, and Italians set up the democratic government that followed. The main allied contribution was some unhelpful meddling by Britain's Winston Churchill, who was obsessed with the rather undemocratic goal of preserving the unpopular Italian monarchy. To this end, Churchill blocked the respected antimonarchist leader Count Carlo Sforza from becoming prime minister in 1944. This action weakened the fledgling democratic regime, which lost the support of Sforza's followers. In the end, however, Italian democrats overcame Churchill's interference. A national referendum voted out the monarchy in 1946, and Sforza made it into the cabinet in 1947. The Americans, clueless about Italian politics, did not meddle at all. As Italian historian Gianfranco Pasquino explains, "the Americans did not have a specific policy for Italy, or any clear-cut design for the shaping of the Italian political system" (1986, 60).

These cases show that the advocates of nation building need to go back and take a close look at what really happened in the postwar political evolution of the defeated powers. In the lore of nation building, it is supposed that American "experts" carried out sophisticated social engineering that made these countries become democracies against their will. For example, the editors of a four-volume survey of nation building, Larry Diamond, Juan Linz, and Seymour Martin Lipset, declare that "[d]emocracy was imposed on Germany, Italy, and Japan, and surprisingly took hold and endured" (1989, xi). This interpretation is not grounded in the facts. As just noted, it is pure invention that the United States "imposed" democracy on Italy. I do not have space here to review the cases of Germany and Japan, where the United States played a large domestic role. It is an open question, however, whether on balance that role was helpful or harmful for democracy. Many historians, political scientists, and journalists at the time concluded that it was destructive. For example, in September 1949, *Commentary* ran an article entitled "Why Democracy Is Losing in Germany" that decried the inept, counterproductive policies of the U.S. military administration (Gurland 1949).

"MAKING THIS UP AS WE GO ALONG"

The recent interventions in Afghanistan and Iraq further illustrate how haphazard and unfocused nation building is in practice. Neither of these efforts has followed any plan, design, or theory for establishing a democracy. In invading Afghanistan, the Bush administration gave little thought to political arrangements that might follow military victory over the Taliban. Less than three weeks before the attack, President Bush asked national-security advisor Condoleezza Rice, "Who will run the country?" It was a moment of panic for her because she had not given the issue any thought (Daalder 2003, 112).

A year and a half later, with the invasion of Iraq, the administration had apparently gained nothing in nation-building expertise. Although the military campaign was a success, the occupation and its administration have been characterized by naïveté and improvisation. In the early stages of the invasion, the U.S. government had neither a policy to check looting nor the forces to do so—policymakers had apparently forgotten the lesson of Panama—and the result was a ravaging of local infrastructure, the rapid formation of gangs of thugs and paramilitary fighters, and a loss of local support for the U.S. effort. The civilian administration was first put in the hands of retired Lieutenant General Jay Garner, who was two weeks late getting to Baghdad and who naively expected to find a functioning government in the country. After one month, the hapless Garner was fired, and Paul Bremer was appointed his replacement as chief administrator. Two months after the invasion, Lieutenant General William Wallace, the Fifth

Corps commander, described the nation-building "technique" that U.S. officials were applying in Iraq: "We're making this up here as we go along" (qtd. in Daalder 2003, 153).

Trying to establish democracy through military occupation is not a coherent, defensible policy. There is no theory on which it is based; it has no proven technique or methodology; and no experts know how to do it. The record shows that it usually fails, and even when it appears to succeed, the positive result owes more to historical evolution and local political culture than to anything the nation builders might have done.

NOTE

1. For example, despite the heavy U.S. military involvement in Kuwait, especially the 1991 liberation of the country from Iraq, the United States has played no active role in trying to shape Kuwaiti politics. Another such "politically neutral" intervention is the British involvement in Oman. The British had troops there from 1951 to 1971, and they played a role upholding the emir against rebels, but they made no effort to shape local politics in a democratic direction.

REFERENCES

Bush, George W. 2003. Speech at the American Enterprise Institute, Washington, D.C., Feb., 26.

Daalder, Ivo H., and James M. Lindsay. 2003. *America Unbound: The Bush Revolution in Foreign Policy.* Washington, D.C.: Brookings Institution.

Diamond, Larry, Juan J. Linz, and Seymour Martin Lipset, eds. 1989. *Democracy in Developing Countries: Latin America.* Boulder, Colo.: Lynne Rienner.

Fishel, John T. 1997. *Civil Military Operations in the New World.* Westport, Conn.: Praeger.

Gurland, A. R. L. 1949. Why Democracy Is Losing in Germany. *Commentary* 8 (September): 222–37.

Haass, Richard N. 2005. Freedom Is Not a Doctrine. *Washington Post,* January 24.

Karatnycky, Adam. 2002. *Freedom in the World: The Annual Survey of Political Rights and Civil Liberties 2001–2002.* New York: Freedom House.

Kristol, William, and Robert Kagan. 1996. Toward a Neo-Reaganite Foreign Policy. *Foreign Affairs* (July–August): 18–32.

Pasquino, Gianfranco. 1986. The Demise of the First Fascist Regime and Italy's Transition to Democracy: 1943–1948. In *Transitions from Authoritarian Rule: Southern Europe,* edited by Guillermo O'Donnell, Philippe C. Schmitter, and Laurence Whitehead, 45–70. Baltimore: Johns Hopkins University Press.

Payne, James L. 2004. *A History of Force: Exploring the Worldwide Movement Against Habits of Coercion, Bloodshed, and Mayhem.* Sandpoint, Idaho: Lytton.

Wiarda, Howard J. 1989. The Dominican Republic: Mirror Legacies of Democracy and Authoritarianism. In *Democracy in Developing Countries: Latin America,* edited by Larry Diamond, Juan J. Linz, and Seymour Martin Lipset, 423–58. Boulder, Colo.: Lynne Rienner.

Acknowledgment: Reprinted from *The Independent Review,* 9, no. 4 (Spring 2005): 563–72. ISSN 1086-1653, Copyright © 2005.

7

Did the United States Create Democracy in Germany?

JAMES L. PAYNE

Do we know how to promote democracy in a troubled land? Do we have a set of policies and practices that administrators can take off the shelf, as it were, and apply in a reasonably straightforward fashion to produce a lasting democracy?

Before the U.S. invasion of Iraq in 2003, many commentators and policymakers seemed to believe that such an established methodology exists. The difficult experience in that country has somewhat dimmed this confidence, but it has by no means destroyed it. Many writers continue to speak of nation building as if it involved a settled technology, like that of building interstate highways. They seem to believe that nation-building experts can go to any country and, regardless of its culture and traditions, successfully impose a democracy. What accounts for this confidence in the efficacy of nation-building expertise?

One important source appears to be the U.S. experience after World War II. Those who today advocate assertive policies of nation building repeatedly cite this era as a golden age of nation building. The United States should invade dictatorships and failed states, they say, and turn them into democracies. How do we know this task is feasible? They answer, "Look at what we did in Germany and Japan."

Writing in the *New York Times Magazine* in June 2005, Michael Ignatieff, a professor of human rights at the Kennedy School of Government at Harvard, urged an "American crusade to spread democracy" around the world. His main evidence for the soundness of this undertaking is the presumed success in Germany. "Freedom in Germany was an American imperial imposition, from the cashiering of ex-Nazi officials and the expunging of anti-Semitic nonsense from school textbooks to the drafting of a new federal constitution" (Ignatieff 2005, 45).

A political analyst for the Rand Corporation, James Dobbins, makes the same claim: "The post–World War II occupations of Germany and Japan were America's first experiences with the use of military force in the aftermath of a conflict to underpin rapid and fundamental societal transformation. Both were comprehensive efforts that aimed to engineer major social, political, and economic reconstruction. The success of these endeavors demonstrated that democracy was transferable" (2003, xiii).

Three leading scholars of democratic development, Larry Diamond, Juan J. Linz, and Seymour Martin Lipset, echo the point. After the victory of the Allied powers in World War II, they say, "Democracy was imposed on Germany, Italy, and Japan, and surprisingly took hold and endured" (1989, xi).

Political scientist Mark Peceny advances the same idea: "In by far the most successful application of this policy [of encouraging democracy] in the history of U.S. foreign policy, U.S. occupation governments transformed Nazi Germany and Imperial Japan into liberal democratic allies in the wake of World War II" (1999, 81).

Even those who oppose nation building agree that the United States did succeed in Germany and Japan. Gary Dempsey, a foreign-policy analyst at the libertarian Cato Institute, criticizes observers who assume that "with enough money, experienced bureaucrats, and military firepower, retrograde states anywhere can be turned into open, self-sustaining, peaceful democracies, as Germany and Japan were after World War II" (2002, 3). Thus, even though Dempsey is critical of the idea that we can easily create democracies, he apparently accepts the premise that Germany and Japan were "turned into" democracies by U.S. action.

The current Bush administration absorbed this view. Two weeks before invading Iraq, the president defended the impending attack by pointing to the post–World War II interventions: "America has made and kept this kind of commitment before— in the peace that followed a world war. After defeating enemies, we did not leave behind occupying armies; we left constitutions and parliaments. We established an atmosphere of safety, in which responsible, reform-minded local leaders could build lasting institutions of freedom. In societies that once bred fascism and militarism, liberty found a permanent home."[1]

These many references to the case of Germany make one curious. What exactly did U.S. administrators do to succeed so well in promoting democracy there? Surely, one supposes, this experience should yield a wealth of valuable lessons for modern-day nation builders to apply elsewhere.

On opening the contemporaneous books and articles about the postwar occupation of Germany, however, we find this assumption of success rudely contradicted. At the time, reporters and scholars did not have a glowing, confident view of U.S. policy. As they saw it, muddled policies and incompetent administration were botching the task of encouraging democracy. Illustrative of the tenor of these writings was an article entitled "Why Democracy Is Losing in Germany" that appeared in *Commentary* in September 1949. "We must face the fact," the author wrote, "that the contradictions, vacillations, and reactionary manifestations of Western occupation policy have appallingly discredited democracy in Germany, both as a political system and an intellectual outlook" (Gurland 1949, 235). A close look reveals that, from the standpoint of democratic nation building, the U.S. occupation of Germany is actually a lesson on what not to do!

DON'T SHAKE HANDS!

In Germany, the Allied effort had two aspects. One was the impact of the *war*. In World War II, Germany's enemies defeated Hitler and in the process revealed to the German people that his pretensions were absurd and colossally destructive. As a result, the national mood in Germany that had enabled Hitler to come to power vanished. In this specific sense, one can say that U.S. action contributed to democracy in Germany: the Allied victory created a tabula rasa that permitted it to emerge.

The Allied effort's second aspect was the military occupation, which extended from victory in 1945 to (for most practical purposes) 1952. As the previous quotations indicate, modern writers assume that skilled and purposeful U.S. officials applied sophisticated nation-building techniques during this period and thereby "imposed" democracy where it otherwise would not have come into existence. This hypothesis is extremely doubtful. The occupation's actual policies and activities from 1945 to 1952 did little to further democracy, and many of them caused positive harm.

Modern writers' first mistake is to assume that the goal of the American occupation in Germany was to make the country a democracy—that it constituted, as Dobbins puts it, a "comprehensive effort that aimed to engineer major social, political, and economic reconstruction." This view is wildly at variance with the facts. Building democracy was *not* the aim of occupation policy. Instead, policymakers aimed to punish Germany and to deny it any war-making potential. Some American leaders advocated a "back to the Stone Age" policy for Germany. One such plan, drawn up by Treasury Secretary Henry Morgenthau and his assistant Harry Dexter White, called for Germany to be dismembered and turned into an agrarian society in which the inhabitants would live by subsistence farming. Other leaders did not go so far, but they all agreed on severe punishment. "If I had my way," President Franklin D. Roosevelt commented, "I would keep Germany on a breadline for the next 25 years" (qtd. in Davidson 1959, 7). From this angry mood came JCS 1067, the Joint Chiefs of Staff directive on U.S. objectives and basic policies that formed the orders of the military government from May 1945 to July 1947. It emphasized not reconstruction or democracy, but harsh treatment of the Germans.

One directive of JCS 1067 that the U.S. military authority attempted to implement was a policy of "nonfraternization." Americans were not to engage in any kind of friendly, normal intercourse with Germans. They were not supposed to shake hands with them, to visit them in their homes, to play games with them, or to converse or argue with them. If they went to a German church, they had to sit in separate, Americans-only pews. The army newspaper *Stars and Stripes* ran many antifraternization slogans and statements such as "Don't fraternize. If in a German town you bow to a pretty girl or pat a blond child…you bow to Hitler and his reign of blood" (qtd. in Davidson 1959, 54). Military police arrested more than a thousand Americans in an effort to sustain the policy of nonfraternization (Davidson 1959, 55). In practice, many Americans ignored the policy and braved punishment to do the sensible, human thing in interacting with the Germans. The nonfraternization policy was gradually relaxed and eventually abandoned. Nevertheless, the policy started the occupation out on the wrong foot if its presumed aim was to win hearts and minds and to teach the German people about democracy.

Other policies exacerbated this wrong-footedness. For example, the United States sought to keep its military and civilian personnel isolated from the Germans in compounds and colonies (often surrounded by barbed wire) known as "Little Americas." At a time when great numbers of Germans were living in rubble, tents, and railway stations, the Americans had a comfortable lifestyle—and it was created at the Germans' expense. U.S. troops seized the best homes and hotels as their living quarters and pushed the German occupants onto the street. For each American family housed in a requisitioned dwelling, eight Germans were made homeless; in Frankfurt alone, Americans requisitioned 10,800 apartments and single-family dwellings (Davidson 1959, 156, 276).

DELIBERATELY WRECKING THE GERMAN ECONOMY

Further setting the stage for resentment were the U.S. economic policies. Although little is known about the requirements for democracy, one important factor suggested by research and common sense is prosperity: destitute people are ready to listen to demagogues who promise bread at the expense of freedom. Therefore, anyone seeking to establish a democracy in a defeated country should make a maximum effort to ensure the local inhabitants' prosperity and well-being. Many Americans today suppose that "we put Germany on its feet after the war," but the truth is more nearly the opposite. U.S. policy was intended to inflict economic privation. As part of the JCS 1067 punishment philosophy, U.S. forces were not supposed to provide ordinary relief. Troops were specifically ordered not to let American food supplies go to hungry Germans. American households were instructed not to let their German maids have leftovers; excess food was to be destroyed or rendered inedible (Davidson 1959, 85). A German university professor pointed out that U.S. soldiers "create unnecessary ill will to pour twenty litres of left-over cocoa in the gutter when it is badly needed in our clinics. It makes it hard for me to defend American democracy among my countrymen" (qtd. in Davidson 1959, 86).

JCS 1067 forbade the occupation authority from taking any "steps looking toward the economic rehabilitation of Germany" (JCS 1067 qtd. in Zink 1957, 253). The Allies placed limits on German industries, freezing the production of steel, machine tools, and chemicals at less than half the prewar rate. Even the production of textiles and shoes was limited to depressed levels. The Allies also pursued a policy of dismantling factories, deliberately destroying hundreds of plants and throwing several hundred thousand employees out of work in the western zone (Davidson 1959, 255). German workers threatened strikes against this practice; even the archbishop of Cologne and his parishioners prayed against this senseless economic destruction (Davidson 1959, 255). Nevertheless, it continued out of sheer bureaucratic inertia until 1950.

The German economy was further burdened by having to pay for the occupation itself, both through arbitrary requisitions of properties, finished goods, and raw materials and through direct payments from German governmental units. One calculation estimated that occupation costs consumed 46 percent of local tax receipts in 1948 (Davidson 1959, 261). German newspapers began to release details of what troops were buying with German taxpayers' money: one ton of water bugs to feed a U.S. general's pet fish, a bedspread of Korean goatskin, thirty thousand bras (the Americans banned the newspaper for publishing this last item—a nice "democratic" touch on the part of the would-be "teachers of democracy").

Another economic factor that kept the country in poverty was the failure to issue currency. This lapse had many reasons, including complications with the Russians and U.S. officials' economic ignorance, but the fact was that for three years, from 1945 to 1948, the Germans had no sound currency, only Hitler's debased old currency and an untrustworthy occupation script. In desperation, locals turned to cigarettes—which consequently became much too valuable as a medium of exchange to smoke. Imagine trying to carry out a high-value sale or to make a future-oriented contract in cigarettes! When a new currency was finally issued in June 1948, economic life began to revive immediately.

Not all American actions were economically injurious to Germany. Some Americans were personally generous, some relief aid was distributed, and the Allies did work to restore basic services. But these positive efforts were not enough to counteract the damage that occupation policies had done to economic life. The Germans were desperately poor in 1945–48 not because of war damage. Studies showed that German industries and facilities were largely intact and that production could have been restored quickly had the Allies been willing to allow it (Zink 1957, 253). But U.S. policy, some of it deliberate, some simply the usual muddle in a government-directed economy, promoted destitution and despair—and thereby earned the resentment of much of the local population.

At this point, some readers may want to ask, What about the Marshall Plan? In June 1947, Secretary of State George C. Marshall announced a sweeping foreign-aid proposal for Europe. As a public gesture of magnanimity, the Marshall Plan was certainly a public-relations success of the first order. It convinced many, in both the United States and Europe, that the United States wanted to aid Europe's economic recovery. Unfortunately, the focus on the Marshall Plan's good intentions has tended to obscure a crucial scientific question: Was the aid decisive in Europe's economic recovery, or was Europe going to recover anyway?

This question, it seems, remains an open one, especially as we are beginning to notice that aid to underdeveloped countries has in many cases brought little positive economic result (see World Bank 1998; Easterly 2006). Foreign aid may well be one of those policies that seems as if it ought to work, yet does not. The money follows bureaucratic and political channels and winds up being wasted or used to prop up uneconomic arrangements. In the case of the Marshall Plan, one notices, for example, that there is no correlation between the amount of aid per capita given to the various European countries and their respective increases in production from 1948 to 1951.[2] This finding suggests no cause-and-effect relationship between aid and increased production. As scholars have looked more closely at this program, doubt has grown about whether the aid was needed or effective (Wexler 1983; Milward 1989; Esposito 1994).

It is especially doubtful that Marshall Plan aid helped Germany decisively because the contribution to that country was relatively low. England and France received $2.7 and $2.2 billion respectively, about $54 per capita, whereas West Germany received only $1.2 billion, or $24 per capita. It seems unlikely that the latter amount, even if used effectively, counterbalanced the negative effect of the U.S. policies of confiscation, economic obstruction, and deliberate destruction.

FIRST PUNISHING, THEN HELPING NAZIS

Democracy was eclipsed in Germany in 1933, when Hitler and the Nazi Party took power. With their defeat in war, however, the mood and motivation that buoyed their followers collapsed. Hitlerism, whatever it was, had been demonstrated to be catastrophically foolish, and the vast majority of Nazi supporters turned away from it. They did not make a reasoned analysis of what was wrong with Nazism; it simply became passé, unattractive, and unhelpful for personal advancement. Therefore, after the war, no positive measures were needed to keep Nazism from coming back.

At the time, policymakers were not sufficiently open-minded to perceive this reality. U.S. officials imagined that those who had acted in the Nazi Party remained deeply committed believers. This view led them to expect "werewolves," or cells of fanatical, violent Nazis who would harass the occupation army in suicide attacks and sabotage (Montgomery 1957, 69). Nothing of the sort happened, but its absence did not cause policymakers to change their views about the Nazis' nature.

Furthermore, heinous deeds had been done in the name of Nazism, and the world wanted to see punishment. Imprisoning the obvious leaders and malefactors would not be enough; all who had put their shoulders to the Nazi wheel must be made to suffer. Many occupation officials on the scene perceived the basic, normal "humanness" of former Nazis, but they could not tell distant audiences that persecution of former Nazis was unwise and unworkable. When General George Patton commented that there wasn't much more difference between German parties than there was between Republicans and Democrats, a storm of protest back home led to his recall.

In the American zone, the process of purging and punishing Nazis started with the requirement that the entire adult population, 13 million people, fill out a detailed autobiographical questionnaire consisting of 150 searching personal questions. In effect, every adult was assumed to be guilty until cleared by a tribunal that decided his or her degree of complicity. Although these tribunals did not follow judicial rules of evidence, they were still slow and cumbersome and could not deal with the caseload in reasonable time. Because no German could hold any job except day laborer without clearance by the tribunal, "millions of capable and politically indifferent Germans had to remain idle or engage in 'ordinary labor' for an indefinite period" (Montgomery 1957, 23). This obstacle to staffing firms and agencies formed, of course, another impediment to economic development.

The denazification process ascribed guilt by association. Germans were punished—fired from their jobs, fined, or sent to jail—not for what they actually did. To convict a person, the tribunals did not have to prove that a defendant killed someone or that he ordered an arrest or caused some other kind of injury. It was enough that the accused was or was alleged to be an active sympathizer. This shadowy protocol encouraged informers to come forward to denounce neighbors—or personal enemies. The public came to feel that thousands of perfectly innocent people were being punished. German politicians, especially Christian Democratic Party leaders, opposed the denazification process, arguing that it resembled Hitler's persecutions in its reliance on the doctrine of "collective guilt." Even the Americans eventually agreed that the effort was a counterproductive failure, and they abandoned the program. Then, in 1951, they made a complete reversal and embraced the idea that Nazis had rights! Amazing as it seems, it was *required by law* that civil servants and teachers who had been removed because of their alleged Nazi attachments be rehired, so scores of thousands were (Montgomery 1957, 66, 81; Davidson 1959, 276). Former Nazis even demanded—and sometimes received—compensation for the wrongs done to them in the denazification process (Montgomery 1957, 69).

The most unfortunate consequence of the U.S. policy of trying to persecute Nazis was that it provoked sympathy for Nazis that they otherwise would not have received. Harvard professor of public administration John D. Montgomery, who made a comprehensive study of the episode, concluded that the denazification policy actually strengthened the neo-Nazis in the postwar years. The process, he concluded, generated "bitterness and resentment [that] gave the sanction of martyrdom to otherwise unsaintly lives or dignified an otherwise degraded ideology by appearing to persecute it" (1957, 150; see also pp. 31, 57, 67, 69).

The U.S. denazification policy was not a brilliant pro-democratic stroke, as modern nation builders imagine. Instead, it was a counterproductive witch hunt, widely recognized at the time as a "fiasco," and it was *abandoned entirely and even reversed by the same occupation authority that had imposed it* (Herz 1948).

EDUCATING FOR FUZZINESS

For centuries, education has been considered important, even essential, to democracy. Unfortunately, this presumed link has never been defined concretely. Is it necessary for citizens to learn arithmetic, spelling, or religious catechism? Should schools teach history, and, if so, which history? There is perhaps no woolier and more contentious subject than "education for democracy."

Occupation policy after World War II reflected the confusion on this topic. Take the matter of textbooks, which Ignatieff (quoted at the beginning of this article) believes to have been so decisive. The German experience clearly proves that textbooks do not matter. Under the Hitler regime,

German schoolchildren had used the Nazi-oriented textbooks for more than a decade, yet all this propaganda and indoctrination failed to produce a cohort of dedicated Nazis: after the war, no significant manifestation of Nazi loyalties appeared in Germany (Montgomery 1957, 69; Davidson 1959, 231–32). Yes, the Allies did away with the offensive Nazi-slanted school textbooks (by using reprinted German textbooks of the pre-Hitler era), and they no doubt felt much better having made the change. It is doubtful, however, that the change had any effect on relevant political attitudes. After all, the postwar German democracy was set up by middle-aged and elderly German adults who were not reading these schoolbooks anyway.

Beginning in 1947, the Americans moved beyond merely restarting the existing German education system and took up the idea of redirecting and reforming it. A good authority on the quality of this reform effort is political scientist Harold Zink, who was a high official in the U.S. occupation, becoming chief historian of the Office of the U.S. High Commissioner in 1950. As a former member of the U.S. occupation establishment, Zink is cautious and forgiving in his treatment of Allied miscues, but even with this bias he gives a damning account of the American education program. The program, he says, was an "incohesive" mélange of "divergent points of view" (1957, 193–94).

The first head of the education section was H. B. Wells, the president of Indiana University, picked because he was a "big name," an administrator skilled at wheedling money from the Indiana legislature, not an authority on elementary or secondary education (Zink 1957, 200). Wells quickly developed a huge staff, composed for the most part of "empire builders," Zink says, "who knew very little about German problems and cared less, but saw in the Education Division an opportunity to gain recognition, build up personal power, and the like" (1957, 202). This staff was directed to draw up plans for "a complete reorganization of German education on American lines." Wells left within a year, and most of these plans, "fortunately for both Germans and Americans," says Zink, "remained on paper and were never executed" (1957, 203).

The next "big name" to head the education branch was Alonzo Grace, a former commissioner of education in Connecticut. Grace began by damning the first three years of the U.S. occupation as "more or less devoid of an educational and cultural relations effort" (Zink 1957, 204). Having spurned the work of his predecessors, he proceeded to enunciate a rambling collection of, according to Zink, "inconsistent" principles and "platitudes" that left most observers bemused. Fortunately this period of "fuzziness" and "too much rather pompous talk" ended in less than a year, and the education program was essentially closed out in 1949 (Zink 1957, 206, 207).

Zink's summary of the occupation effort in education is telling: "Because of the time factor and the lack of detailed knowledge of German institutions, many ill-conceived programs were set up which had no chance of succeeding and squandered large amounts of public funds. There was duplication of effort, conflict, and an immense amount of sheer waste of effort" (1957, 202).

POLITICAL ENGINEERING

Democracy is a political arrangement, so it is of interest to see how the institutions of democratic German government came into being. Were they created and imposed by the Allies on an apathetic or resisting people, or did the Germans themselves take the lead? The evidence strongly supports the latter interpretation. The Christian Democratic Party—soon to become the ruling party in West Germany—was founded by a group of thirty-five German political leaders in Berlin two weeks *before* U.S. military forces even reached the city. On their own, they drew up a declaration of principles, rejecting Nazi ideas such as the primacy of the state and asserting the importance of individuals and families (Davidson 1959, 93). The Americans did not officially authorize the formation of parties in Berlin until August 1945, more than a month *after* the four main ones had been formed.

If anything, the U.S. occupation harassed and delayed the formation and functioning of political parties. The Americans required parties to go through a cumbersome licensing process in order to operate in each local region; they banned the use of party symbols, armbands, and parades; in Bavaria, they banned a democratic monarchist party (Zink 1957, 336–37; Davidson 1959, 95–96). The U.S. authority on political parties and elections, Richard M. Scammon, summed up the impact on political party activity: "Interference by occupation authorities was not infrequent in the earliest days of German political activity, and many of these interferences seem on later examination to have been improper and arbitrary" (qtd. in Zink

1957, 337). Scammon attributed the mischief more to ineptitude ("lack of understanding") than to a deliberate intention to impair the formation of democratic parties.

Constitution writing is another area in which the U.S. occupation is often given credit (again, see Ignatieff's statements, cited earlier), but here, too, the record indicates a doubtful effect. In the writing of constitutions for German state-level governments, U.S. officials "kept close touch with the work," but, official historian Zink says, "it cannot be fairly stated that the constitutions were their brain children" (1957, 180).[3] He says the same about the national constitution, drafted in 1949: "Definitely a German product" (1957, 186). Historian Eugene Davidson echoes this opinion: "it was mainly a German document" (1959, 237).

If setting up a democracy were an intricate, specialized undertaking, then it would be unrealistic to expect an army of occupation to do it very well, or perhaps to do it at all. We must bear in mind that most post–World War II occupation officials were military officers with no particular expertise in social science, diplomacy, or constitutional theory. For example, the head of the occupation, General Lucius Clay, had come up through the army engineers, working on rivers and harbors projects. He had "almost no background in political matters" (Zink 1957, 68). According to Zink, the staff officers who ended up in the occupation administration tended to be of an inferior quality because the best officers were kept in the active military combat units, not released to serve in the occupation branch. Many had "little self-control, indifferent moral standards, and a record of failure in their domestic relations and social groups at home" (1957, 8–9). Very few spoke German. The occupation officials were, at best, run-of-the-mill army personnel; in many cases, says Zink, they were "deadwood" (1957, 208, 210). Therefore, it is droll to behold today's nation-building theorists attribute to them superior powers to engineer a major social and political transformation.

Did the U.S. occupation impose democracy on Germany? On this point, we need go no further than the conclusion of political scientist and occupation chief historian Harold Zink. He reports, as noted earlier, that the objective of preparing Germany for democracy was not a serious goal of the occupation and was never given serious attention by the Joint Chiefs of Staff. This "vague or perhaps meaningless" objective was included in the Potsdam Declaration (signed with the Soviet Union) merely "because it sounded well" (1957, 326). Zink scorns the idea that the United States might have had a coherent program for building democracy: "The transplanting of democratic political institutions to Germany would be most uncertain at best, but when such a goal was coupled with a vengeful program emphasizing denazification, the imposition of a low living standard on the German people, nonfraternization, the destruction of German industry, and the like, it would seem to have little or no concrete significance" (1957, 327).

DEMOCRACY BY DESIGN OR BY EVOLUTION?

The record shows, then, that from the standpoint of promoting democracy, the U.S. occupation of Germany was extraordinarily inept. Yet, despite the miscues, democracy emerged in Germany. How do we explain this result? A full answer is beyond the compass of this article, but I can sketch out the beginnings of an explanation.

There are, it seems, two broad theories about how democracy comes into being. One is that it is the product of social engineering. In this view, democracy is an elaborate machine with many parts—constitutions, electoral systems, civic organizations, and so forth—and experts are needed to craft and assemble these parts. Nation builders tend to favor this model because it validates their role. They are like the highway engineers who believe that highways can be built anywhere and that they have the skills to build them.

Belief in this "design" model of democracy accounts for the misperception about what happened in postwar Germany. The commentators have reasoned backward, supposing that because democracy can come about only by design, then skilled, purposeful nation builders must have been at work on the scene.

An opposing model of political development views democracy as an organic, natural outgrowth in a society that has reached a certain stage of cultural evolution. It cannot be imposed from the outside if the society is not "ready" for it. When conditions are propitious, it will happen more or less naturally, without any experts or social engineers to create it.

What cultural condition makes a nation "ready" for democracy? The factor I would propose is a variable that has been strangely neglected in the study of democracy: moderation of the amount of leadership political violence. Where political leaders are inclined to use violence against each other—violence in the form of political murders, gang attacks, and armed revolts—democracy cannot survive. It will tend to collapse into civil war or a repressive dictatorship.

From this perspective, democracy is not at all complicated. It may take many complex forms, but the core concept is elementary: leaders have decided not to employ force against each other. As a result, they necessarily turn to nonviolent methods, such as counting heads (elections), to settle their disputes. In this "cultural" model, democracy is simply the default mode of government where leaders are peaceful, and any group of friends and neighbors can start it up spontaneously.[4]

This sort of development, I suggest, is what happened in Germany. Long before World War II, Germany had evolved a basically nonviolent politics. Even before 1850, democratic forms of government were emerging, with elections and legislative bodies, and participants had long transcended the custom of political murder. By 1871, the country was a democracy, with universal manhood suffrage and a national parliament. The Hitler regime of 1933 thus represented a bizarre departure from a long democratic tradition. It was a regime in which thugs and murderers intimidated and displaced the normal political class.

After the war, the country reverted to its peaceful political tradition. Hitler's ideas were thoroughly discredited, his thugs disappeared, and the nonviolent democratic leaders of the prewar era came forward. They simply did what came naturally: started political parties, organized campaigns, drew up constitutions, and staffed the government. I believe the same interpretation applies to Japan, Austria, and Italy. Allied policies did not create democracy in these countries. Instead, the deviant, violent leaders of the prior regime departed the scene, leaving a cadre of leaders who were not inclined to use force against each other. Given this precondition, democracy came into being naturally.

It will be some time before we can fully assess this interpretation of how democracy comes about. Nevertheless, it seems clear, as a number of scholars are now observing, that we need to broaden our theories to include the cultural dimension of the process (see, e.g., Carothers 2002). After all, it is clear that the overwhelming majority of military interventions that have sought to promote democracy have failed.[5] These many failures suggest that democracy involves cultural factors not amenable to direct manipulation by policymakers.

NOTES

1. Speech at the American Enterprise Institute, February 26, 2003.
2. I have computed this correlation from data given in Wexler 1983, 63, 67, 94.
3. General Lucius D. Clay makes the same point in his book *Decision in Germany* (1950, 89).
4. For a fuller exposition of this approach to democracy as an outgrowth of a "low-violence" society, see Mueller 1995, 156–59; Payne 2004, 81–99, and 2005.
5. For a review of the nation-building record, see Payne 2006.

REFERENCES

Carothers, Thomas. 2002. The End of the Transitional Paradigm. *Journal of Democracy* 13, no. 1 (January): 5–21.

Clay, General Lucius D. 1950. *Decision in Germany.* Garden City. N.Y.: Doubleday.

Davidson, Eugene. 1959. *The Death and Life of Germany.* New York: Knopf.

Dempsey, Gary T. 2002. *Old Folly in a New Disguise: Nation Building to Combat Terrorism.* Cato Institute Policy Analysis no. 429, March 21. Washington, D.C.: Cato Institute.

Diamond, Larry, Juan J. Linz, and Seymour Martin Lipset. 1989. *Democracy in Developing Countries.* Vol. 4, *Latin America.* Boulder, Colo.: Lynne Rienner, 1989.

Dobbins, James. 2003. *America's Role in Nation-Building: From Germany to Iraq.* Santa Monica, Calif.: Rand.

Easterly, William. 2006. *The White Man's Burden: Why the West's Efforts to Aid the Rest Have Done So Much Ill and So Little Good.* New York: Penguin.

Esposito, Chiarella. 1994. *America's Feeble Weapon: Funding the Marshall Plan in France and Italy, 1948–1950.* Westport, Conn.: Greenwood Press.

Gurland, R. L. 1949. Why Democracy Is Losing in Germany. *Commentary* 8 (September): 227–37.

Herz, John H. 1948. The Fiasco of Denazification in Germany. *Political Science Quarterly* (December): 569–94.

Ignatieff, Michael. 2005. Who Are Americans to Think That Freedom Is Theirs to Spread? *New York Times Magazine,* June 26, 42–47.

Milward, Alan S. 1989. Was the Marshall Plan Necessary? *Diplomatic History* 13 (spring): 231–53.

Montgomery, John D. 1957. *Forced to Be Free: The Artificial Revolution in Germany and Japan.* Chicago: University of Chicago Press.

Mueller, John. 1995. *Quiet Cataclysm: Reflections on the Recent Transformation of World Politics.* New York: HarperCollins.

Payne, James L. 2004. *A History of Force.* Sandpoint, Idaho: Lytton.

———. 2005. The Prospects for Democracy in High-Violence Societies. *The Independent Review* 9, no. 4 (Spring 2005): 563–72.

———. 2006. Does Nation Building Work? The Prospects for Democracy in High-Violence Societies. *The Independent Review* 10, no. 4 (spring): 597–608.

Peceny, Mark. 1999. *Democracy at the Point of Bayonets.* University Park: Pennsylvania State University Press.

Wexler, Imanuel. 1983. *The Marshall Plan Revisited: The European Recovery Program in Economic Perspective.* Westport, Conn.: Greenwood Press.

World Bank. 1998. *Assessing Aid: What Works, What Doesn't, and Why.* Policy Research Report. New York: Oxford University Press.

Zink, Harold. 1957. *The United States in Germany 1944–1955.* Princeton, N.J.: D. Van Nostrand.

Acknowledgment: Reprinted from *The Independent Review,* 11, no. 2 (Fall 2006): 209–221. ISSN 1086–1653, Copyright © 2006.

8

A Matter of Small Consequence

U.S. Foreign Policy and the Tragedy of East Timor

JERRY K. SWEENEY

When East Timor resurfaced as a journalistic destination, most Americans were hard put to find it on a map. Later, when the Clinton administration took official notice, some were wont to label the U.S. interest yet another example of a meritorious intervention, similar to the one in Kosovo. Others, familiar with East Timor and its problems, suspected the new U.S. involvement was the product of a guilty conscience. I myself recalled an observation from the film *Bull Durham*. Annie Savoy (played by Susan Sarandon) opines to the audience in the opening credits: "A guy will listen to anything if he thinks it's foreplay." The United States was never, in any wise, interested in the well-being of the East Timorese. The United States was not inclined to listen to what they had to say, especially if their grievances were justified. East Timor was and will be nothing more to the United States than a means to ephemeral ends involving a third party.

THE PORTUGUESE CONNECTION

Our tale begins in 1942, when the successes of German submarine warfare led the Allied High Command to realize that a successful campaign against the U-boats would require an airbase in the Portuguese Azores. This realization placed Washington in a good news/bad news situation. The bad news was that Portugal was a neutral nation in 1942. The good news was that Lisbon was party to an ancient alliance with the British, a U.S. ally. Britain and Portugal had avowed their friendship in 1373, and they concluded a formal treaty of alliance in 1386.

Thus, in the fullness of time, U.S. aircraft based in the Azores put paid to the efforts of the German navy. Despite the success of the antisubmarine campaign, however, the Department of War was disconsolate. In the first instance, the U.S. presence in the Azores was under the auspices of the Royal Air Force. Not surprisingly, the War Department preferred a wholly owned U.S. subsidiary. In addition, the existing facility at Lajes could not be expanded to handle an increase in air traffic incident to the invasion of Europe or Japan. Finally, there was no doubt that a second airfield would be beneficial during bad weather. In consequence, at the end of 1943, Washington was committed to the establishment of a base independent of British control.

Enter from stage left the Portuguese colony of East Timor, which the Japanese had occupied in the early months of 1942 as part of their drive on Australia. Despite regular protests by Lisbon, the Japanese remained obdurate. The Portuguese government believed that if it did not liberate the colony before the end of the Pacific War, Portugal might lose control of it in a general postwar settlement. This situation created what seemed a match made in heaven. The United States would provide the logistical support necessary to liberate East Timor, and Lisbon would authorize a U.S. base in the Azores. Of course, when sovereign states negotiate, there's many a slip betwixt the cup and the lip.

The Portuguese were not inclined to risk the ignominy that had resulted from their resort to arms during World War I. Portugal had left that conflict as a discarded and useless country. By 1943, however, Portuguese neutrality was proving quite profitable. If Lisbon managed to liberate East Timor, Portugal not only would survive the war unscathed, but would recover a lost colony in the bargain. In the minds of most Portuguese, the empire was vital to the nation's existence as a sovereign state. Without the empire, Portugal was perceived as little more than a hodgepodge of ethnic remnants strung along a coastal plain. In fact, more than one outside observer noted that the Portuguese were almost pathologically suspicious concerning the empire, and national dismay set in when even a rumor of foreign annexation was afoot. In addition, it was widely believed that the loss of the colonies would presage the end of the authoritarian state created by Antonio de Oliveira Salazar in 1933 (Guimaraes 1993–94; Sweeney 1997). However, any firm commitment to the liberation of East Timor most assuredly would affect operations designed to defeat the Japanese. Therefore, the Americans sought to fashion an agreement that would allow a facility in the Azores with a minimal obligation to support the Portuguese liberation of Timor.

Both sides played their cards carefully, notwithstanding the fact that the United States was the five-thousand-pound gorilla at the table. A bargain was struck and the necessary documents exchanged on November 28, 1944. Once construction of an airfield on the island of Santa Maria was under way, U.S. officials, not unreasonably, believed the Luso-American connection was on solid ground. They were dismayed, therefore, when East Timor emerged as an item in the negotiations over a postwar aviation agreement. Fortunately for the United States, Japan's surrender on August 15, 1945, rendered the matter moot.

Admittedly, a slight contretemps developed over who should accept the surrender of the Japanese forces on the island. The British and the Australian governments insisted that Lisbon could not accept the surrender of Japanese troops because Portugal was a neutral state. London dismissed the resulting Portuguese protests as perfunctory. Washington, for its part, repeatedly requested that London find a way to satisfy Portugal's nationalistic sentiments, clearly seeking to convince Lisbon that it accepted all the obligations implicit in the Santa Maria agreements. The United States reaped an enormous harvest from a series of otherwise innocuous diplomatic notes. The deadlock over the aviation agreement was broken within a month, when the Portuguese reversed their former position on several key points. Unfortunately for the American taxpayer, the newly created base in the Azores was a casualty of the aviation negotiation: Portugal paid $859,000 for a facility and equipment worth an estimated $2,200,000.

In the decades following the war, the Luso-American connection focused on the U.S. facility in the Azores. So long as the ability of military aircraft to cross the Atlantic remained limited, the airbase was crucial to the defense of the United States. An alternative route by way of Newfoundland and England was considered less desirable because of erratic weather patterns. Additional proof of the value of the Azores base came forth in October 1973. In view of the enormous equipment losses suffered by the Israeli Defense Force during the Yom Kippur War, Washington initiated an emergency resupply operation. Unfortunately, that effort could succeed only if the planes refueled in the Azores. Not surprisingly, the Portuguese government demurred, but the U.S. secretary of state read them the riot act. The U.S. planes landed in the Azores, and Portugal became subject to the retaliatory oil embargo imposed by the Organization of Petroleum Export-ing Countries (OPEC) on October 21, 1973. The Azores were valuable, but Lisbon learned that Washington's forbearance had limits.

Portugal profited considerably from the Luso-American connection, so much so that, unlike its neighbor to the east, it became a founding member of the North Atlantic Treaty Organization (NATO). When the issue of the dictatorial nature of the Portuguese government was raised in an executive session of the U.S. Senate, a State Department representative responded that "if it is a dictatorship, it is because the people freely voted for it" (Kaplan 1984, 109–10). As for East Timor, the State Department deemed the colony of so little consequence that it did not even achieve the status of unnoticed. Sumner Welles spoke for countless future U.S. diplomats when he avowed that the territory should be independent but that the process would take a thousand years (Louis 1978, 237). Of course, over time some Americans questioned the need to concern themselves with Portugal or its colonial empire when the whole of Western civilization was presumably at stake. A nation thoroughly convinced of the overweening importance of its own interests found it difficult to recognize another's needs or to attempt to un-derstand the complexities of another's internal politics.

THE CRUMBLING PORTUGUESE EMPIRE

Questions about the future of European colonialism and a seemingly ag-gressive Soviet Union posed an insuperable dilemma for the United States. Precedent and ideological consistency mandated a national response that condemned colonialism in all its manifold versions. Nonetheless, most Cold Warriors averred that they must not allow the past to endanger inter-allied relations or overseas bases. Thus, Washington was wont to assume a rhetorical anti-colonial posture while underwriting the colonial aspirations of its allies. This effort to split the difference between the dreams of indig-enous peoples and the interests of colonial powers was frustrating, albeit apparently necessary. Of course, the United States was not alone in this approach. Despite the obvious propaganda value, the principle of self-deter-mination was seldom acknowledged or widely applied by the USSR before the mid-1950s. The United States on occasion did tilt to one side or the other, as it did when it offered early support to racist regimes in Rhodesia and South Africa. Washington was further induced to assist in maintaining the Portuguese empire. Despite an official embargo imposed by Congress, the United States transferred substantial quantities of dual-use equipment to Portugal for its colonial campaigns. Neither side anticipated, however, a situation that would force Washington to choose between conflicting imperial commitments.

The wars Portugal fought in Angola and Mozambique were as bitter and as unsuccessful as most such campaigns in the postwar decades. Moreover, the wars severely damaged the Portuguese economy. Indeed, the African wars were a significant factor in the coup d'etat that installed a new government in Lisbon on April 25, 1974. Therefore, the new regime was driven toward colonial disengagement. Because pervasive and vocal independence movements existed in the several African colonies, those territories had to be placed on the road to independence.

What then about the rest of the empire? Although Portugal and China agreed with regard to the future of Macao, East Timor was another matter altogether. The colony was relatively tranquil, and a continued Portuguese presence there would not require a significant financial outlay. The Japanese occupation had not sparked nationalist movements such as those that had emerged in Indonesia, Burma (Myanmar), and Malaya. Furthermore, Portuguese Timor was also distinct in colonial Southeast Asia in that it had no underground communist movement—a situation owing, in equal parts, to the efficiency of the Portuguese secret police and to the lack of an educated native elite. Mayhap, Lisbon might retain one last remnant of its imperial past. However, much to Lisbon's dismay, East Timor also fell prey to the independence virus.

EAST TIMORESE INDEPENDENCE
AND INDONESIAN ABSORPTION

In May 1974, three political movements emerged in East Timor, representing the plausible options open to the colony: continuation of colonial status, union with neighboring Indonesia, and immediate independence. The groups were, respectively, the Uniao Democratica de Timor (UDT), the Associacao Popular Democratica de Timor (APODETI), and the Frente Revolucionaria de Timor Leste Independente (FRETILIN). Independence was easily the most popular alternative. The continuation of the status quo and union with Indonesia placed a distant second and third. Lisbon had severe reservations about the viability of an independent East Timor but authorized the colonial governor to open negotiations. The result was a new constitution and a timetable for an independent East Timor. At this juncture, the UDT attempted a coup de main on August 11, 1975. The conflict that ensued gave rise to the departure of the Portuguese government and the apparent victory of those who supported immediate independence. Thus, on November 28, 1975, the world was informed of the existence of a new state: the Democratic Republic of East Timor.

What happened next was to some degree inevitable. Postcolonial governments have been wont to implement programs for socioeconomic reconstruction. Unfortunately, when the immediate neighbor is in a post-revolutionary, if not reactionary, phase, this process invites retribution. Prior to the emergence of the East Timorese republic, the Indonesian struggle for independence had brought Ahmed Sukarno to power as that nation's first constitutional president. Unfortunately for him, Sukarno was perceived as too dependent on the Indonesian Communist Party. This situation provoked discontent within the Indonesian army. In consequence, a military junta mounted a coup d'etat in 1965. The United States and Australia enthusiastically greeted this triumph of unrepresentative democracy, viewing Indonesia as having been safely removed from the path of falling dominoes.

Which is a roundabout way of saying that the Indonesian government of President Raden Suharto was wary of an independent East Timor. Although the new nation was officially nonaligned, might not the Timorese, in pursuit of aid to alleviate the effects of Portuguese colonialism, seek assistance for whatever quarter? In 1974, the idea that East Timor might become the Cuba of the South Pacific was not considered a delusion born of extremist politics. Yet another factor influencing Indonesia was the possibility of propinquitous unification. A colonial fiat had divided the island of Timor between Portugal and The Netherlands in 1895. When Indonesia gained its independence, West Timor was included. Surely the indigenous residents of East Timor might one day seek to create a united Timor.

Whatever the reason, in the early hours of December 8, 1975, the Indonesian armed forces moved against the people of East Timor. International protests and United Nations resolutions proved ineffective. Indonesia continued to absorb the briefly independent nation. It must be noted at this point that convincing evidence exists to support the assertion that a faction within the Indonesian military had planned the annexation of East Timor as early as 1969 (Taylor 1999). In any event, on July 17, 1976, President Suharto announced the incorporation of East Timor as Indonesia's twenty-seventh province, whereupon the United States sought to possess the pastry while consuming the same.

The Indonesian action placed the United States on the horns of a strategic dilemma. The Azores remained an essential aspect of the U.S. defense posture. Despite the advent of in-flight refueling, the facility retained its importance because tanker aircraft themselves must frequently land. Furthermore, a combination of heavy cargo and a strong headwind severely degrades the ability of even a C-141 to cross the Atlantic without refueling. Once that aircraft has been replaced with the C-17, the Lajes facility may become less important. (Of course, aircraft crews faced with midflight emergencies will undoubtedly continue to appreciate its existence.)

Indonesia offered commensurate rewards to the United States—to wit, the Ombai-Wetar Straits that lie north of Timor. The extremely deep channels of the straits provide undetected access for submarines between the Pacific Ocean and the Indian Ocean. Any nation deploying missile-bearing submarines will appreciate the strategic significance of the waterway. Submarines passing through the Straits of Malacca must surface, and they are therefore susceptible to detection by satellite surveillance. The use of Lombok or Selat Sunda straits adds at least eight days to a submarine's travel time from one ocean to the other.

Washington concluded that placing control of a choke point in the hands of a proven anticommunist government was preferable to the alternative. The leaders of an independent East Timor, whoever prevailed, might favor the United States. Nevertheless, the probability that East Timor might be so inclined had to be balanced against the certainty that Raden Suharto was a client of long standing.

President Gerald Ford and Henry Kissinger met with Suharto the day before the invasion of East Timor began. Indonesian communications intercepted by U.S. intelligence organizations reveal that President Suharto was concerned that the takeover might jeopardize U.S. aid. Central Intelligence Agency and Defense Intelligence Agency reports further indicate that Suharto wished to look Ford and Kissinger *in the eye* and to obtain their approval of the operation (Chomsky 1980; Nairn 1992–93; Pilger 1994) Both parties obviously were satisfied in that U.S. aid to Indonesia continued apace.

As for the East Timorese, they joined that ever-lengthening list of agenda items placed in diplomatic limbo by the members of the United Nations (UN). The UN's only positive action was to recognize Portugal as the legal administrator of East Timor. Portugal broke diplomatic relations with Indonesia and requested UN sanctions with the view of returning Timor to its preinvasion status. The matter appeared annually on the UN agenda, and both Portugal and Indonesia carefully monitored each vote. The United States abstained from voting. When The Netherlands raised the issue of human rights violations in East Timor in 1992, Indonesia, with the approval of the World Bank, rejected Dutch aid. Portugal was able to scupper an agreement between the Association of Southeast Asian Nations (ASEAN) and the European Community in 1993, but most European countries viewed the issue as a bilateral problem and conducted business as usual.

East Timor is heavily dependent on subsistence agriculture and a tenuous transportation infrastructure. The island is also host to a plethora of tropical ailments. In consequence, the Indonesian invasion and the resistance thereto proved catastrophic, with more than 10 percent of the population dying of causes directly attributable to the invasion. Many of the deaths were at the hands of the Indonesian army, but the largest group died of famine and disease. Exact figures are impossible to give because access to East Timor was severely restricted after the invasion and subsequent reports were sometimes affected by political bias. Moreover, although allegations of extraordinary atrocities surfaced on both sides, independently verifiable evidence was difficult to obtain. Nevertheless, none of this mattered much in the larger scheme of things. Indonesia was given a free rein within its national borders. Most nations live in glass houses, so it is hardly surprising that they tend to support a ban on rocks.

THE CABLE NEWS NETWORK FACTOR
AND U.S. FOREIGN POLICY

There matters might have remained, save for the coming of Cable News Network (CNN) diplomacy and the time of falling dictators. Nations that once accepted the tyrant's lash became at least nominally independent, as the likes of Ferdinand Marcos, Anastasio Somoza, Augusto Pinochet, Jean-Claude Duvalier, and even the odious Idi Amin relinquished the reins of power. The retribution school avowed that such discredited despots should be hounded through the streets until a suitable lamp post was located. This group was wont to insist that if vengeance be left to providence, it must be expeditious and broadcast on cable! Conversely, the pragmatic, less-sanguinary school asserted that seeing a monster off was more important than a visceral vindication. This faction was of a mind that thieves are more inclined to surrender when giving up does not result in being drawn and quartered. In any event, the realization that it was safe to dismount the tiger hardly went unnoticed within the ranks of remaining autocrats. Nor did those in power fail to note what occurred when their fellow despots faced opposition from groups whose images raced around the globe.

In the closing decades of the twentieth century, television—especially as broadcast by organizations such as CNN—bid fair to become a dominant factor on the foreign-policy scene. At first, television was conceived as little more than a newspaper with pictures. The coverage of the U.S. effort in South Vietnam disabused not a few journalists of that notion. Newspaper photographs were static, whereas television imagery was dynamic. For decades, print editors had affirmed: if it bleeds, it leads. That hoary mantra now became the question: have we got film? Are pictures available that tell a story through sound and movement?

Generations of American children were told to clean their plates because others were starving elsewhere. As the century drew to an end, Americans in the sanctity of their living rooms could see the starving children. When war broke out in South Korea in 1950, Americans scrambled to find an atlas. In 1992, their grandchildren watched real-time images from Somalia and Kazakhstan. The world became an omnipresent feature in American life. It demanded attention and a response. And therein lay the rub. Absent evocative images, the inclination of television networks to cover a story is severely compromised. Now the medium had become the message. When containment gave way to a renewed world order, these two contrasting developments came together in a deleterious, yet propitious manner for East Timor.

For more than a century, Americans followed George Washington's advice: they avoided foreign entanglements in pursuit of the creation of a powerful nation. They patiently awaited the day when the world would see the wisdom of the American way. With the end of World War II, however, the nation abandoned its position as a beacon in the darkness and set forth looking, as John Quincy Adams once phrased it, for monsters to destroy. Adams also opined, on the same occasion, that if the nation engaged in an active foreign policy, it might control the world, but it would no longer rule its own spirit.

Then came the Soviet threat and the vicissitudes of a bipolar world. Everything Americans held dear was in some wise threatened. So threats were given priority, budgets unbalanced, resources exploited, and allies acquired. Still, the American crusade against the Evil Empire was resolved in an unexpected manner. The Soviet Union was not vanquished. Instead, it melted away like a sand castle at high tide, leaving behind an inchoate democracy of uncertain purpose or life span. Americans found they had made history, but not in the manner they had intended.

A return to the undiluted past was out of the question. Isolation was incompatible with the demands of a global marketplace. Meanwhile, Vietnam, El Salvador, and a host of other warm places put paid to the idea of remaking the world in the American image. Perhaps a tincture of both policies would suffice. Selective engagement might allow the United States to elaborate tailored solutions, thereby avoiding the knee-jerk reactions that allowed the Vietnam incursion. Admittedly, this approach did not achieve total acceptance. Nonetheless, the newly elected Clinton administration was seemingly committed to a new approach. A White House panel avowed that the first question in any foreign-policy debate was: what's in it for us? (*New York Times,* September 9, 1999).

Of course, it might be argued that this view was "deja vu all over again." Throughout the Cold War, the United States meddled incessantly around the globe in support of its self-interest. Certain lines, however, were never seriously compromised. The existence of the Soviet Union served to constrain U.S. actions. Such was no longer the case. The United States was now free to thrash about unhindered, yet if it was free from outside limitations, it was not devoid of fissures in the fabric of American society. The Gulf War engendered reservations about the nature of the American dream. One response was to abjure the lure of Satan. Any contact between the unregenerate and the regenerate must be avoided. The United States was without flaw and must remain sacrosanct. What some saw as a sickness, however, others viewed as a life-affirming experience. The resulting culture wars threatened to tear the nation apart.

The rest of the world was amused and bemused. Americans used to possess all the answers. Now they were thoroughly at odds with themselves, and any consensus was by the boards. Thus did a normally fractious people descend into unprecedented depths of disputatious acrimony. Americans at one time could be relied on to behave in a predictable fashion. They might be a day late and a dollar short, but they would arrive. Then they would save the world to one extent or another. Now it was questionable if the Americans would join the party at all. Or, if they did arrive, might they not leave early once the televised images proved unfavorable?

Televised images goaded the United States toward involvement in Bosnia and Kosovo. Televised footage of the famine in Somalia was undoubtedly a factor in the decision to send U.S. forces to East Africa, and those selfsame images, this time of Americans killed and injured, provoked the U.S. withdrawal. Television could incite both action and reaction. Only one question remained. What would happen when something evil occurred and no provocative images flickered into American households? The world got a glimmer of an answer when the government of Rwanda began to exterminate its minority Tutsi population. Although U.S. officials did not conspire with murderers in Rwanda, a compelling case might be made that they most certainly did little to obstruct them (Power 2001).

EAST TIMOR—STILL BENEATH U.S. NOTICE

Then came the May 3, 1994, presidential decision directive establishing the parameters of U.S. involvement in a United Nations peacekeeping operation. Henceforth the United States would pursue cafeteria intervention. Americans would support operations to help the embattled inhabitants of some nations but not others. Moreover, the United States would not resolve claims to sovereignty with regard to their intrinsic merits; instead, it would handle such problems with reference to geopolitical calculations. Presidential Decision Directive 25, titled *Reforming Multilateral Peace Operations* (U.S. Department of State 1996), in words reminiscent of Casper Weinberger, stipulated clear criteria. First, a clear threat to U.S. security must exist. Second, there must be substantial public support for intervention. Third, other countries must participate under UN supervision. Fourth, the United States must be assured that long-term nation building would not be necessary.

In the end, it all came together. A regional economic crisis placed Indonesia's crony capitalism in default, and the economic situation produced riots that found their way onto countless television screens. Faced with seemingly incontrovertible proof that Raden Suharto had lost his grip, his foreign supporters turned away. The Indonesian tree of state obviously required a measure of pruning. Therefore, the house of cards so painstakingly created by Suharto tumbled with his resignation on May 21, 1998. Suharto left for internal exile, and Vice President B. J. Habibie stepped to the fore. Then, for reasons presumably manifold, if still inexplicable, President Habibie announced that he would allow the people of East Timor to hold a referendum, the results of which, he asserted, would determine the destiny of the fractious province. Perhaps Habibie believed the referendum would yield a safe majority for Indonesia, or he might have been bowing to pressure from Indonesia's international financial donors. It is even conceivable that he believed it was time to cut the country's losses.

In 1862, Abraham Lincoln used the words *free* and *Negro* in the same sentence in the Emancipation Proclamation. Whatever else happened after that, there was no possibility that chattel slavery would survive the war. Such was also the case when Habibie coupled the words *referendum* and *East Timor*. Few, if any, among the Indonesian governing elite imagined the East Timorese would elect to associate with their oppressor. Unfortunately, all that was on offer was a plebiscite. Nothing was said about whether the process would be without incident. As the world knows, East Timor was racked with violence before the referendum. Moreover, when the East Timorese opted for independence, their country was subjected to devastation on a thoroughly disgusting scale.

Where then stood the city on the hill? Absent compelling electronic images or strategic considerations, the United States found small initial profit in affairs Timorese. The international press did provide voluminous coverage of the aftermath of the independence referendum, but televised images were sparse in the United States. Americans could read about the travail of the Timorese people, but images of the carnage were unavailable. Maybe the networks decided that graveyards do not make exhilarating images. Then, after international peacekeepers had entered East Timor, the world's media found other avenues to explore.

Portugal and its Atlantic islands had mattered. Indonesia had mattered. East Timor was a speed bump on the road leading to stability elsewhere (Mufson 1999). Reporters for the *New York Times* averred that the United States was disposed to put its relationship with Indonesia ahead of its concern over the fate of East Timor (Becker and Shenon 1993). James Foley, a State Department spokesman, in late August 1999 and Secretary of Defense William Cohen in a press briefing on September 8, 1999, seemingly validated such views (Alcorn 1999). Only when the Australian government expressed official concern about conditions in East Timor did Washington find time to consider the problem.

Some insist the Australian government was engaged in damage control after decades of backing the Suharto regime (Hainsworth and McCloskey 2000). There was also the matter of the extensive oil deposits located south of the island of Timor.

East Timor signed a lucrative development agreement with Australia on July 3, 2001 ("Australia sees reason," *The Economist,* July 7, 2001, 41). In any event, once Canberra expressed an interest in East Timor, diplomatic antennas in Washington began to quiver. Governments will listen, but only if they think an advantageous obligation may eventuate. Indeed, the most important motivation behind the affairs of nations is not the threat of force but services rendered and debts redeemable. If Indonesia imploded, the United States must be on good terms with the only power that might support its regional endeavors in the future (Hartcher 1999).

Was the United States moved by a guilty conscience or inspired to meritorious intervention in the affairs of East Timor? I am disposed to support a third alternative: it was simply taking care of business. Americans have a penchant for following the course of least resistance. It is, I submit, a significant ingredient in their national success. Unfortunately, that same propensity is a source of shame when Americans sacrifice peoples and nations on the altar of the greater good. The United States was not after merit, nor was it consumed by guilt regarding East Timor. Washington saw no reason to exhibit even a modicum of testicular fortitude. The past was precedent, prologue, and too much of a burden to shift. East Timor and its people had never been deemed worthy of interest, and so they must remain. What truly mattered was whether the United States might gain some momentary advantage elsewhere. The diplomatic foreplay emanating from Canberra will surely yield desirable results. Australia will someday be reminded that no good deed goes unpunished.

REFERENCES

Alcorn, Gay. 1999. Too Late to Send Armed UN Force. *Sydney Morning Herald,* August 25.
Becker, Elizabeth, and Philip Shenon. 1999. With Other Goals in Indonesia, U.S. Moves Gently on East Timor. *New York Times,* September 23, 1A.

Chomsky, Noam. 1980. A Curtain of Ignorance. *Southeast Asia Chronicle* 74 (August): 4.

Guimaraes, Fernando J. Andersen. 1993–94. The Collapse of the New State and the Emergence of the Angolan Civil War. *Camoes Center Quarterly* 5 (winter): 9–16.

Hainsworth, Paul, and Stephen McCloskey, eds. 2000. *The East Timor Question: The Struggle for Independence from Indonesia.* London: I. B. Tauris.

Hartcher, Peter. 1999. The ABCs of Winning U.S. Support. *Australian Financial Review,* September 13.

Kaplan, Lawrence S. 1984. *The United States and NATO.* Lexington: University Press of Kentucky.

Louis, William Roger. 1978. *Imperialism at Bay: The United States and the Decolonization of the British Empire, 1941–1945.* New York: Oxford University Press.

Mufson, Steven. 1999. West's Credibility at Stake, Laureate Says. *Washington Post,* September 9, 17A.

Nairn, Allan. 1992–93. Tragedy in East Timor: A Roundtable Discussion. *Camoes Center Quarterly* 4 (autumn–winter): 12–24.

Pilger, John. 1994. The West's Dirty Wink. *The Guardian,* February 12, at http://pilger.carlton. com/timer/articles/48734 and 48735.

Power, Samantha. 2001. Bystanders to Genocide: Why the United States Let the Rwandan Tragedy Happen. *Atlantic Monthly* 288, no. 2 (September): 84–108.

Sweeney, J. K. 1997. Portugal and the United States. In *The Romance of History: Essays in Honor of Lawrence S. Kaplan,* 217–20. Kent, Ohio: Kent State University Press.

Taylor, John G. 1999. *East Timor: The Price of Freedom.* London: Zed Books.

U.S. Department of State. Bureau of International Organizational Affairs. 1996. *Reforming Multilateral Peace Operations.* Presidential Decision Directive 25. Available at: www.fas.org /irp/offdocs/pdd25.htm.

Acknowledgment: Reprinted from *The Independent Review,* 7, no.1 (Summer 2002): 91–102. ISSN 1086-1653, Copyright © 2002.

PART III
Debating the Democratic Peace

9

Democracy and War

TED GALEN CARPENTER

R.J. Rummel, professor of political science at the University of Hawaii, has justifiably acquired a reputation as an outstanding scholar of violence perpetrated by the political state. His book *Death by Government* (New Brunswick, N.J.: Transaction Publishers, 1994) is a detailed, searing, and compelling indictment of the mass murder (more than 169 million victims) committed by governments during the twentieth century.

Rummel has also long been a proponent of the "peaceful democracies" thesis: that democracies are markedly less prone than are authoritarian or totalitarian states to resort to violence in the conduct of their external relations and that democracies never (or almost never) fight other democracies. In *Power Kills: Democracy as a Method of Nonviolence* (New Brunswick, N.J.: Transaction Publishers, 1997), he provides the most systematic development of that thesis to date. Unfortunately, his reach greatly exceeds his grasp.

The realist faction of foreign policy scholars—especially the so-called structural realists, who argue that conflict is inherent in an international system that has no central authority and is made up of nation-states with conflicting interests—is Rummel's principal target. The realists are wrong across the board, he contends.

> Wrong with regard to war and lesser international violence. Wrong about civil collective violence. Wrong about genocide and mass murder. There is one solution to each and the solution to each case is the same. It is to foster democratic freedom and to democratize coercive power and force. That is, mass killing and mass murder carried out by government is a result of indiscriminate, irresponsible Power at the Center. (p. 3)

In addition to that general conclusion, Rummel asserts that several key propositions about democracy and violence have been "uncovered or verified." Among the more important are the following: "Well established democracies do not make war on and rarely commit lesser violence against each other" (p. 4). "The more two nations are democratic, the less likely war or lesser violence between them" (p. 5). "The more a nation is democratic, the less severe its overall foreign violence" (p. 5). Indeed, Rummel contends that for "theoretical reasons" he "would expect no violence between democracies at all" (p. 101).

He advances (with varying degrees of conviction) three explanations for the peaceful nature of democracies. The first-level explanation is that the publics in democratic societies generally prefer to avoid war. Rummel argues that although that factor (emphasized by other scholars) has some validity, it must be viewed with caution. He acknowledges that "democratic peoples have become jingoistic on occasions and enthusiastically favored war....They can also be aggressive today, pacific tomorrow." (p. 132).

Rummel attaches greater importance to the second-level explanation: the influence of democratic institutions and culture. "Where by virtue of their institutions democratic people must, to maintain democracy, negotiate and compromise rather than fight, this becomes part of the cultural heritage" (p. 138).

Moreover, he states,

> since we deal with others through a cultural matrix, it is also natural for democratic people to perceive other regimes in these terms, to believe that all basic issues between nations can be settled by people sitting down at a table and talking them out, and to tolerate the existence of other regimes and ideologies that do not openly threaten one's democratic way of life. (p. 38)

The converse is equally true: totalitarian regimes see other regimes as being as ruthless, duplicitous, and brutal as themselves, and they act accordingly, thereby intensifying the cycle of violence.

Even more significant than the impact of democratic political culture, Rummel contends, is the third-level explanation: the operation of a "social field" based on diversity and individual freedom. "This spontaneous social field of constantly interacting individuals and groups, all pursuing their own interests, is a field of continuous *nonviolent* conflict" (p. 165; emphasis in original). In other words, the way to minimize violence, both domestic and international, is to decentralize power by strengthening civil society and constraining the role of the state.

It is a truism of science (even social science) that extraordinary claims require extraordinary evidence. Because Rummel affirms not only that democracies are on balance more peaceful than authoritarian and totalitarian systems but that a global system consisting entirely of democracies would produce a world without war, he faces a daunting burden of proof. In *Power Kills*, he fails to provide the necessary evidence.

Rummel does a credible job of making the case that there is a continuum of violence: as one moves from democratic states to authoritarian and then totalitarian ones, the level of violence, both domestic and international, increases. Even on that point, however, both his methodology and his arguments are sometimes dubious. For example, he attaches great weight to the fact that historically the less democratic a regime, the higher the number of battle deaths. Such data are designed to show both that democratic governments are less inclined to put their people through the meat grinder of war and that democratic populations and institutions are less tolerant of battlefield casualties.

Both propositions may well be true, but battle-death figures hardly provide compelling evidence. There are several possible alternative explanations for the markedly lower battlefield fatalities among democratic states. Most obvious, democracies have been on the winning side in most wars during the twentieth century—an important consideration because the losing side typically suffers disproportionately. The meager number of U.S. fatalities in the Persian Gulf War, for example, would appear to have had more to do with the superiority of American military technology and the abysmally stupid strategy of Saddam Hussein (a static defense in open desert terrain) than with the virtues of American democracy. Similarly, military superiority was the most probable reason that U.S. forces inflicted far more casualties than they incurred in the Korean and Vietnam conflicts.

Equally questionable are Rummel's assertions that wars between democracies (if such events occurred at all) would be less violent than those between authoritarian states and that wars between totalitarian states are, and will inevitably be, the most violent. Again, other factors can influence, and perhaps even determine, the magnitude of warfare. If the Cold War between the United States and the Soviet Union had ever turned hot, the struggle involving such a mixed dyad (one democratic state and one totalitarian state) would have been enormously destructive. Indeed, it would have been far worse than the war between China and Vietnam in 1979, even though both belligerents were totalitarian. The reason is self-evident: the United States and the Soviet Union had huge, capable military forces (including thousands of nuclear weapons). By comparison, Chinese and Vietnamese military forces were relatively puny in their destructive capacities.

Such examples illustrate a more general failing in *Power Kills*. Rummel repeatedly seems oblivious to or casually dismissive of alternative explanations of the phenomena he examines. Nowhere is that tendency more evident than in his core thesis—that democracies do not wage war against other democracies.

In making that case, Rummel relies heavily on the work of other "democratic peace" scholars, such as Bruce Russett and Michael Doyle, as well as on his own research. Unfortunately, their scholarship usually mirrors the weaknesses in Rummel's. Quoting liberally from such studies to "refute" the arguments of realists, therefore, produces a less-than-compelling case.

For example, Rummel favorably cites Doyle's observation about Italy's abrupt decision to switch alliances as World War I began.

> Italy, the liberal member of the Triple Alliance with Germany and Austria, chose not to fulfill its obligations under that treaty to support its allies. Instead, Italy joined in an alliance with Britain and France, which prevented it from having to fight other liberal states and then declared war on Germany and Austria. (p. 177)

Rummel proceeds to emphasize the point that "Italy changed from the side it was obligated to fight on to line up with the democracies" (p. 177).

At the least, both scholars have engaged in egregious oversimplification. Many reasons prompted Italy's decision, but few historians would maintain that a sense of democratic solidarity was the dominant motive. Italian leaders had far more mundane considerations—most notably the desire to detach large portions of Austro-Hungarian territory in the southern Tirol and the northwestern Balkans. It is revealing that London and Paris, Rome's new democratic allies, did not merely appeal to the Italian leaders' sense of democratic solidarity; they explicitly assured the Italians that their territorial claims would be recognized in the event of an Allied victory.

That same tendency to minimize or ignore factors other than the existence of democracy as an explanation for the apparent lack of wars among democratic states appears throughout the book. Rummel is almost contemptuous of the important article in which the RAND Corporation's Christopher Layne examined a number of military "near collisions" between democratic states ("Kant or Can't: The Myth of the Democratic Peace," *International Security* 19 [Summer 1994]: 5-49). Those included the U.S.–British confrontation over the *Trent* affair in 1861, the Anglo-American crisis over the Venezuela boundary dispute in the mid-1890s, and the British–French war scare over control of the Nile River (the so-called Fashoda incident) in 1898. Layne's overriding point is that in every case, the bulk of the evidence indicates that the parties pulled back from the brink of war not because of domestic pressures against fighting another democracy but because of realist strategic calculations. For example, French leaders concluded that they could not win a war against Britain, and British leaders in the 1890s concluded that Wilhelmine Germany posed a more serious long-term threat to British interests than did American preeminence in the Western Hemisphere.

Rummel dismisses Layne's treatment as subjective conjecture, emphasizing that the only pertinent fact is that in all those cases the countries involved in the crises *"did not fight"* (p. 42, emphasis in original). But the probable reasons for a phenomenon are at least as important as its existence. And no robotic invocation of statistical data on the alleged lack of armed combat between democracies ought to spare a scholar from the need to engage in such analysis. (After all, one can establish a strong statistical correlation between the crowing of roosters and sunrise. It would, however, be manifestly absurd to assume that the former caused the latter.)

The need to consider probable reasons for a phenomenon becomes even more apparent with another of Layne's examples, the French military occupation of Germany's Ruhr region in the early 1920s. A case in which one democratic country forcibly seized the most economically valuable portion of its democratic neighbor's territory should have elicited an extended discussion from Rummel. The mere fact that Weimar Germany did not militarily resist the occupation is hardly the salient point. The contemporary and historical records are quite clear that German leaders recognized their country's military impotence and realized they could not prevail. To contend that the lack of a war in that situation supports the proposition that democracies do not fight other democracies borders on perversity.

Unfortunately, Rummel's failure to adequately discuss the Ruhr incident is not an aberration. Throughout the book he avoids the "hard cases" that might cast doubt on the peaceful democracies thesis. One example is the Boer War of the late 1890s, a British bid to conquer the Orange Free State and the Transvaal. That conflict produced shocking acts of brutality on both sides. Because Britain was indisputably democratic (Rummel concedes that point) and the Boer states were, in his lexicon, "oligarchic republics" (politically democratic within a restricted electorate—in this case, whites only) and were perceived as democratic by the British, the war ought to be a troubling episode for Rummel and like-minded scholars. Yet he barely mentions it.

Rummel's treatment of America's War Between the States is little better. In cursory discussion he states that no major power recognized the Confederacy as an independent state and he asserts that it was not a real democracy in any case because only white males could vote and President Jefferson Davis was not directly elected. The inconvenient matter that Southerners considered their new confederacy democratic (which it was by the standards of the day) and that most Northerners did not dispute that view (they merely regarded it as beside the point) is simply ignored. The willingness of democratic Americans to wage an enthusiastic internecine slaughter fairly cries out for a more serious discussion. If a democratic people could do that to their own, how confident can we be that two democracies divided by culture or race (e.g., the United States and Japan) would recoil from doing so? At the very least, proponents of the democratic-peace thesis cannot assume that the point is self-evident.

A third hard case virtually ignored by Rummel is the western front in World War I—the bloody struggle between Britain and France on one side and Wilhelmine Germany on the other. Layne and other scholars have made solid arguments that Germany was a democratic state, as it had an elected parliament with significant powers, vigorously contested elections involving multiple parties, broad suffrage, and a reasonably free press. Although it also had some autocratic features, so did Britain and France.

World War I tends to give democratic-peace theorists intellectual indigestion, and for good reason. If Wilhelmine Germany is acknowledged to have been democratic, World War I alone is probably enough to falsify the democratic-peace thesis, given the extent of the bloodletting on the western front. (To argue otherwise would risk creating the social science equivalent of the old joke "Other than that, Mrs. Lincoln, how was your evening?") Of course, Rummel may have had irrefutable evidence that Wilhelmine Germany was not democratic, but if so his readers were entitled to see it.

To have engaged that issue, however, would have required him to be far more explicit about the features of a democracy and why certain countries during the nineteenth and twentieth centuries were or were not democratic. Instead, we get a vague and slippery treatment of that topic. Frequently, it is not clear whether Rummel is applying his own definition or that of one of his democratic-peace colleagues. Nor is it always clear whether certain political features are indispensable or to what extent the definition of a democracy depends on the norms of the era being discussed. That unsystematic approach produces erratic and arbitrary designations. For example, Rummel asserts that Britain did not become a liberal democracy until 1884 (p. 109). Why was that year so important? Because the franchise was then extended to agricultural workers. But why did that measure make Britain a democracy even though women (half the adult population) were not granted the vote until several decades later?

Rummel is so determined to prove his thesis about peaceful democratic solidarity that he virtually ignores conflicting evidence. Sometimes that tendency produces embarrassing overstatements clearly at odds with the facts. He asserts at one point that "with the spread of democracy around the world, armies and secret services would be less and less needed. *Indeed, with near universal democratization, they could be eliminated altogether*" (p. 17; emphasis in original). But both present and former U.S. intelligence officials acknowledge that democracies routinely spied on one another, even during the Cold War, when they confronted a dangerous mutual security threat. (The Jonathan Pollard case, in which Israel conducted espionage against the United States, is merely one celebrated example.) Indeed, democratic intelligence services sometimes did more than spy. Another episode barely mentioned by Rummel was the successful CIA effort to overthrow the elected governments of Iran (1953) and Guatemala (1954). Those incidents cast further doubt on the democratic-peace thesis; if officials in the United States were willing to mount covert operations to overthrow two sister democracies—and bring highly authoritarian regimes to power in both instances—why should we assume that they would have recoiled from using military force?

Moreover, intramural democratic espionage has not abated with the end of the Cold War. As the *Wall Street Journal's* John Fialka, Cato Institute research fellow Stanley Kober, and others have shown, espionage (particularly economic espionage) has actually increased since the end of the Cold War—precisely the opposite of what Rummel would have predicted. Within weeks of the publication of *Power Kills,* U.S. Navy intelligence analyst Robert Kim was convicted of passing classified information to South Korea, not only another democracy but a U.S. military ally.

In the broadest sense, the argument that the world would be better off if all countries had strong civil societies and were governed by decentralized, democratic regimes is correct. It would almost certainly be a more peaceful world. But that is not the same as claiming that universal democracy is a panacea that will banish war. That democracies have *never* waged war against other democracies remains highly debatable despite the categorical assertions presented in this book. Likewise, Rummel's analysis does not establish that the absence of armed conflict between democracies since World War II (a rather brief period in any event) is due to the factors he identifies rather than other influences—for example, the existence of a powerful totalitarian threat that inhibited intrademocratic squabbles. Rummel makes an array of extraordinary claims, but he ultimately fails to prove his case.

Acknowledgment: Reprinted from *The Independent Review,* 2, no. 3 (Winter 1998): 435–41. ISSN 1086-1653, Copyright © 1997.

10

Democracy and War: Reply

R. J. RUMMEL

I write here in response to Ted Galen Carpenter's negative review (*The Independent Review* 2 [Winter 1998]) of my book *Power Kills: Democracy as a Method of Nonviolence* (New Brunswick, N.J.: Transaction, 1997). In that book I bring to bear all the published systematic quantitative and historical evidence I could find and have generated on five propositions about the inverse relationship between democracy and collective violence. The propositions are that democracies (1) don't make war on each other, (2) limit bilateral violence, (3) are least warlike, (4) are most internally peaceful, and (5) don't murder their own citizens. These overwhelmingly supported propositions led me to a concluding and summary proposition: democracy is a method of nonviolence.

But empirical findings, no matter how sophisticated, are insufficient unless supported by a consistent theory. Therefore, I devoted about half the book to presenting alternative theories for explaining the nonviolent nature of democracy, concluding that the best way of understanding it is in relation to the spontaneous society that freedom (liberal democracy) creates. This idea is similar to F. A. Hayek's notion of a spontaneous order, described in his three-volume work *Law, Legislation, and Liberty* (Chicago: University of Chicago Press, 1973, 1976, 1979) and is well known to libertarians. It is a free market writ large: of the economy, society, and politics within an overarching legal framework of civil liberties and political rights. A spontaneous society creates cross-pressures and an exchange culture in which negotiation, compromise, and tolerance reduce the tendency toward violence found in more hierarchically organized societies. Moreover, the natural bonds and linkages that develop between such societies (e.g., trade, social, and cultural exchanges, treaties), and the perception that the other society is like one's own, favoring negotiation and compromise, reduces the possibility of violence between them.

Now for Carpenter's review.

1. *Rummel's "core thesis" is that democracies do not make war on each other* (p. 437). No, the core thesis, as indicated by the title of the book, is that power kills. This thesis sums up all five of the book's propositions, whereas Carpenter mistakenly focused his review on only one of them.

I'm perplexed that he completely ignores the most important propositions and evidence of the book, which show that democracies are most internally peaceful and don't murder their own citizens. If the importance of each proposition is understood in terms of the number of people killed in the indicated violence (and the resulting or correlative misery), then it is critical that far more people are killed in domestic collective violence than in international wars. For example, millions more people were killed in the Teiping Rebellion in China alone than died in battle in World War I and World War II. In our century, governments have murdered about four times the number killed in combat in all the domestic and foreign wars. Stalin alone is responsible for the murder of millions more than the combat deaths of both world wars together. Therefore, even if *Power Kills* dealt only with domestic violence and democide (genocide and mass murder), the findings would be an incredible testament for freedom, because they show that promoting democratic freedom will eliminate or reduce to a minimum by far the largest category of deaths from collective violence.

2. *Overall, Rummel "fails to provide the necessary evidence"* (p. 437). I don't understand what Carpenter means by evidence. To me evidence for a general hypothesis, such as "A does not do B," comprises all, or an appropriate sample of, the cases in which A does or does not do B over the relevant time period, the significance (possible randomness) of the cases, the historical context and understanding of the cases, and the findings on the same or similar hypotheses by other researchers and scholars. These are the sorts of evidence I brought to bear on the five hypotheses (propositions). The data I drew on, mine and those of others, cover all wars, going back to the ancient Greeks, in which democracies may have been involved; and for democide in this century, all democide and regimes. Moreover, my colleagues and

I have subjected these data to both traditional and quantitative analyses. The overall result is that different investigators with different data collected under different definitions of democide, violence, war, and democracy and applying different methodologies verified the five propositions.

Perhaps Carpenter means the kind of evidence that would satisfy a historian. But I did review such evidence elsewhere and referenced a number of historical and qualitative studies, as listed for criticism 6 considered below. I also referenced the historical analyses of others, such as that of the historian Spencer Weart (*Never at War* [New Haven: Yale University Press, forthcoming]), who scoured written ancient and modern historical records to find a case in which democracies clearly made war on each other, including those proposed by Carpenter, and found none.

In sum, no other general propositions of international relations and foreign policy have been so widely tested and thoroughly supported by empirical analysis. Indeed, as a result, some are now asserting that the lack of war between democracies is an iron law of international relations, so well established that further research should focus on democratization. In fact, one publisher's reader recommended that my book not be published because it contained nothing new.

3. Rummel fails to consider alternative explanations or factors. Neither do I understand this criticism. Consider some of the alternative explanations and factors that I or those I cited tested for with respect to one or another of the five propositions: geographic distance or size, small number of democracies, economic development, culture, power parity or lack thereof, ideology or religion in general and specific ideologies and religions in particular (e.g., communism, Islam, Christianity), war or revolution (possibly accounting for democide), population density, resources, education, and technology (a factor Carpenter believes important), among others. I think that my colleagues and I have covered the most popular alternative explanations and factors, even those that most analysts consider only remotely possible.

I have also considered alternative theories, including those that account for sociopolitical violence by social distances, in-group perception, cross-pressures, economic forces, and concomitant values as well as those that emphasize the natural peacefulness of people, political bonds and interests, and the role of power. Yet Carpenter writes that I am "oblivious to or casually dismissive of alternative explanations" (p. 437).

4. Rummel fails to consider cases of war between democracies. Those mentioned are the American Civil War, the Boer War, and World War I. These and other possible cases have been carefully considered and dismissed by my colleagues, such as Bruce Russett in *Grasping the Democratic Peace* (Princeton: Princeton University Press, 1993), James Lee Ray in *Democracy and International Conflict* (Columbia: University of South Carolina Press, 1995), and the aforementioned Spencer Weart. Space does not allow a consideration of all these possible exceptions, but let me focus on the war between Germany and the democracies that Carpenter writes "tends to give democratic-peace theorists intellectual indigestion" (p. 439). In my view, this possible counterexample is easily disposed of. Consider: the Chancellor of Germany served at the whim of the Kaiser, by whom he was appointed and dismissed. Moreover, the Kaiser had considerable power over foreign affairs, and the army was effectively independent from control by the democratically elected Reichstag. For all practical purposes, in foreign policy Germany was autocratic, without a democratic leash, and thus World War I hardly contradicts the proposition that democracies don't war on each other.

5. Rummel does not consider cases where democracies almost went to war. Carpenter mentions several such cases and focuses on the 1898 Fashoda Incident, a war scare between France and Great Britain over control of the Nile River. But note that negotiation between both sides was respectful and straightforward, neither side seeking to end up dominant; and both sides thought they could count on the other side to be reasonable. Indeed, in his book (chap. 13) Weart quotes a French diplomat as saying that France assumed "England would never initiate hostilities." Rather than raising questions about the proposition that democracies don't make war on each other, this crisis supports it by illustrating why war crises do not escalate to war among democracies.

6. Rummel robotically invokes statistical data (p. 438). What? Should I not throw a wide net for statistical evidence? Or organize such evidence by proposition, dates, and methods? This criticism is a strange one for a libertarian, because so many libertarian policy recommendations are based on economic statistical evidence. In any event, the "robotically" presented systematic evidence shows that power kills.

The context for this criticism is Carpenter's discussion of incidents such as Fashoda and the claim that I should have engaged these cases. But a book can cover in depth only so much; gaps must be filled by reference to other work. Carpenter ignores that on the most important democide proposition I also did extensive historical and qualitative analyses. In *Death by Government* (New Brunswick, N.J.: Transaction, 1994), I wrote case studies of each of fourteen cases in which a regime murdered at least one million people. I also wrote separate histories of the Soviet democide (*Lethal Politics* [New Brunswick, N.J.: Transaction, 1990]), Chinese democides (*China's Bloody Century* [New Brunswick, N.J.: Transaction, 1991]), and that by Nazi Germany (*Democide* [New Brunswick, N.J.: Transaction, 1993]). Moreover, I presented all the democide estimates, their sources and qualifications, and the qualitative considerations underlying them in my *Statistics of Democide* (Charlottesville: Center of National Security Law, Law School, University of Virginia, 1997). On the war propositions, I wrote five volumes of *Understanding Conflict and War* (Beverly Hills, Calif.: Sage, 1975–1981). In sum, far from robotically invoking statistical data, I have immersed myself deeply in historical and qualitative analyses before coming to my conclusions.

7. Rummel assumes that correlation means causation (pp. 438–39). This invocation of Statistics 101 misses the essence of the results. Fundamentally, the theory, described earlier, led to hypotheses that were then tested and re-tested, and the results were replicated by others. The theory dominates, the five hypotheses (propositions) flow from it, and the hypotheses have been extensively tested empirically, qualitatively, and historically.

8. Rummel gives a "vague and slippery treatment" of democracy (p. 440). This criticism is yet another I do not understand. I have tried to define democracy carefully, for without a precise definition I could not collect data on democracy or understand the results of my analysis. Moreover, in chapter 8 ("What Is to Be Explained") I extensively detail the meaning and nature of democracy, carefully delineating it from authoritarian and totalitarian regimes and placing the three types of regimes within the space of a political triangle that encompasses the variation among them. Moreover, as noted in the book, this analysis is informed by several factor analyses of political variables I carried out in *Statistics of Democide* and elsewhere.

Carpenter is most concerned about my applying a contemporary defini-tion of democracy to previous centuries. The problem here is the historical limitation on equal rights and the franchise, for instance, before women achieved equal rights or slavery was eliminated. For previous centuries the definition of democracy was loosened to include the criterion of at least two-thirds of the males having equal rights (as long as the lower classes were not excluded) while the other requirements were maintained, such as open competitive elections. Consider, first, that democracies so defined in previous centuries, such as the United States in 1800 and democratic clas-sical Athens, saw themselves as democratic, called themselves democratic, and were perceived by other nations as democratic. Second, even with this looser definition, well-established democracies so defined still did not make war on each other. "Well established" means that a regime had been demo-cratic long enough to have become stable and for democratic practices to have become established.

The fundamental question about any definition is: does it work? Does it define something in reality that systematically predicts something else? If we have defined an x such that its value regularly predicts the value of y, and our theory explains this relationship, then that definition of x is a useful and important one. Both my definition of contemporary democracies and the limited definition of earlier democracies allow a prediction of continuous peace (nonwar) between the nations so defined. If one does not agree that these nations are democracies, fine. Call them x-cracies. We then can say that x-cracies do not make war on each other. And by universalizing x-cracies we can expect an end to war.

9. Rummel ignores conflicting evidence, such as that the United States carried out covert action against other nations, even democracies (p. 440). Covert ac-tion is not war (military action) and is therefore irrelevant to the propo-sitions. But Carpenter did catch me in a misstatement about a world of democracies eliminating the need for secret services. I had in mind covert violence against hostile nations, but my statement does not come through that way. There would be a place for spies in a democratic world, just as there is a place for corporate spies in a free market. But in such a world hostile enemies would be absent, the expectation of war gone, and thus a secret war unnecessary.

But what about past American covert action? This occurred during the

Cold War as part of the largely successful policy to contain communism, particularly Soviet power. Mistakes were made, actions were taken that in hindsight embarrass democrats. Even then, however, there was no military action between democracies.

Still, a deeper explanation may be advanced. Democracies are not monolithic; they comprise many agencies, some of which operate in secrecy and are really totalitarian subsystems connected only at the top to democratic processes. The military, especially in wartime, and the secret services, such as the CIA, are examples. These nearly isolated islands of power operate as democratic theory would lead us to expect. Outside of the democratic sunshine and processes, they take actions that, were they subject to democratic scrutiny, would be forbidden. The solution to this problem is more sunshine and greater democratic control.

10. Rummel ignores that the peace among democracies since World War II may be due to a "powerful totalitarian threat" (p. 441). The data are not limited to the postwar period. As mentioned, other tests have been done for different years, including 1816 through 1960. It may be true that the Cold War has accounted for the particular lack of war between democracies since World War II, but what about the other periods? Further, set aside the statistics and consider Europe, the historical cauldron of war, and what has happened there since the end of the Cold War. Unity, not hostility, has continued to grow. And, incredibly, those old enemies, France and Germany, have even considered forming a common army. Moreover, having become democratic, the former enemy states of Eastern Europe have sought integration into a united Europe.

And finally Carpenter's conclusion:

11. "Rummel makes an array of extraordinary claims, but he ultimately fails to prove his case" (p. 441). But Carpenter ignores most of the book and concentrates on the proposition that democracies do not make war on each other. The title of his review, "Democracy and War," should have been "Power Kills." Moreover, even with respect to the one proposition on which he focused, his criticisms do not make sense, are incorrect, or are irrelevant, as I have shown here.

I would have thought that Carpenter, a vice president of the Cato Institute, a libertarian think tank, would be overjoyed by what I have shown about freedom. Not only does freedom promote greater economic and social welfare and happiness, as libertarians believe, but it also promotes life and security. To the best of our knowledge, its universalization would end war and virtually eliminate other forms of collective violence, particularly the most pervasive and greatest cause of violent death—democide. Wielders of unchecked political power have killed people by the hundreds of millions. Freedom would have saved nearly all of them and averted the attendant suffering and misery.

Acknowledgment: Reprinted from *The Independent Review*, 3, no. 1 (Summer 1998): 103–8. ISSN 1086-1653. Copyright © 1998.

11

Democracy and War: Rejoinder

Ted Galen Carpenter

Professor Rummel continues his tradition of creative historical revisionism. Given the amount of space he devoted to the peaceful-democracies thesis in his book, it is misleading—at the very least—for him now to argue that that was merely one of five propositions. It is by far the most prominent theme of his book; unfortunately, it is also the weakest.

Rummel's other objections are no more compelling. He invokes the work of yet another historian to "prove" that democracies never make war on each other. That invocation does little to remedy one of the more intractable problems with the democratic-peace theory: so much of the thesis depends on arbitrary coding decisions by the analysts involved. Whenever such scholars do not ignore the hard cases—as Rummel did repeatedly in *Power Kills*—they massage the evidence until it supports the conclusion that at least one of the parties to a conflict was not a real democracy. It is a safe bet that if war ever erupts between Greece and Turkey, Rummel and his colleagues will discover that one or both regimes failed to meet their purity test for being "well established" democracies—a vacuous standard that can mean anything the writers want it to mean.

Nowhere is the arbitrary quality of coding decisions more evident than in Rummel's latest comments about Wilhelmine Germany. He notes that the Kaiser "had considerable power over foreign affairs, and the army was effectively independent from control by the democratically elected Reichstag. For all practical purposes, in foreign policy Germany was autocratic, without a democratic leash, and thus World War I hardly contradicts the proposition that democracies don't war on each other."

That observation is revealing in several respects. First, Rummel appears to be conceding that in domestic policy Germany *was* democratic—which raises the interesting question of why such democratic values and institutions did not carry over into the arena of foreign policy. Second, "for all practical purposes" the British and French governments also conducted foreign affairs as a policy fiefdom virtually immune from parliamentary input, much less control. Indeed, that situation elicited a complaint voiced frequently and loudly by members of parliament in both countries. One also wonders what Rummel would say about President Harry Truman's decision to send U.S. troops to wage the Korean War without even making the pretense of seeking congressional authorization. Where was the "democratic leash" in that case? Or perhaps the United States wasn't a "well-established" democracy in 1950.

The weakest portion of Rummel's reply, however, is his attempt to deal with the embarrassing point that during the Cold War the United States government overthrew democratic regimes in other countries. Rummel attaches great importance to the idea that covert action is not war—something that will come as a tremendous comfort to the people of Iran, Guatemala, and other countries that were saddled with thuggish dictatorships courtesy of Washington's foreign policy. The point that Rummel studiously ignores is that U.S. policy exhibited extreme hostility to democratic regimes that were not deemed "friendly" to the United States. Indeed, the hostility was sufficient to sustain the objective of extinguishing such regimes. Rummel's flaccid, Clintonesque apologia ("mistakes were made") does not erase that sizable blemish on his portrait of democratic solidarity.

It would be wonderful if Rummel were correct that universal democracy would bring universal peace. There is too much evidence, however, that democratic states can act—and in many instances have acted—in a violently aggressive manner. It is a sobering reality, for example, that Britain and the United States in the nineteenth century were simultaneously democratic and aggressively expansionist. Rummel's vision of a world of peaceful democracies is enticing, but like all utopian visions it exists only in the realm of fantasy.

Acknowledgment: Reprinted from *The Independent Review,* 3, no.1 (Summer 1998): 109–10. ISSN 1086-1653, Copyright © 1998.

12

Stealing and Killing

A Property-Rights Theory of Mass Murder

STEPHEN W. CARSON

> *[H]e who would get me into his power without my consent,*
> *would use me as he pleased, when he had got me there, and*
> *destroy me too when he had a fancy to it.*
> — John Locke, *Second Treatise of Civil Government*

In the study of mass murder by governments, R. J. Rummel stands tall. His theory, which focuses our attention on the role of the state, is a giant step forward from previous theories that focused on "cultural-ethnic differences, outgroup conflict, misperception, frustration-aggression, relative deprivation, ideological imperatives, dehumanization, resource competition, etc." (Rummel [1994] 1997a, 19). Rummel has expressed his theory in a number of different ways over decades of work in this area. Oversimplifying somewhat for now, I characterize his theory as a *regime-type theory:* at one extreme, totalitarian dictatorships are the most deadly; authoritarian regimes are still deadly but less so; and, at the other extreme, democracies are the least deadly (see figure 1).

Besides presenting a theory that puts the state at center stage, Rummel has also made two other major contributions to this area of study. First, he has attempted to make the first full accounting of twentieth-century mass murder. No earlier investigators, for example, had tried to come up with a number for total Nazi mass-murder victims because they had focused on particular groups—Jews, Gypsies, and so forth. His most recent estimate is that 262 million civilians were killed by governments in the twentieth century.[1] Second, using what he learned about the number of government killings, he has emphasized the importance of understanding *democide* (his

Figure 1

Deaths (in millions) from Democide Compared to Deaths from International War

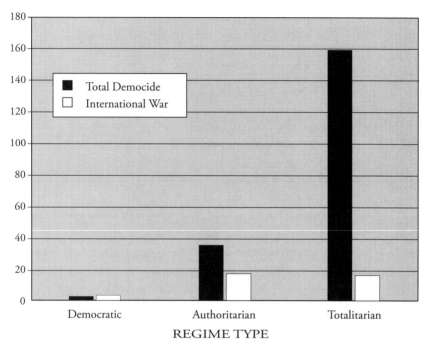

Source: Rummel [1994] 1997a, 14.

term for mass murder of civilians by government) by pointing out that as horrendous as combat deaths were in the twentieth century, the truth is that many more noncombatants were murdered.

In this chapter, I present an alternative theoretical approach, a *property-rights theory,* for understanding how governments came to slaughter unarmed civilians by the millions and tens of millions. The questions that Rummel and I are trying to answer are, first, How does a government gain the capability to murder millions of civilians? And, second, What, if anything can be done to prevent such monstrous crimes? Rummel focuses on the structure of government, pointing to the centralization of power in an authoritarian or dictatorial ruler as the primary problem and to "political freedom" and decentralization of power through democracy as the solutions. The property-rights approach, by contrast, points to systematic invasions of private-property rights as the primary enabling acts and to defense of those rights as the solution. My proposed approach implies that, contra Rummel, democracy is not part of the solution but rather part of the problem because both democratic ideology and democratic practice undermine private-property rights.

Although in broad terms the regime-type theory and the property-rights theory are complementary, they give rise to different conclusions in many respects. So I must proceed to criticize Rummel's work. First, however, I want to honor Rummel and orient the reader to this difficult and painful topic by quoting a powerful passage from his book *Death by Government:*

> A systems approach to politics still dominates the field [of political science]. Through this lens, politics is a matter of inputs and outputs, of citizen inputs, aggregation by political parties, government determining policy, and bureaucracies implementing it. Then there is the common and fundamental justification of government that it exists to protect citizens against the anarchic jungle that would otherwise threaten their lives and property. Such archaic or sterile views show no appreciation of democide's existence and all its related horrors and suffering. They are inconsistent with a regime that stands astride society like a gang of thugs over hikers they have captured in the woods, robbing all, raping some, torturing others for fun, murdering those they don't like, and terrorizing the rest into servile obedience. This exact characterization of many past and present governments, such as Idi Amin's Uganda, hardly squares with conventional political science. ([1994] 1997a, 26)

ADVANTAGES OF A PROPERTY-RIGHTS THEORY
OF DEMOCIDE

Before getting into the theory, let us think about why a property-rights approach is worthy of consideration. What does this theory offer that can supplement or amend Rummel's regime-type theory?

First, focusing on the regime type is not helpful in understanding cycles of mass murder under the same regime type—for example, the peaks and valleys of mass murder by the government of the USSR, a totalitarian dictatorship from beginning to end. A property-rights approach, however, not

Figure 2
Soviet Democide

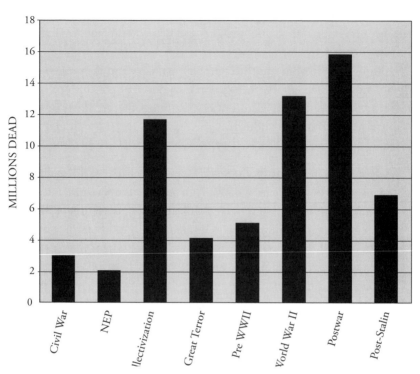

Source: Rummel 1990, 9.

only suggests that a totalitarian regime would be murderous but also shows where the peaks and valleys of killing will be: the peaks would correspond to determined efforts to collectivize (that is, to massive assaults on private-property rights), and the valleys would correspond to retreats from collectivization (for example, to the New Economic Policy [NEP] period in the USSR). See figure 2.

Similarly, in the case of China, a focus on regime structure would merely indicate that China has been under a Communist dictatorship for more than fifty years. A property-rights approach, in contrast, calls our attention to the significant changes in property rights in China in recent years and predicts that large-scale democide is unlikely, despite the regime type's being nominally the same as the one during the Great Leap Forward.

A property-rights approach gives us more insight into the dynamic of how a state gains murderous strength and the people become weak, so that the state can kill so many people. If a devil asked Rummel, "How do I murder tens of millions of people?" Rummel would have to answer, "Establish a totalitarian dictatorship." To which the devil would respond, "Fine, but how can I put myself in a position to do so?" The property-rights theory then explains that the path to mass murder and the path to a powerful, centralized state is the same and that the key is to attack private-property rights.

Socialism: From the perspective of the property-rights theory, it seems clear why the greatest mass murderers were avowed socialists instead of, say, right-wing military dictators such as Francisco Franco. Attacks on private-property rights in socialist regimes were not a side effect of another goal, such as defending the country, suppressing a dissident religious group, or attacking a particular race. Such attacks expressed the socialists' explicit and avowed ideological aim. It comes as no surprise then that the revolutionary socialists (socialists who really meant business) attacked private-property rights repeatedly in deadly waves of "collectivization," "de-kulakization," "Great Leaps Forward," and so forth.

Imperialism: The property-rights theory helps us to understand how the same type of regime can behave one way "at home" and another way abroad. At home, the regime may face resistance at every turn from long-established property-rights traditions. Abroad, the regime does not face these constraints in dealing with the "natives." A recent case in point is the gun grabbing by the U.S. forces in Iraq, in contrast to the still relatively well-armed population of the United States itself (Rockwell 2003).

Democracy: Where the regime-type theory holds up democracy as the solution to mass murder, war, and other types of regime violence, the property-rights theory argues that because the principle of democracy (at least in the modern sense) has nothing to do with the protection of private-property rights and in practice undermines such rights (Hoppe 2001, 95–106), it promotes such violence. The relevance to democide is illustrated by events in Germany, where, as F. A. Hayek argued, a period of democracy laid the groundwork for a dictator to emerge: "In Germany, even before Hitler came into power, the movement [toward centralized economic planning] had already progressed much further. It is important to remember that, for some time before 1933, Germany had reached a stage in which it had, in effect, had [*sic*] to be governed dictatorially....Hitler did not have to destroy democracy; he merely took advantage of the decay of democracy and at the critical moment obtained the support of many to whom, though they detested Hitler, he yet seemed the only man strong enough to get things done" ([1944] 1994, 75–76).

Regime Change: The regime-type theory has been used as a justification for "regime change," a policy of sanctions, military invasion and occupation, and other means intended to change an undemocratic regime into a more democratic one. The reasoning is all too familiar: "you have to break some eggs to make an omelet." In this case, the omelet is democracy, which it is hoped will result in less democide and a more peaceful regime, thus justifying in the long run all the short-term "collateral damage" and other destruction.

Joseph Stromberg explains why the means of imperialistic war is incompatible with the proposed goal of constructive change: "In all probability, revolution from the outside is the most costly and counterproductive, not to mention least revolutionary, approach to revolution. The characterization of the War as Revolution raises the very important issue of 'modern "Bonapartism," that is,…a confusion between a war of conquest and revolutionary war.'…Imperialist war strengthens statism and destroys the material welfare of the people. As such, it is profoundly antirevolutionary, no matter how it unsettles the defeated enemy society" (1979, 39).

The property-rights theory encourages instead an increase in justice, which is to say an increased respect for private-property rights, or, to put it another way, a decrease in robbery. Nothing in this perspective suggests that a wave of injustice, such as "liberating" a country's population by means of "shock and awe" aerial bombardments, can serve as the path to justice. In pointing out this advantage of the property-rights theory, I do not mean to be topical in a frivolous way. A theory of decreasing mass murder that encourages mass murder has a serious defect.

A PROPERTY-RIGHTS THEORY OF DEMOCIDE

What stands out about democide in the twentieth century is not the discrete "crimes of passion," such as the killings in Tiananmen Square, but the systematic, bureaucratic killing that took place over years. Not only is this aspect of state murder horrifying to contemplate, but it also explains how the killing occurred on such a stupendous scale: killing millions of people took a long time. This aspect of democide seems especially amenable to economic—or, more precisely, praxeological—analysis because the systematic killing took place over time, used resources, and even involved something like capital investment (for example, to build concentration camps). But mass killing is not a market phenomenon, so rather than turning to the familiar praxeology of cooperation, which starts with the mutual gains realized in peaceful exchange, we must turn to the analysis of the dark side of human action: the praxeology of aggression.

The Praxeology of Aggression

Murray Rothbard presents the fundamentals of a praxeology of aggression in "Fundamentals of Intervention," the second chapter of his book *Power and Market*. He starts with a simple two-person situation: an aggressor and a victim. We know, first, that aggression causes a loss of utility for the victim (Rothbard 1970, 13), but causes an ex ante gain of utility for the aggressor (14). When aggression is not incidental but systematic or even institutionalized (such as state aggression), broader consequences result. Social conflict is created in the scramble to go from being the victim to being the aggressor (14). Furthermore, as John C. Calhoun pointed out, this scramble gives rise to the creation of antagonistic "classes" (14). Finally, "the indirect consequences are such that many interveners themselves will lose utility ex post" (23).

Systematic Aggression and Time Preference

Hans-Hermann Hoppe argues that systematic aggression against property changes the time horizon for individuals. Because incentives for producing for the future are reduced, future income and consumption are also reduced, which results in a rise in time preference ([1993] 2006, 36). Hence, "the length of the production structure will necessarily be shortened, and a decrease in the output of goods produced must result" (44 n. 9). Furthermore, taxation discourages time-consuming but productive efforts to earn income and encourages instead short time horizon methods, including stealing or legally seizing goods through politics (43–44). To summarize Hoppe's points, systematic aggression against property results in increased time preference (short-term consumption becoming more preferred to long-term consumption); decreased output of goods; and the more aggressive scrambling for money obtained by ordinary and political (legal) theft—all of which implies as an upshot a more and more shortsighted and violent scramble over an increasingly smaller pie. Thus, aggressions against external property are problematic in several ways.

First, such aggressions constitute a violent attack on a person through an attack on the things the person owns. When they are "legal," then a property owner's resistance to them will result in official violence directly against his person. This point deserves emphasis because political attacks on private-property rights have been widely glorified as idealistic and socially minded for more than a hundred years. Much as rape needs to be viewed primarily as a violent act rather than as a sex act, so aggression against property needs to be viewed primarily as a violent act rather than as a manifestation of idealism if we are to understand its role in mass murder.

Second, successful aggression against private-property rights removes the use of the property from the rightful owner's control. Loss of property has numerous consequences, but those most relevant to democide are loss of the ability to protect oneself, as when one's guns or other means of self-defense are taken, and loss of the ability to be productive and hence of the ability to command resources for consumption.

Third, a successful expropriation empowers the aggressor. Owing to control of the property acquired through aggression, the aggressor will probably have enhanced capability to perpetrate even more aggressive violence.

Fourth, a successful theft may reduce the incentive to reacquire property because the victim perceives such accumulation as pointless—the property will just be taken again; hence, time preference increases.

Aggression Against External Property Necessary for Systematic Democide

Systematic stealing disarms the victims and empowers the aggressors. By "disarms," I mean not only that it takes weapons away, but also, and perhaps more important, that it takes away the resources used to sustain and defend their lives.

Is this theory just a tautology: "violence is a predictor of violence"? No, the thesis is specifically that aggression against external property usually *precedes* aggression against person. Moreover, aggression against external property *enables* aggression against person by transferring resources from victim to aggressor, lowering the time preference of both, creating conflict where there was harmony, and so forth. Because democide usually takes place over long periods, the victims must be prevented from running away and from effectively defending themselves. Thus, attacks on property are essential to a successful democide—to keep the victims helpless and foreclose their alternatives.

Claim Number 1: *Aggression against external property is a necessary condition for systematic democide.*

To deny this claim implies support for the alternative claim that in at least some cases systematic democide was *not* preceded by aggression against external property. The first difficulty with this counterclaim pertains to explaining how the murderers came by the resources to kill on a large scale over time without first stealing. One logical possibility is that the murderers used their own justly acquired property. Though not strictly impossible, this scenario is extremely unlikely and, I think, historically unprecedented.

A second difficulty pertains to explaining how the victim population is rendered powerless to flee, defend itself, or hire others for its defense without having first been looted or disarmed. One possible response is that the victim population has been "disarmed" ideologically; that is, although they have the resources to defend themselves, they do not choose to do so because they have been convinced that the regime may legitimately kill them. Such an unusual situation verges on mass suicide, a different phenomenon from the one at issue here.

Socialism: Production, Distribution, and Calculation

In the case of a Communist system, the attack is mounted not simply on external property, in general—the sort of attack illustrated by a bandit raid or by income taxation—but on the means of production in particular. Ludwig von Mises's ([1920] 1975) socialist-calculation argument demonstrates that where capital is socialized, calculational chaos will ensue. At the extreme, the economy will break down altogether, and the advantages of the division of labor will be lost for the most part. This consequence alone may be enough to account for the murderous famines that invariably accompany all concerted efforts to socialize.

Mises argues that it is impossible for a government to take over an economy fully and run it rationally. A full government takeover can only destroy an economy. We see this outcome in the British Empire's camps in Kenya, the Soviet work camps, the Nazi work camps, and so forth. These forced-labor projects exhibit the ultimate subordination of people to "the plan," and the workers, rather than being extremely productive for the state, often simply perished from starvation, disease, and abuse. There have been, then, real instances of full communism in which the means of production were truly socialized, money was abolished, the entrepreneur had no role, and everyone was guaranteed work—indeed, was compelled to work. The concentration camps, also known as "death camps," constituted the fullest practical realization of the Marxist economic program. Hoppe summarizes the economic effects of socialization as including a drop in the rate of investment, wasteful use of capital, and a "drop in the general standard of living" (1988, 25, 26, 28).

We can say even more, however, based on our understanding of "distribution" in the market. Rothbard writes: "'Personal distribution'—how much money each person receives from the productive system—is determined, in turn, by the functions that he or his property performs in that system. There is no separation between production and distribution, and it is completely erroneous for writers to treat the productive system as if producers dump their product onto some stockpile, to be later 'distributed' in some way to the people in the society. 'Distribution' is only the other side of the coin of production on the market" ([1962] 2004, 624). Or, as Hoppe puts it, "From the standpoint of the natural theory of property, there are not two separate processes—the production of income and then, after income is produced, its distribution. There is only one process: in producing income it is automatically distributed; the producer is the owner" (1988, 45).

An attack on people's ability to produce differs from merely stealing someone's output for the day. A person who has lost his productive capacity has lost the ability to demand consumer goods in the market—another reason why socialism has been deadly on such a huge scale. Socialism's victims are left without the means to draw goods to themselves to meet their basic needs. They become entirely dependent on bureaucratic distribution, which, as the calculation argument suggests, will be ineffective even if the regime intends to feed them. If the regime decides to starve them, however, it can do so with deadly effectiveness.

Claim Number 2: *Aggression against people's means of production is even deadlier than generalized aggression against external property; socialism is more dangerous than mere looting.*

Socialism: Public Slavery

Another aspect of the socialization of the means of production is that everyone becomes an "employee" of the state. What jobs they may take, whether they work, their rewards and punishments—all are determined by the state. As Hayek writes, "Economic control is not merely control of a sector of human life which can be separated from the rest; it is the control of the means for all our ends" ([1944] 1994, 101).

The people become slaves in fact, if not officially, but they become slaves of an unusual sort. Hoppe explains that just as socialized capital is depleted, so also socialized labor receives "lowered investment, misallocation, and overutilization" (1988, 30). Misallocation results from the lack of a competitive market for labor and the consequent absence of market prices for labor because independent entrepreneurs are eliminated. One pictures the schoolteachers and skilled craftsmen working in the killing fields under the watchful eyes and guns of the Khmer Rouge. Overutilization results because with the workers' income largely subject to the caretakers' control, these partial, temporary owners have an incentive to use up the labor without regard for the long-term consequences. In public slavery, the worker has no resale value. In the extreme, laborers are worked to death, as many millions were in the twentieth century.

In *Democracy: The God That Failed,* Hoppe starkly explains the nature of this "public" slavery, as compared with private slavery, in a long footnote in which he contrasts "the case of private slave ownership, as it existed for instance in antebellum America, with that of public slave ownership, as it existed for instance in the former Soviet Union and its Eastern European empire":

> Just as privately owned slaves were threatened with punishment if they tried to escape, in all of the former Soviet empire emigration was outlawed and punished as a criminal offense, if necessary, by shooting those who tried to run away. Moreover, anti-loafing laws existed everywhere, and governments could assign any task and all rewards and punishments to any citizen. Hence the classification of the Soviet system as slavery. Unlike a private slave owner, however, Eastern-European slave owners—from Lenin to Gorbachev— could not sell or rent their subjects in a labor market and privately appropriate the receipts from the sale or rental of their "human capital." Hence the system's classification as public (or socialist) slavery.

Without markets for slaves and slave labor, matters are worse, not better, for the slave, for without prices for slaves and their labor, a slave owner can no longer rationally allocate his "human capital." He cannot determine the scarcity value of his various, heterogeneous pieces of human capital, and he can neither determine the opportunity-cost of using this capital in any given employment, nor compare it to the corresponding revenue. Accordingly, permanent misallocation, waste, and "consumption" of human capital results.

The empirical evidence indicates as much. While it occasionally happened that a private slave owner killed his slave, which is the ultimate "consumption" of human capital, socialist slavery in Eastern Europe resulted in the murder of millions of civilians. (2001, 24–25 n. 25)

Claim Number 3: *Successful socialization of the means of production reduces the people to slaves whose lives the regime has neither the incentive nor the ability to preserve.*

Gun Control and Democide

In *Death by "Gun Control,"* Zelman and Stevens argue that gun control has preceded all the mass murders of the twentieth century. They summarize their thesis in what they call the "Genocide Formula": "Hatred + Government + Disarmed Civilians = Genocide" (2001, 25). As they explain further,

> How does "gun control" relate to genocide? As explained in this book, "gun control" schemes try to make it unpopular and then relatively rare for private citizens to own and use firearms. Anti-gun laws make it more costly and risky to have guns. Anti-gun rhetoric weakens the spirit of people to be armed.
>
> Licensing, registration and safety-inspection laws do more than discourage firearm ownership. By enforcing these laws the government creates a list of people who could possibly resist tyranny and oppression. As shown in this book, evil governments use such lists to locate, disarm, and eliminate firearms owners from the population.
>
> When the firearms are confiscated and the defense-minded people gone, only the defenseless unarmed people remain. The third ele-

ment of the Genocide formula—the only one that the people can directly control—is in place. (29–30)

This important argument fits very well into a property-rights approach to democide. I would emphasize, however, that stealing the means of production is perhaps even deadlier. People who still can demand goods on the market, owing to their ability to produce, can procure new means of defense.

The deadliest combination is gun control and socialization. Take away people's means of defense and their ability to acquire another means of defense, and they are left truly defenseless before the power of the state.

Ideology and Democide

So far I have argued that a massive invasion of private-property rights, especially the right to produce, is a prerequisite for democide, but I have not considered how this invasion comes about. How does a regime that ultimately rests on popular opinion get away with such horrendous actions? Ideology holds the key.

Ideology's role in democide must be considered carefully, however. Violators of external property rights do not always embrace an explicitly anti-property ideology, as the Communists did. For example, the deadly economic sanctions against Iraq were not explicitly justified by an antiproperty ideology, but in the name of democracy, freedom, and regime change. The socialists were especially deadly, though, because they precisely and consciously aimed their attacks at property rights. As we examine ideologies with elements of socialization, we should expect to find some of this same lethal effect, though not as much as in outright socialism.

Attacks on property also go by other names besides *socialism. Militarism,* which includes the subordination of private-property rights to the state's military machine, played a deadly role not only in the Nazi regime, but also, we are learning, in Mao's regime, as Mao focused on building up military power (Chang and Halliday 2005). He was willing to take food from the mouths of the Chinese people for this purpose, and he often did so. Ideologies that announce their devotion to the race, to the nation, and even to freedom and democracy can also result in attacks on private-property rights.

The property-rights approach to democide gains credibility when we recognize that the twentieth century, a time of such colossal mass murders, was also a time of ideological rejection of classical liberalism's strong devotion to the protection of private-property rights—an ideological rejection, it should be noted, that was popular in all regimes by the middle of the century, even in those that were nominally committed to "freedom." It is no coincidence, however, that the century's deadliest regimes were explicitly socialist and featured an announced ideology of enmity toward private-property rights.

Socialism leads to dictatorship. Hayek ([1944] 1994) argues that a regime that massively invades private-property rights will tend toward dictatorship as a side effect. George Reisman explains more forcefully "why socialism, understood as an economic system based on government ownership of the means of production, positively requires a totalitarian dictatorship" (2005). These arguments do not tell us whether socialism or dictatorship plays the larger role in facilitating mass murder. We may well note, however, that throughout history many regimes sought the kind of power over society that was finally achieved only by regimes with an ideological and practical commitment to the elimination of private-property rights.

War and Democide

According to Rummel, "[m]ost democides occur under the cover of war, revolution, or guerilla war, or in their aftermath" ([1994] 1997a, 22). "Over the life of a regime the more disposed it is to be involved in deadly foreign and domestic wars, the more likely it will commit democide, whether or not carried out during these wars. This is because totalitarian power not only underlies democide and genocide, but also because this power underlies as well the occurrence and intensity of war" (1997b, 93, 95).

From the perspective of the property-rights approach to democide, war plays a causal role in empowering a regime and in compromising property rights. Modern "democratic" war, in particular, has made massive taxation and conscription leading features of the state. "War is the health of the state," as Randolph Bourne pointed out: the state gains strength, and the people who are subject to it become correspondingly weaker. "Government interference with business and socialism," writes Mises, "create[s] conflicts for which no peaceful solution can be found....What has transformed the limited war between royal armies into total war, the clash between peoples, is not technicalities of military art, but the substitution of the welfare state for the laissez-faire state" ([1949] 1998, 819–20). During wartime, we are likely to see the warfare state, swollen with stolen men and goods, commit genocide against "foreigners." "Given his natural human aggressiveness," Hoppe asks, "is it not obvious that [the state ruler] will be more brazen and aggressive in his conduct toward foreigners if he can externalize the cost of such behavior onto others?" (2001, 241).

RUMMEL'S REGIME-TYPE THEORY OF DEMOCIDE

Rummel presents a moving target. I criticize his theory here for putting so much stress on the way the government is structured (as a dictatorial, authoritarian, or democratic system) rather than on what the government actually does (specifically to private-property rights). Yet in his 1983 paper "Libertarianism and International Violence," he distinguishes "political freedom" and "freedom," defining the latter as political freedom plus economic freedom. In that paper, at least, he puts great weight on economic freedom as a contributor to avoiding violence.

In his 1997 book *Power Kills,* however, he places heavy stress on democracy ("political freedom") and makes little or no mention of the role of property rights or economic freedom: "There is one solution to each [war, civil collective violence, genocide, mass murder], and the solution in each case is the same. It is to foster democratic freedom and to democratize coercive power and force. That is, mass killing and mass murder carried out by government is a result of indiscriminate, irresponsible Power at the center" (3).

Elucidating how this relationship works, he states that in the deadly, dictatorial regime, "Their culture is one of command, and unquestioning obedience and their modus operandi is naked power." He contrasts this situation with the democratic society, which he describes as a spontaneous order whose "primary mode of power is exchange, its political system is democratic, and this democratic government is but one of many groups and pyramids of power in the social field....Of necessity such an exchange-based order produces a culture of exchange, that is norms of negotiation, accommodation, concessions, tolerance, and a willingness to accept less than one wants" (1997b, 7). Summarizing the two opposites in his schema, Rummel states:

At the most fundamental level, then, we have an opposition between Freedom and Power. It is an opposition between the spontaneous society and the society turned into a hierarchical organization. It is an opposition between social field and antifield. This is not to deny the importance of culture and cross-pressures and the influence of public opinion in explaining the democratic peace. It is to say that they are social forces whose presence or absence is best understood in terms of the freedom of a democratic, spontaneous society or the commanding power of one that is tightly organized. (1997b, 8).

THE THEORIES COMPARED

We might agree for the most part with Rummel's static picture of the two types of regime. Respect for private-property rights will lead to a more decentralized, spontaneous society, whereas systematic invasions of private-property rights will lead to centralization and, at the extreme, to dictatorship. Yet we are left with little sense of the dynamics of how either regime gets to such a place. Rummel's enthusiastic endorsement of democracy leaves little room in particular for understanding, as I see it, how democracy actually contributes to the deadly move toward the massive invasion of property rights.

To summarize, the points of agreement between Rummel's regime-type theory of democide and my property-rights theory are:

- "What about cultural-ethnic differences, outgroup conflict, misperception, frustration-aggression, relative deprivation, ideological imperatives, dehumanization, resource competition, etc.? At one time or another, for one regime or another, one or more of these factors play an important role in democide" (Rummel [1994] 1997a, 19). Yet none of these factors applies to all democides.
- The state's power is the common denominator: "Power is a necessary cause for war or democide" (Rummel [1994] 1997a, 20).
- "Most democides occur under the cover of war, revolution, or guerilla war, or in their aftermath" (Rummel [1994] 1997a, 22).

The points of disagreement are:

- The regime-type theory points to democracy as the solution to democide. The property-rights theory points to respect for private-property rights as the solution.
- The regime-type theory points to a dictatorial form of government as the main cause of democide. The property-rights theory points to massive invasions of private-property rights as the main cause both of a dictatorial form of government and of democide.
- Although Rummel spends little time on pre-twentieth-century history, his classification of regimes suggests that monarchies would be classified as authoritarian and that they should be expected to be more murderous than democracies but less so than totalitarian dictatorships. The property-rights theory judges each regime by its respect for private-property rights and notes that many European monarchies historically were far more respectful of such rights than modern democracies have been; therefore, we would expect those monarchical regimes to have been less murderous than democracies.
- Rummel tends to excuse or rationalize democide by democracies (by the United States, in particular), for obvious reasons. The property-rights theory does not view democracies through such rose-colored glasses. The millions killed in Vietnam, the million killed by economic sanctions against Iraq, the millions killed as a result of covert U.S. operations, the violence by France in Algeria—these incidents are no surprise for the property-rights theorist, who recognizes the power that the perpetrating democratic regimes possessed, owing to massive amounts of stolen property and the lack of respect these regimes had for (certain) foreigners. Moreover, the property-rights theorist accepts Hoppe's point that democratic regimes, being public governments, take a short-term caretaker view that results in sometimes treating lives as cheap.
- The regime-type theory explains that the twentieth century's deadliest regimes were socialist because they were totalitarian dictatorships. The property-rights theory explains that their deadliness sprang directly from their socialism.

NOTE

1. Rummel describes his recent revisions to his originally published estimate of 174 million on his blog, at http://freedomspeace.blogspot.com/.

REFERENCES

Chang, Jung, and Jon Halliday. 2005. *Mao: The Unknown Story.* New York: Knopf.

Hayek, F. A. [1944] 1994. *The Road to Serfdom.* Chicago: University of Chicago Press.

Hoppe, Hans-Hermann. 1988. *A Theory of Socialism and Capitalism: Economics, Politics, and Ethics.* Boston: Kluwer Academic.

———. 2001. *Democracy: The God That Failed.* New Brunswick, N.J.: Transaction.

———. [1993] 2006. *The Economics and Ethics of Private Property.* 2d ed. Auburn, Ala.: Ludwig von Mises Institute.

Locke, John. [1664] 1993. *Two Treatises of Government.* London: Everyman/J. M. Dent.

Mises, Ludwig von. [1920] 1975. Economic Calculation in the Socialist Commonwealth. In *Collective Economic Planning,* edited by Friedrich A. Hayek, 87–130. Clifton, N.J.: Kelley.

———. [1949] 1998. *Human Action.* Scholars Edition. Auburn, Ala.: Ludwig von Mises Institute.

Reisman, George. 2005. Why Nazism Was Socialism and Why Socialism Is Totalitarian. Available at: http://www.mises.org/story/1937.

Rockwell, Llewellyn H. 2003. Anatomy of the Iraqi State. Available at: www.lewrockwell.com/rockwell/anatomy-iraqi-state.html.

Rothbard, Murray N. 1970. *Power and Market.* Kansas City, Kans.: Sheed Andrews and McMeel.

———. [1962] 2004. *Man, Economy, and State.* 2d ed. Auburn, Ala.: Ludwig von Mises Institute.

Rummel, R. J. 1983. Libertarianism and International Violence. *Journal of Conflict Resolution* 27, no. 1 (March): 27–71.

———. 1990. *Lethal Politics: Soviet Genocide and Mass Murder since 1917.* New Brunswick, N.J.: Transaction.

———. [1994] 1997a. *Death by Government.* New Brunswick, N.J.: Transaction.

———. 1997b. *Power Kills: Democracy as a Method of Nonviolence.* New Brunswick, N.J.: Transaction.

Stromberg, Joseph N. 1979. The War for Southern Independence: A Radical Libertarian Perspective. *Journal of Libertarian Studies* 3, no. 1: 31–53.

Zelman, Aaron, and Richard W. Stevens. 2001. *Death by "Gun Control": The Human Cost of Victim Disarmament.* Hartford, Conn.: Mazel Freedom Press.

Acknowledgment: Reprinted from *The Independent Review,* 11, no. 3 (Winter 2007): 381–95. ISSN 1086-1653, Copyright © 2007.

PART IV

Free Trade as a Peace Strategy

13

Commerce, Markets, and Peace
Richard Cobden's Enduring Lessons

EDWARD P. STRINGHAM

The progress of freedom depends more upon the maintenance of peace and the spread of commerce and the diffusion of education than upon the labour of Cabinets or Foreign Offices.
—Richard Cobden

In a 1944 review of F. A. Hayek's *Road to Serfdom*, George Orwell declared, "Capitalism leads to dole queues, the scramble for markets, and war" (1968, 119). Indeed, if we look at the past century, we see significant advances in markets, but we also see an era plagued by war. Do capitalism and conflicts go hand in hand? Are the military and markets complements? Indeed, many conservative advocates of markets also passionately support the military, and many people who oppose war also oppose markets. Nineteenth-century writer Richard Cobden, however, maintained that the military and markets were substitutes: more military entails less market. Although the ideas in *The Political Writings of Richard Cobden* (1903) are a century and a half old, Cobden considered many arguments for military intervention still made today. He discussed whether military spending was beneficial to the economy, to commerce, and to peace, and in all three cases he answered no. Both conservatives and left liberals can learn much from Cobden's discussion of commerce, markets, and peace. As he demonstrated, the advocate of markets must be an advocate of peace.

COSTS OF MILITARY SPENDING

Cobden began his 1835 pamphlet *England, Ireland, and America* with a quote from George Washington's farewell address to the American people: "The great rule of conduct for us in regard to foreign nations is, in extending our commercial relations, to have with them as little political connection as possible" (1903, 3).[1] Whereas Washington made the political case for trade with all and entanglements with none, Cobden outlined an economic case.[2]

Cobden emphasized first the opportunity costs of military spending. Unlike later economists influenced by Keynes, he did not fall victim to the "broken window" fallacy (Hazlitt 1996). He recognized that each million the government spent was necessarily a million (or more) not spent by private parties. When the government devotes resources to armies and navies, those resources have an opportunity cost. He referred to military spending, "every farthing of which goes, in the shape of taxation, from the pockets of the public" (197).

Cobden did not view all government expenditures as promoting the public good. He regarded British military spending as a drain on the economy. As the government consumes more resources, fewer resources can be devoted to private wealth-generating activities.[3] Government agents may gain from increased public spending, but the public loses. Cobden drew a distinction between the interests of the productive class and the interests of government. "Our history during the last century may be called the tragedy of 'British intervention in the politics of Europe'; in which princes, diplomatists, peers, and generals, have been the authors and the actors—the people the victims; and the moral will be exhibited to the latest posterity in 800 millions of debt" (196). When the state directs resources, its beneficiaries certainly gain, but unfortunately the public foots the bill.

Cobden maintained that the productive citizens did not profit from Britain's activities around the globe. He wanted to educate members of the business class that they had to pay for all of the government's projects.

[I]f it could be made manifest to the trading and industrious portions of this nation, who have no honours or interested ambition of any kind at stake in the matter, that whilst our dependencies are supported at an expense to them, in direct taxation, of more than five millions annually, they serve but as gorgeous and ponderous appendages to swell our ostensible grandeur, but in reality to complicate and magnify our government expenditure, without improving our balance of trade. (24–25)

When the government creates programs around the world, the bureaucracy can only grow. Although this activity may look good for government, the average person receives little benefit when government exerts its influence abroad.

Although the public's benefits are murky, its costs are crystal clear. Cobden recognized that taxes constitute a weight on the economy and that decreasing military spending abroad would result in significant savings: "[W]e know of nothing that would be so likely to conduce a diminution of our burdens, by reducing the charges of the army, navy, and ordnance (amounting to fourteen millions annually), as a proper understanding of our relative position with respect to our colonial possessions" (24). Although England's international affairs were conducted under the pretext of enhancing the public good, Cobden believed that much of public policy benefited only special interests: "The honours, the fame, the emoluments of war belong not to [the middle and industrious classes]; the battle-plain is the harvest-field of the aristocracy, watered with the blood of the people" (34).

At the time of Cobden's writings, Britain had more than ten times more ground soldiers than the United States maintained and a significantly larger navy as well (82–84). Cobden viewed Britain's military expenditures as wasted resources. Rather than encouraging commerce, the army and navy were a drain on the economy. As Robert Higgs (1992) has argued, the "prosperity" brought about by military spending is an illusion.

Making an elementary institutional comparison of England and the United States, Cobden hypothesized that American enterprise had become so important in such a short time because it was relatively unburdened by heavy taxes: "[N]o person possessing sound reason will deny that we, who find it necessary to levy upwards of thirty millions annually upon the necessaries of life, must be burdened with grievous disadvantages, when brought into commercial competition with the untaxed labour of the inhabitants of America" (81–82). The Americans had followed "a policy from which so much wealth, prosperity, and moral greatness have sprung. America…is a spectacle of the beneficent effects of that policy which may be comprised in the maxim—As little intercourse as possible betwixt Governments, as much connection as possible between the nations of the world" (215).

Cobden's hypothesis seems to be corroborated by recent empirical work by James Gwartney, Robert Lawson, and Walter Block (1996), which indicates that the greater the government spending in an economy, the worse the economic performance. The panel data analyzed by Malcolm Knight, Norman Loayza, and Delano Villanueva also indicate that military spending retards economic growth. These analysts hypothesize that "military spending adversely affects growth; namely, through crowding out human capital investment and fostering the adoption of various types of trade restrictions" (1996, 27–28).

The key to a successful economy is not heavy military spending but heavy reliance on markets. Cobden argued: "It has been through the peaceful victories of mercantile traffic, and not by the force of arms, that modern States have yielded to the supremacy of more successful nations" (79). He upheld the Americans' lesser military spending as a model to be followed: "The first, and, indeed, only step towards a diminution of our government expenditure, must be the adoption of that line of foreign policy which the Americans have clung to, with such wisdom and pertinacity, ever since they became a people" (103–4). Cutting back government spending is the easiest way to improve economic performance.

COMMERCE AS A JUSTIFICATION FOR WAR?

Although all able economists recognize military spending as costly, these costs may be necessary for the existence of markets. If so, opposing military spending would amount to opposing markets, as many conservatives contend. This line of argument has a long history. For example, in the seventeenth century King William III declared, "The necessity of maintaining the maritime strength of the country, and of giving adequate protection to the extended commerce of my subjects, has occasioned some increase in the estimates for the naval branch of public service" (qtd. in Cobden 1903, 217). Cobden recognized that arguments in favor of military outlays were made in the name of business: "still more popular, pretence for wars and standing armaments, the protection of our commerce" (217).

Although commerce certainly has beneficent characteristics and war does not, perhaps society has to take the bad with the good. The only choice might be to accept both markets and militarism or to oppose both. Cobden recognized the popularity of this view: "[A] proposal to reduce our armaments will be opposed upon the plea of maintaining a proper attitude, as it is called, amongst the nations of Europe. British intervention in the state policy of the Continent has been usually excused under the two stock pretences of maintaining the balance of power in Europe, and of protecting our commerce" (196). To Cobden, however, this union was a false marriage: markets and military do not go hand in hand. He found the commercial justification for military spending to be spurious:

> [W]e confess ourselves to be much more at a loss to understand what is here meant by the protection of commerce through an increase in the navy estimates. Our commerce is, in other words, our manufactures; and the first inquiry which occurs necessarily is, Do we need an augmentation of the naval force, in order to guard our ingenious artisans and industrious laborers, or to protect those precious results of their mechanical genius, the manufactories of our capitalists? (217–18)

The success of an economy depends on the achievements of free enterprise, which do not depend on military spending.

We can see this reality by looking at where the government devotes military resources. Discussing how much trade occurred between England and the United States, Cobden asked, "Now, what precaution is taken by the Government of this country to guard and regulate this precious flood of traffic?" (223). Although the commerce certainly had great importance, the merchants who conducted it were for the most part on their own. With great passion, Cobden argued that commerce did not depend on the navy:

> How many of those costly vessels of war, which are maintained at the expense to the nation of many millions of pounds annually, do our readers suppose, are stationed at the mouths of Mersey and Clyde, to welcome and convoy Liverpool and Glasgow the merchant ships of New York, Charleston, and New Orleans, all bearing the inestimable freight of cotton wool, upon which our commercial existence depends? Not one! (223–24)

Similarly, he asked about the army: "What portion of our standing army, costing seven millions a year, is occupied in defending this more than Pactolus—this golden stream of trade, on which floats not only the wealth, but the hopes and existence of a great community? Four invalids at the Perch

Rock Battery hold the sinecure office of defending the port of Liverpool!" (224). The world is too big for any nation to police every mile of it, so merchants were left to themselves.

> But our exports to the United States will reach…more than ten millions sterling, and nearly one half of this amount goes to New York:—what portion of the Royal navy is stationed off that port to protect our merchants' cargoes? The appearance of a King's ship at New York is an occurrence of such rarity as to attract the especial notice of the public journals; whilst, all along the entire Atlantic coast of the United States—extending, as it does, more than 3,000 miles, to which we send a quarter of our whole yearly exports—there are stationed two British ships only, and these two have also their stations at the West Indies. No! this commerce, unparalleled in magnitude, between two remote nations, demands no armament as its guide or safeguard. (224)

The trade between the nations was immense, but British merchants simply could not depend on their navy to defend their every journey. The British military, although significant, was not devoting its resources to protecting merchants.

Why then are so many arguments for the military made in the name of commerce? One reason is the legacy of mercantilism, under which the government played an active role attempting to manage the economy. This intervention included the establishment of foreign trading monopolies by law. Because the government maintained these commercial monopolies with armed forces, the discussion of commerce and the military went hand in hand. Cobden explained:

> Whilst our trade rested upon our foreign dependencies, as was the case in the middle of the last century—whilst, in other words, force and violence were necessary to command our customers for our manufacturers—it was natural and consistent that almost every king's speech should allude to the importance of protecting commerce of the country, by means of a powerful navy. (222)

To Cobden, however, mercantilist policies conflict with free trade. The military should not be used to enforce monopolies.

Cobden favored abandoning military conquest for the benefit of "commerce" and adopting instead a system of free trade. The entire military involvement with commerce was unnecessary, so superfluous spending could be cut without harming the market. He asked, "But will any one who understands the subject pretend to tell us that our trade will suffer by such a change?" (86).

> [W]e are to infer that it is the principle of the government that the extension of our trade with foreign countries demands for its protection a corresponding augmentation of the royal navy. This, we are aware, was the policy of the last century, during the greater part of which the motto, "Ships, Colonies, and Commerce," was borne upon the national escutcheon, became the watchword of statesmen, and was the favourable sentiment of public writers; but this, which meant, in other words— "Men of war to conquer colonies, to yield us a monopoly of their trade," must now be dismissed, like many other equally glittering but false adages of our forefathers, and in its place we must substitute the more homely, but enduring maxim—Cheapness, which will command commerce; and whatever else is needed will follow in its train. (221)

The simple solution is to implement policies friendly to business. Triumph in the world market hinges on successful private enterprise, which depends not on military superiority but on lower costs. By cutting the military drastically, the savings can be passed on to productive enterprise. "By this course of policy, and by this alone, we shall be enabled to reduce our army and navy more nearly to a level with the corresponding burdens of our American rivals" (104).

Not only does free trade require little military backing, but, moreover, markets should substitute for the military. Replacing military relations with commercial relations would lead to significant tax savings, as well as to more peace. "[B]esides dictating the disuse of warlike establishments, free trade (for of that beneficent doctrine we are speaking) arms its votaries by its own pacific nature, in that eternal truth—*the more any nation traffics abroad upon free and honest principles, the less it will be in danger of wars*" (222, emphasis in original). Thus, rather than creating antagonistic relationships, trade encourages peaceful relations between nations. Nothing encourages cooperation so much as a mutually advantageous enterprise. The key then is the promotion of commerce, especially at the expense of the military. Cobden kept returning to the theme: "Where, then, shall we seek for a solution of the difficulty, or how account for the necessity which called for the increase of our naval strength? The commerce of this country, we repeat, is in other words its manufactures" (218). Manufacturing, not naval strength, is the key to prosperity.

Cobden believed that trade would flourish as long as manufacturers lowered their costs. Like economists who focus on the principle of comparative advantage, he argued: "In a word, our national existence is involved in the well-doing of our manufactures....Are we asked, How is this trade protected, and by what means can it be enlarged? The reply still is, By the cheapness of our manufactures" (219). When trading partners specialize according to their comparative advantage, they produce increased output and consumption for all traders.

LIBERTY AS JUSTIFICATION FOR WAR?

The dilemma concerning international trade is that it requires more than one party. If one country adopts policies inimical to markets, it reduces others' opportunities for trade. Can liberating such a country benefit both its citizens and its liberators? Citizens would have their government overthrown, and the liberators would have newfound trading partners, so might the outcome be a win-win situation? Cobden considered such justifications for military involvement abroad, recognizing that appeals for military involvement were made in the name of promoting good: "We shall here be encountered with a very general prepossession in favour of our maintaining what is termed a rank amongst the states of the Continent—which means... that England shall be consulted before any other nations presume to quarrel or fight; and that she shall be ready, and shall be called upon, to take a part in every contention, either as mediator, second, or principle" (194). Cobden favored the preservation of peace, but he disputed that military involvement was an effective means to that end. In his view, military intervention served the interest of neither the intervening nation nor the distant country.

Cobden made a case first by appealing to the self-interest of his fellow citizens. He argued that a country embroiled itself in other people's affairs only at its peril. "Our sole object is to persuade the public that the wisest policy for England, is to take no part in these remote quarrels....We shall claim the right of putting the question upon a footing of self-interest. We do not, for a moment, imagine that it is necessary for us to show that we are not called upon to preserve the peace and good order of the entire world" (127). Although many problems exist in the world, becoming involved in each one would be futile. "Upon what *principle,* commercial, social, or political—in short, upon what ground, consistent with common sense—does the foreign secretary involve Great Britain in the barbarian politics of the Ottoman Government, to the manifest risk of future wars, and the present pecuniary sacrifice attending standing armaments?" (211, emphasis in original). Moreover, not only are such endeavours costly, but they risk full-fledged war. Why should a country be surprised when it is attacked after its government has involved itself in far-off concerns? Cobden believed countries that do not maintain an international military presence would be less at risk.

Even though other governments may well be in the wrong, why chance the further muddying of already roiled waters? Viewing British involvement with foreign nations as a problem, Cobden argued that the British had no business interfering in overseas politics. "If we go back through the Parliamentary debates of the last few reigns," he observed, "we shall find this singular feature in our national character—the passion for meddling in the affairs of foreigners" (195). With sufficient problems at home, why worry about the entire world's problems? "Public opinion must undergo a change; our ministers must no longer be held responsible for the every-day political quarrels all over Europe" (33). Intervention struck Cobden as counterproductive: "Again we say (and let us be excused the repetition of this advice, for we write with no other object but to enforce it), England cannot survive its financial embarrassment, except by renouncing that policy of intervention with the affairs of other States which has been the fruitful source of nearly all our wars" (104).

A second type of argument for military involvement abroad is humanitarian. Yes, military intervention entails costs, but when a country is blessed with more liberty, compassion requires helping others to attain such liberty. Cobden recognized this line of argument:

England...sounded like filling the office of Justice herself to one of the globe. Of course such a post of honour could not be maintained, or its dignity asserted, without a proper attendance of guards and officers, and we consequently find that at about this period of our history large standing armies began to be called for...[and] supplies solicited by the government from time to time under the plea of preserving the liberties of Europe. (196–97)

Although Cobden favored liberty throughout Europe, he did not believe that British military action could establish it.

Cobden also questioned whether war can advance markets. As Robert Higgs (1987) has demonstrated with regard to U.S. history, war always leads to an increase in government power. Although arguments for militarism are often made under the pretext of promoting liberty, wars actually diminish freedom. Simply deposing and replacing a country's leaders will not lead to more liberty. Cobden wrote: "[L]et it never be forgotten, that it is not by means of war that states are rendered fit for the enjoyment of constitutional freedom; on the contrary, whilst terror and bloodshed reign in the land, involving men's minds in the extremities of hopes and fears, there can be no process of thought, no education going on, by which alone can a people be prepared for the enjoyment of rational liberty" (35–36). Liberty requires enlightenment, which can come about only by means of education and persuasion, not military force.

Public opinion must undergo a change toward respecting private-property rights; otherwise, a market economy cannot function. Cobden described how the French were having so many difficulties precisely because of war: "[A]fter a struggle of twenty years, begun in behalf of freedom, no sooner had the wars of the French revolution terminated, than all the nations of the continent fell back into their previous state of political servitude, and from which they have, ever since the peace, been qualifying to rescue themselves, by the gradual process of intellectual advancement" (36). Cobden viewed the transition to liberty as a learning process that cannot be imposed by brute force. As Ludwig von Mises observed, "It [liberty] cannot be accomplished by a despotic regime that instead of enlightening the masses beats them into submission. In the long run the ideas of the majority, however detrimental they may be, will carry on" (1962, 93). If we want markets, the public has to be convinced, not forced, to support them.

Because war does not advance liberty, foreign nations must be left to sort out their own affairs, no matter how difficult their problems. A desire to step in and control the situation is a natural feeling, but Cobden opposed such intervention. Rather than trying to fix every problem using might, England should stay out:

> With France, still in the throes of her last revolution, containing a generation of young and ardent spirits, without resources of commerce, and therefore burning for the excitement and employment of war; with Germany, Prussia, Hungary, Austria, and Italy, all dependent for tranquility upon the fragile bond of attachment of their subjects to a couple of aged paternal monarchs; with Holland and Belgium, each sword in hand; and with Turkey, not so much yielding to the pressure of Russia, as sinking beneath an inevitable religious and political destiny—surely, with such elements of discord as these fermenting all over Europe, it becomes more than ever our duty to take natural shelter from a storm, from entering into which we could hope for no benefits, but might justly dread renewed sacrifices. (35).

Precisely at a time of so much discord, the best policy is nonintervention. Rather than venturing into the storm, a nation, instead, should focus on free trade. "Let us imagine that all our ambassadors and consuls were instructed to take no further share in the domestic concerns of European nations…to leave all those people to their own quarrels, and to devote our attention, exclusively, after the example of the Americans, to the commercial interests of their country" (85–86). Rather than acting as the world's policeman, England should devote its energy to commerce. Let others attend to their problems.

Would eschewing foreign political squabbles be tantamount to abandoning everyone else and refusing to help those in need? To Cobden, the answer was no. He believed that the English economy had been able to become freer only when it was unfettered with foreign involvement.

> Those who, from an eager desire to aid civilisation, wish that Great Britain should interpose in the dissensions of neighbouring states, would do wisely to study, in the history of their own country, how well a people can, by force and virtue of native elements, and without external assistance of any kind, work out their own political regenera-

tion: they might learn too, by their own annals, that it is only when at peace with other states that a nation finds the leisure for looking within itself, and discovering the means to accomplish great domestic ameliorations. (36)

Cobden recommended laissez-faire as the most humanitarian course of action. A policy of nonintervention would actually help other nations more than activist policies. "England, by calmly directing her undivided energies to the purifying of her own institutions, to the emancipation of her commerce…would, by thus serving as it were for the beacon of other nations, aid more effectually the cause of political progression all over the continent than she could possibly do by plunging herself into the strife of European wars" (35). Serving as a model for foreign nations would help them far more than becoming embroiled in their conflicts.

Consider the trade between the United States and England in the nineteenth century. Despite the lack of political reunification, peaceful relations existed because the private sectors of the two economies were so closely connected. "England and America are bound up together in peaceful fetters by the strongest of all ligatures that can bind two nations to each other, viz., commercial interests; and which, every succeeding year, renders *more impossible,* if the term may be used, a rupture between the two" (78, emphasis in original). Much of England's manufacturing depended on raw materials imported from the United States. When groups are interdependent, aggression is less likely. Where no trade exists, in contrast, both countries have less to lose by resort to warfare.

Conflict often occurs where trade barriers are present. Have embargoes ever brought about more cooperation or produced more liberty? Empirical evidence demonstrating the effectiveness of these policies is scant. Government interference with trade jeopardizes peace. With each new trading relationship under free trade, a bond comes into existence between otherwise separate parties. By expanding trade around the globe, nations develop more such peaceful relations. In this realm, government relations are superfluous.

England…has…united for ever two remote hemispheres in the bonds of peace, by placing Europe and America in absolute and inextricable dependence on each other; England's industrious classes, through the energy of their commercial enterprise, are at this moment influencing the civilization of the whole world, by stimulating the labour, exciting the curiosity, and promoting the taste for refinement of barbarous communities, and, above all, by acquiring and teaching to surrounding nations the beneficent attachment to peace. (149)

Cobden was right: trade is the great panacea. To promote a world of peace, we must promote a world of free markets.

CONCLUSION

Military buildups and the projection of military force abroad in the name of markets have a long history, but nineteenth-century writer Richard Cobden met these arguments head-on. Military spending is not a boost to the economy; rather, it entails significant costs. A government's campaigns abroad increase the risk of war and increase the burden on taxpayers. Despite claims to the contrary, the military is not helpful for commerce. National success depends on private enterprise, not on military might. Armed forces must play an active role in regulating commerce under mercantilism, but not under free trade. The bulk of commercial activity does not depend on the military at all. The key is to create an atmosphere in which businesses are free to innovate and lower costs—a policy that would benefit all nations. A nation can advance liberty more effectively by adhering to the principles of free trade and serving as a beacon than by going to war. Free trade promotes international cooperation and thereby promotes peace. Contrary to widely prevailing views, markets and war do not go hand in hand. The market promotes peace.

NOTES

1. Cobden 1903 hereafter cited parenthetically by page number only.
2. Although Cobden was not a pacifist on principle, he opposed military spending on economic grounds (Bresiger 1997, 48).
3. As Baumol (1990) has emphasized, in economies where too much entrepreneurial spirit is devoted to government rather than to the market, fewer beneficial innovations will occur.

REFERENCES

Baumol, William. 1990. Entrepreneurship: Productive, Unproductive, and Destructive. *Journal of Political Economy* 98: 893–921.

Bresiger, Gregory. 1997. Laissez Faire and Little Englanderism: The Rise, Fall, Rise, and Fall of the Manchester School. *Journal of Libertarian Studies* 13: 45–79.

Cobden, Richard. 1903. *The Political Writings of Richard Cobden.* London: Fisher Unwin.

Gwartney, James, Robert Lawson, and Walter Block. 1996. *Economic Freedom of the World: 1975–1995.* Vancouver: Fraser Institute.

Hazlitt, Henry. 1996. *Economics in One Lesson.* San Francisco: Laissez Faire Books.

Higgs, Robert. 1987. *Crisis and Leviathan: Critical Episodes in the Growth of American Government.* New York: Oxford University Press.

———. 1992. Wartime Prosperity? A Reassessment of the U.S. Economy in the 1940s. *Journal of Economic History* 52: 41–60.

Knight, Malcolm, Norman Loayza, and Delano Villanueva. 1996. The Peace Dividend: Military Spending Cuts and Economic Growth. *International Monetary Fund Staff Papers* 43: 1–37.

Mises, Ludwig von. 1962. *The Ultimate Foundation of Economic Science.* Princeton, N.J.: Van Nostrand.

Orwell, George. 1968. *The Collected Essays, Journalism, and Letters of George Orwell.* Vol. 3. Edited by Sonia Orwell and Ian Angus. New York: Harcourt, Brace and World.

Acknowledgment: Reprinted from *The Independent Review,* 9, no. 1 (Summer 2004): 105–16. ISSN 1086-1653, Copyright © 2004. This chapter is adapted from the essay that won second prize (faculty division) in the 2003 Olive W. Garvey Fellowship Program for the Independent Institute, Oakland, California.

14

The Diffusion of Prosperity and Peace by Globalization

ERICH WEEDE

Capitalism and economic freedom promote peace. Globalization can be understood as a process of market expansion and market integration, as the universalization of capitalism. After a short discussion of the political economy of globalization, I turn to the frequently overlooked security benefits of globalization. The diffusion of prosperity, free trade, and democratization is part of the story. Quantitative studies provide a great deal of evidence for a causal chain running from free trade via prosperity and democracy to the avoidance of military conflict, as well as for another causal relationship between trade or economic openness and conflict avoidance. After a review of the quantitative literature and a discussion of some methodological issues, I illustrate the capitalist peace by historical examples and contemporary applications. At the end, I consider how the capitalist peace may be "exported" from Western societies to poor and conflict-prone nations and regions.

THE POLITICAL ECONOMY OF GLOBALIZATION

The process of globalization had already begun in the late nineteenth century. Before World War I, trade and foreign investment were fairly globalized. Because of low political obstacles to international migration, labor markets actually were more globalized at the beginning of the twentieth century than at its end. The two world wars and the Great Depression between them interrupted the process of global market integration for about half a century. Thereafter, the process regained force and speed. Now, inexpensive, fast, and reliable communication and transportation enable producers of goods and some service providers in low-wage countries to challenge high-cost producers in rich countries on their home turf, but technological innovation resulting in falling prices and rising speed of intercontinental communication and transportation is not the only determinant of globalization. Political decisions in rich and poor countries alike contribute strongly to globalization, too. Tariffs and, to a lesser degree, nontariff barriers to trade have been reduced. Many countries try to find and exploit their comparative advantage, to realize economies of scale and gains from trade by looking for buyers and sellers everywhere. If trade between countries is truly free, then it promises to enrich all nations.

Since the publication of Adam Smith's *Wealth of Nations* ([1776] 1976), we have known that the size of the market limits the division of labor and that the division of labor boosts innovation and productivity. In principle, globalization is the logical endpoint of the economic evolution that began when families switched from subsistence farming and household production to production for the market. As long as globalization is not yet completed—and it certainly is not yet—gains from trade remain to be realized by further market expansion. Because globalization adds to competitive pressure, however, it causes resentment, and because globalization springs from technological innovation and political decisions that promote free trade, these innovations and decisions attract resentment, too. The world is already globalized enough that national resistance does limited damage. Except for the United States, national resistance is more likely to contribute to a country's decline than to derail the process of globalization.

Free trade is vulnerable. If foreigners are perceived as a cause of the need to adjust, then attacking free trade becomes politically attractive. After all, no politician benefits from the affection of foreigners who cannot vote. Of course, economists who insist on the benefits of free trade (even if your trading partner does not practice free trade) are right. Benefits include serving customers better at lower prices, but also faster growth of total factor productivity (Edwards 1998; OECD 2003, 89). The benefits of free trade, however, tend to be dispersed widely, whereas its costs (for example, certain bankruptcies and job losses) tend to be concentrated and more visible. Therefore, the political case against free trade may become very strong despite the weakness of the economic argument.

Who in rich Western societies is affected most by globalization? Although unskilled labor is much less expensive in poor countries than in rich countries, this difference does not necessarily provide poor countries and poorly paid labor there with a competitive advantage. Frequently, even unskilled labor is much more productive in rich countries than in poor ones. If the wage gap is neutralized by a countervailing productivity gap, unit labor costs are not affected by international differences in pay. If unskilled labor in rich countries is overpaid compared to unskilled labor in poor countries, however, then free trade reduces the demand for rich-country labor that is used intensively in the production of importable goods—that is, for low-skilled labor used in producing goods that compete with Western imports. The wages of low-skilled Western workers may suffer from downward pressure because their services have become more easily substitutable than previously (Rodrik 1997). This process might result in growing volatility of earnings and income inequality, as in the United States, or high unemployment, as in much of Continental Europe. Of course, unemployment is most likely to result from a combination of fierce international competition and rigid labor markets at home. Otherwise, trade is more likely to affect the composition of employment than its amount (Irwin 2002, 71).

Analysts dispute the degree to which either trade or technological progress has caused the predicament of unskilled labor in the West. Although the majority view (for example, Krugman 1996) blames most of it on technological progress, this conclusion is not entirely satisfying because technological progress is frequently inferred from estimated production-function residuals rather than from direct measurement. An outspoken minority (for example, Wood 1994, 166–67) puts most of the blame on free trade and estimates that approximately 9 million manufacturing jobs might have been lost in rich countries by 1990 and many more by now. The complementary gain of 23 million jobs in poor countries may satisfy humanitarian impulses, but it does not help Western politicians to win elections. In the past three years, one out of six manufacturing jobs has been lost in the United States ("Flying on One Engine" 2003, 30). Although trade is almost certainly not the primary determinant of this job loss or of increased wage inequality (Irwin 2002, 99), some Americans look for scapegoats. Because China has a larger trade surplus with the United States than even Japan does, China bashing has become popular in America.

With regard to the expansion of economic freedom and secure property rights, globalization provides reason for hope. Globalization ties politicians' hands and prevents them from pursuing politically attractive but self-defeating policies, such as those that created the welfare state and its disastrous effects on incentives to produce goods or services for others. As Vanberg has observed, "competition among jurisdictions offers citizens and jurisdiction-users effective protection against exploitation, be it in favor of privileged groups or of those who hold the reins of political decision-making power" (2000, 106). Where markets are significantly larger than political units, stifling the markets by political controls and by undermining economic freedom becomes more difficult than elsewhere. In my view (Weede 1996, chap. 4, and 2000, inspired by Jones 1981), even the rise of the West and the comparative stagnation of the great Asian civilizations until the mid- or late twentieth century is owing to political fragmentation and disunity in Europe in contrast to the huge centralized empires in China, India, or the Middle East. Capital and even labor to a lesser degree could exit from oppressive rule in the West, thereby mitigating its incidence. By contrast, Asian emperors or sultans were not forced to respect the property rights of merchants and producers.

Because globalization may require Western welfare states to accept either widening income inequality or high unemployment (given their fairly rigid labor markets), protectionism remains a politically attractive cure. In politics, competition does not guarantee a movement toward greater efficiency or economic freedom. For special interests—owners and workers of enterprises threatened by foreign competition, and politicians willing to serve them rather than the much bigger, but silent constituency of consumers—academic support may be crucial in legitimating their claims (Bhagwati 1991, 6). Even if material well-being were one's only concern, it would be extremely important to resist the protectionist temptation. Protectionism harms consumers, reduces the speed of wealth-enhancing structural change, and diminishes opportunities for employees to move to better-paid jobs producing for global markets.

THE SECURITY BENEFITS OF GLOBALIZATION

A Survey of Empirical Studies

Although neither "realist" theorizing about interstate politics (Waltz 1979; Mearsheimer 2001) nor critical treatments of globalization (Gray 1998; Kapstein 1999) recognize it, a strong and beneficial link exists between globalization and the avoidance of war. In my view, the economic benefits of globalization and free trade are much less important than the international security benefits. The quantitative literature (summarized by Weede 1996, chap. 8, and 2000, chap. 11) comes fairly close to general agreement on the following four propositions from economics, political sociology, and international relations.

First, democracies rarely fight each other (Russett 1993; Russett and Oneal 2001). This finding does not necessarily imply that democracies fight fewer wars than do other regimes. It is even compatible with the view widely shared until recently that the risk of war between democracies and autocracies might be even higher than the risk of war between autocracies. I agree with critics of the democratic peace that we do not yet understand fully *why* democracies rarely fight each other and whether normative or institutional characteristics of democracies matter most. Explaining the democratic peace between Western democracies as "an imperial peace based on American power" (Rosato 2003, 599) is not justified, however. Admittedly, I held this view thirty years ago (Weede 1975). Then I explained peace among U.S. allies by their common ties or even by their subordination to the United States. Later, however, I discovered that autocratic U.S. allies, in contrast to democratic U.S. allies, fought each other or against democratic U.S. allies, as the football war in Central America and the Falklands War illustrate. Thus, I became a convert to the democratic-peace proposition. John Oneal, in unpublished analyses carried out in Bonn in 2003, found that although the democratic-peace proposition consistently calls the imperial-peace proposition into question, controlling for an imperial peace does not subvert the democratic-peace proposition.

Second, prosperity, or high income per capita, promotes democracy (Burkhart and Lewis-Beck 1994; Lipset 1994; Przeworski et al. 2000; Boix and Stokes 2003; Rajapatirana 2004).

Third, export orientation in poor countries and open markets in rich countries (that is, trade between rich and poor countries) promote growth and prosperity where they are needed most, in poor countries (Greenaway and Nam 1988; Dollar 1992; Edwards 1998; Lindert and Williamson 2001, 37; Dollar and Kraay 2002; Rajapatirana 2004).

Fourth, bilateral trade reduces the risk of war between dyads of nations (Oneal and Russett 1997, 1999; Russett and Oneal 2001). As to *why* trade contributes to the prevention of war, two ideas come to mind. First, war is likely to disrupt trade. The higher the level of trade in a pair (dyad) of nations is, the greater the costs of trade disruption are likely to be. Second, commerce might contribute to the establishment or maintenance of moral capital (Ratnapala 2003), which has a civilizing and pacifying effect on citizens and statesmen. In the context of this article, however, answering the question of why trade affects conflict-proneness or providing the answer with some microfoundation is less important than establishing the effect itself in empirical research.

Although some writers have questioned or even rejected the "peace by trade" proposition, their criticisms are not convincing. Beck, Katz, and Tucker (1998) raised the serious technical issue of time dependence in the time-series cross-section data, but Russett and Oneal (2001; see also Oneal 2003 and Oneal and Russett 2003b) responded to the objections raised against their earlier work and demonstrated that those objections do not affect their substantive conclusions. For a while, Hegre's (2000) study seemed to necessitate a qualification of the "peace by trade" proposition. He found that the pacifying effect of trade is stronger among developed countries than among less-developed countries. More recently, however, Mousseau, Hegre, and Oneal corrected this earlier finding and reported: "Whereas economically important trade has important pacifying benefits for all dyads, the conflict-reducing effect of democracy is conditional on states' economic development" (2003, 300). Gelpi and Grieco (2003) suggested another qualification. In their view, trade no longer pacifies relations between autocratic states. According to Mansfield and Pevehouse (2003), another modification of the "peace by trade" proposition might be required. The institutional setting, such as preferential trade agreements, matters. It is even conceivable that other forms of economic interdependence, such as cross-border investments, exercise some pacifying impact. Foreign direct investment (FDI) certainly promotes prosperity, growth, and democracy (de Soysa and Oneal 1999; de Soysa 2003), but the conceivable pacifying impact of FDI still lacks sufficient empirical investigation.

The most radical criticism comes from Barbieri (2002), according to whom bilateral trade *increases* the risk of conflict. As outlined by Oneal and Russett (2003a, 2003b; Oneal 2003; Russett 2003), her conclusion results from disregarding the military power of nations—that is, their different capabilities to wage war across considerable distances. Should we really proceed on the presumption that war between Argentina and Iraq is as conceivable as between the United States and Iraq or between Iran and Iraq? Of course, trade has no pacifying effect on international relations wherever the risk of conflict is extremely close to zero to begin with. Even this inadequate handling of the power and distance issue by itself does *not* suffice to support her conclusions. If the military-conflict variable is restricted to those conflicts that resulted in at least one fatality, then trade is pacifying, whether power and distance are adequately controlled or not. Moreover, Barbieri (2003) herself found some pacifying effect of economic freedom and openness to trade on the war involvement of nations. In spite of the attempted criticism of Russett and Oneal's findings, the "peace by trade" proposition stands and enjoys powerful empirical support.

Another issue also must be considered. Barbieri's (2002) measures are based on dyadic trade shares relative to national trade, whereas Russett and Oneal's measures are based on dyadic trade shares relative to the size of national economies. Gartzke and Li (2003) have demonstrated—arithmetically as well as empirically—that trade shares relative to national trade may rise when nations are *dis*connected from world trade. Nations may concentrate most of their trade on a few partners and remain rather closed economies. If Barbieri's and Oneal and Russett's measures of bilateral trade and their effects are simultaneously considered, then Barbieri's trade shares exert a conflict-enhancing effect and Oneal and Russett's trade dependence exerts a conflict-reducing effect. This finding of Gartzke and Li's study not only replicates the substantive findings of both main contenders in the debate about trade and conflict, but it remains robust whether one relies on the Oneal and Russett data or on the Barbieri data, whether one includes all dyads or only dyads for which there is some risk of military conflict to begin with. If one is interested in finding out whether more trade is better or worse for the avoidance of military conflict, then it seems more meaningful to focus on a measure that is related to openness at the national level of analysis, as Oneal and Russett (1997, 1999, 2003a, 2003b; Russett and Oneal 2001) have done, than on a measure that may be high for fairly closed economies, as Barbieri (2002) has done.

Actually, the pacifying effect of trade might be even stronger than the pacifying effect of democracy (Oneal and Russett 1999, 29, and 2003a, 160; Gartzke 2000, 209), especially among contiguous pairs of nations, where conflict-proneness is greater than elsewhere. Moreover, trade seems to play a pivotal role in the prevention of war because it exerts direct and indirect pacifying effects. In addition to the direct effect, there is the indirect effect of free trade as the consequent growth, prosperity, and democracy reduce the risk of militarized disputes and war. Because the exploitation of gains from trade is the essence or purpose of capitalism and free markets, I label the sum of the direct and indirect international security benefits "the capitalist peace," of which "the democratic peace" is merely a component.[1] Even if the direct "peace by trade" effect were discredited by future research, economic freedom and globalization would still retain their crucial role in overcoming mass poverty and in establishing the prerequisites of the democratic peace. For that reason, I (Weede 1996, chap. 8) advocated a capitalist-peace strategy even before Oneal and Russett (1997, 1999) convinced me of the existence of a directly pacifying effect of trade. An Asian statesman understood the capitalist peace intuitively even before it was scientifically documented and established. According to Lee Kuan Yew, "The most enduring lesson of history is that ambitious growing countries can expand either by grabbing territory, people or resources, or by trading with other countries. The alternative to free trade is not just poverty, it is war" (qtd. in "Survey: Asia" 1993, 24).

On Theory and Causality

My survey of the literature may appear vulnerable to a powerful and simple charge. In essence, the quantitative evidence referred to seems to consist of associations between variables and an arbitrary causal interpretation of them. Certainly, one should not infer causation from association or correlation, but this generally accepted insight does not mean that causation and correlation are independent of each other. From my epistemological perspective (influenced by Lakatos 1968–69 and Popper 1959), the proper procedure is the following. *Hypothetical causal* propositions provide the starting point of empirical research. From such propositions and ceteris paribus assumptions we may deduce which associations, correlations, or regression coefficients between variables to expect—that is, whether the relationship should be positive, zero, or negative. Empirical evidence may either support or contradict our expectations. Although certitude about possession of the truth seems beyond the capabilities of human inquiry, growth of knowledge is conceivable by the successive elimination of errors.

Although an association between the two variables X and Y is equally compatible with the alternative propositions that X causes Y, that Y causes X, that Z causes X and Y—and, conceivably, with more complicated models, too—this argument cannot be generalized to standard multiple-regression models. In general, estimation of partial effects on X and on Y presuppose controlling some other determinants of X that do not affect Y and some other determinants of Y that do not affect X. Taking a partial effect of X on Y as evidence that there is likely to be an equally strong effect of Y on X is not permissible. Of course, the specification of regression equations assumes a causal structure without proving its existence, but final proofs and certainty are not characteristics of empirical science. What is possible is to demonstrate a better or worse fit of propositions and observable reality. Although the evidence adduced in the literature cannot and does not prove that prosperity causes democracy or that dyadic democracy or trade causes peace, this evidence does not support reverse causality, such as democracy causing prosperity or growth, or peace causing democracy or trade. These questions require different research designs from the ones applied in the studies discussed earlier. Therefore, these issues are beyond the scope of this review.

There is also another complication. As illustrated by the debate about the effects of trade and economic interdependence on the avoidance of military conflict, full accordance of empirical studies and verdicts with theories is the exception rather than the rule, if it ever happens at all. Therefore, some philosophers of science (for example, Kuhn 1962 and Lakatos 1968–69) have criticized the idea of falsification and warned against premature rejection of propositions. If "anomalies" or "falsification" are more or less ubiquitous, then our task is no longer simply to choose between theories that have been falsified and therefore deserve rejection and those that are compatible with the facts and therefore deserve to be accepted until evidence against them turns up. Rather, our task is to choose between competing theories—for example, about the conflict-reinforcing or conflict-pacifying effect of trade—and to pick those that fit the data relatively better than others. So the claim advanced in this review of the literature cannot be that the empirical evidence fits the capitalist-peace idea perfectly, but merely that the evidence fits it much better than it fits competing explanations of military conflict and notions about the negative effect of capitalism or the irrelevance of democracy on the avoidance of conflict and war.

Admittedly, the nonexperimental evidence referred to here provides weaker support than experimental evidence in the natural sciences does. In the experimental sciences, two things are under much better control than in the nonexperimental sciences, including econometrics: first, the temporal precedence of presumed causes before their hypothesized effects; and, second, other determinants of the phenomenon under study and their possibly distorting effects. Still, weak or "correlational" evidence is better than none. Moreover, certain precautions are possible and routinely applied in the research discussed here. An association between an independent variable X observed at a certain time and a dependent variable Y observed *later* provides some support for the proposition that X causes Y, but none for Y causing X. Granger causality tests elaborate on this basic idea and provide further reassurance about the compatibility of causal theory and observable data (see Burkhart and Lewis-Beck 1994 for the prosperity-democracy link and Oneal, Russett, and Berbaum 2003 on the "causes of peace").

Some Illustrations of the Capitalist Peace

Before discussing illustrations of the capitalist peace, I should consider a standard historical objection against it. Certainly, economic interdependence, including trade, between the Western powers and the central European powers before World War I was quite strong. Nevertheless, World War I occurred. What does this evidence imply about the capitalist peace in general and about "peace by trade" in particular? First, it reminds us that all macropolitical propositions—and certainly those discussed here—are probabilistic instead of deterministic statements. We should always expect exceptions. Second, "peace by trade" is not the only component of capitalist-peace theory applicable here. Another is "peace among democracies." The democratic character of Germany and its allies before World War I is debatable. By contemporary standards, even the democratic character of the United Kingdom before World War I is not beyond suspicion because of franchise limitations. So World War I is not a clear exception to the democratic component of the capitalist peace. Third, no one should believe that trade and democracy, or the capitalist peace, suffice to explain the presence or absence of military disputes and war. At most, we can claim that "capitalist-peace theory" summarizes some known pacifying effects, but it does not summarize conflict-promoting variables and their effects (Russett 2003). As quantitative researchers documenting the pacifying effects of democracy and trade have found again and again (for example, Oneal and Russett 1997, 1999; Russett and Oneal 2001), power balances matter, too. Before World War I, the balance of power between the opposing coalitions was fairly even. There were no pacifying preponderance effects. Although one cannot claim World War I to be a case demonstrating the value of capitalist-peace theory, neither does it undermine the theory seriously.

It may be argued that the different long-term effects of the settlements of World Wars I and II derive from failure or success in applying a capitalist-peace strategy to the losers of the war. After World War I, France, which determined the peace settlement more than any other nation, failed to promote a capitalist peace. Immiseration and desperation in Germany contributed to Hitler's ascent to power and indirectly to World War II, in which France had to be saved by its allies. After World War II, the United States pursued a capitalist-peace strategy toward the vanquished and succeeded in making allies out of Germany and Japan.

If the West were afraid of the downside of globalization—that is, its inherent tendency to undermine the status quo and thereby Western or U.S. hegemony—or if the West turned protectionist, then its policies would look like white racism from the outside. Protectionism in the West would condemn many non-Westerners to poverty for longer than unavoidable. Protectionism might turn Huntington's (1996) "clash of civilizations" into a self-fulfilling prophecy.

Peace by trade is at least as important as peace by democracy. Trade (because of its contribution to prosperity) underwrites democracy and thereby the democratic peace where it prevails. Moreover, it does not suffer from a geopolitical complication that affects peace by democratization. According to the best research, the risk of war between democracies is much lower than elsewhere, but the risk of war between a democracy and an autocracy is higher than elsewhere, at least in recent decades. Although Russett and Oneal (2001, 116) no longer accept this view, I am not convinced that they are correct. To me, findings from a separate analysis of disputes in the Cold War period (Oneal and Russett 1997) look more persuasive than an analysis of data beginning in 1885 that combines relationships from the multipolar pre–World War II period, the bipolar Cold War period, and the beginning of the unipolar period thereafter. Some of the findings reported by Russett and Oneal (2001, 113)—namely, the qualitatively different alliance effects on militarized disputes found in the multipolar and bipolar periods of observation—cast doubt on the wisdom of imposing the same causal structure on different periods of world politics (Gowa 1999).

If we accept, as I do, the idea that democracy causes peace only among democracies, then democratization does not contribute everywhere to peace. Imagine the democratization of a nation located in the middle of a deeply autocratic area. Its democratization would generate a number of autocratic-democratic dyads and thereby increase the risk of war. By contrast, the democratization of a nation surrounded by democracies would certainly be desirable. The democratic peace should first be extended from its North Atlantic core area to contiguous areas. Geographical compactness of the democratic bloc is a prerequisite for the pacifying effects of democracy to apply. Promoting democracy in Poland first and in Uzbekistan much later is not only more desirable, but also more feasible than the reverse order would be. Furthermore, an imposition of democracy in poor and politically unstable countries, as currently being attempted in Afghanistan and Iraq, is at least as likely to produce hostility as democratization and stability.

Israel and Taiwan illustrate the ambivalence of democratization as a tool of pacification. Israel is democratic, but it has been surrounded by autocratic regimes for a long time. Although an autocratic Israel would not necessarily be safe from autocratic neighbors, making a deal between two autocracies—on, say, the Golan Heights— might be easier than making a deal between a democracy and an autocracy. Or, consider Taiwan. Until recently the mainland and Taiwan considered themselves to be parts of China. Now Taiwan is a democracy, and the mainland remains an autocracy. The democratization of Taiwan certainly raised obstacles against an elite deal on unification between two ruling classes.

Fortunately, however, the democratization of Taiwan has already refuted the idea that Confucian or Sinic civilization is incompatible with democracy. If the Chinese economy prospers, if China outgrows poverty, then mainland China may become a democracy in two or three decades. Some promising developments are already observable. Village elections have been held for about a decade (Rowen 1996). Some cadres already have been voted out of office. In 2003, lowly neighborhood committee leaders were elected in parts of Beijing and other big cities ("A Qualified Vote" 2003, 54). Moreover, China trains more lawyers than before, and the Chinese are beginning to perceive the economic benefits of the rule of law (Pei 1998). Instead of publicly criticizing China's poor human-rights performance, it seems more effective to support China in joining the capitalist world economy and in establishing some legal foundations for a future transition to democracy that China will voluntarily pursue for the sake of its economic ambitions.

As Zakaria observes, "To implement its agreements with the WTO, the government has made wide-ranging reforms of Chinese law, creating stronger economic and civil rights" (2003, 84). By contrast, post-Soviet Russia provides a vivid illustration of the limited value of electoral democracy without the rule of law.

According to Mousseau, Hegre, and Oneal (2003), "peace by trade" in contrast to "peace by democratization" applies regardless of the level of economic development of nations. Moreover, the democratic-peace component of the capitalist peace is constrained by the geopolitical need to avoid leapfrogging in the extension of democracy or tiger-coat patterns of democracy and autocracy. The "peace by trade" component of the capitalist peace, however, suffers from no such limitation. It seems to be a rare case of a desirable end that is attainable by a desirable means. By contrast, protectionism engenders less wealth and more war. Although one might argue that globalization or the resulting inequality destabilizes democracies and promotes internal conflict and violence, there is little empirical evidence to support this view (de Soysa 2003; Fearon and Laitin 2003; Hegre, Gissinger, and Gleditsch 2003; Weede 2003; World Bank 2003).

WHAT CAN BE DONE TO PROMOTE A CAPITALIST PEACE?

Rummel (1994) has pointed out that autocracy—itself frequently the result of rebellion, civil war, and revolution—killed even more people than interstate war, rebellion, or revolution in the twentieth century. Even if an autocratic peace within or between nations should exist—in spite of studies (Peceny, Beer, and Sanchez-Terry 2002; Fearon and Laitin 2003, 85) that call these claims into question—the autocratic cure looks even bloodier than the diseases of war and civil war.[2] Therefore, the preservation of democracy where it already exists and the establishment of democracy elsewhere must be part of the solution to the problems of rebellion, political violence, and war. Because the empirical studies discussed earlier have demonstrated some fairly strong effects of democracy on the avoidance of war between democracies, and because the pacifying effects of democracy on rebellion and civil war within states can also be documented (Muller and Weede 1990; Hegre et al. 2001), democracy and democratization are not only ends in themselves but also instruments in combating political violence.[3] What can be done to promote and underwrite democracy?

According to Lipset (1994) or Boix and Stokes (2003), the viability of democratic regimes and the likelihood of transitions to democracy depend on the level of economic development. The more prosperous a country is, the more likely it is to become and to remain a democracy. Because this proposition has been supported strongly by cross-national studies, much better than any other conceivable determinant or prerequisite of democracy, we may argue that the promotion of democracy necessitates providing a helping hand to poor countries. This help can be provided in different ways.

First, prosperous countries influence the legal foundations for capitalism or economic policies elsewhere. How much this influence matters was demonstrated during the Cold War by the divided nations, where one part was influenced by the Soviet Union and the other part by the United States. Economies benefiting from U.S. influence, such as West Germany, South Korea, and Taiwan, did much better than East Germany, North Korea, or mainland China, which were inspired by the Soviet model. After China began to abandon socialist practices and converted to creeping capitalism in the late 1970s, it quadrupled its income per capita in two decades and almost closed a sixteen-to-one gap in income per capita with Russia (Weede 2002). The idea of advice should not be conceived too narrowly. By providing a model for emulation, successful countries implicitly provide advice to others. In general terms, the best institutional and policy advice may be summarized as "promote economic freedom" (Berggren 2003; Kasper 2004). Cross-national studies (Dollar 1992; Edwards 1998; Haan and Siermann 1998; Haan and Sturm 2002; Weede and Kämpf 2002) demonstrate that economic freedom or improvements in economic freedom increase growth rates.[4] Economic openness or export orientation is part of the package of economic freedom.

Second, prosperous and democratic countries may provide open markets for exports from poor countries. Without a fairly open U.S. market, neither Japan nor the nations of western Europe would have overcome the terrible legacies of World War II as quickly as they did. Without a fairly open U.S. market, the East Asian economic miracles might never have happened. South Korea and Taiwan might still be poor and ruled by autocrats instead of being fairly prosperous and democratic.

Third, rich and democratic countries may provide FDI to poor countries. Even the nominally still communist regime in the People's Republic of China has understood the importance of FDI. Moreover, FDI not only promotes growth and prosperity, but also directly contributes to democratization (de Soysa and Oneal 1999; Burkhart and de Soysa 2002; de Soysa 2003).

Fourth, rich and democratic countries may provide economic aid. By and large, big economies, such as the United States or Japan, provide relatively much less aid than small Scandinavian economies, such as Norway or Sweden. But barriers to imports from poor countries are the lowest in the United States and the highest in Norway. Whereas European assistance to poor countries is provided by governments for the most part, U.S. private giving may be 3.5 times as large as U.S. official development assistance (Adelman 2003, 9). Rich-country subsidies to agricultural producers, which harm poor countries, are much greater than development aid. Whereas European Union aid per African person is approximately $8 dollars, subsidies per European Union cow are $913 (UNDP 2003, 155–60). The theoretical case for aid, however, has always been weak (Bauer 1981). Aid may strengthen governments and undermine free markets. This risk is much greater with government-to-government aid than with private giving, which rarely selects the state as recipient. Certainly, foreign aid does not promote democracy (Knack 2004).

Econometric studies have not demonstrated that aid generally increases growth rates. In recent studies, one finds either a curvilinear relationship between aid and growth (Hansen and Tarp 2000), which suggests that some aid may be useful but too much of it may be harmful, or a conditional effect, which suggests that positive aid effects depend on a proper policy environment in the recipient nation and that otherwise aid is simply wasted (Burnside and Dollar 2000). Or one finds that the effectiveness of aid depends on its bilateral rather than multilateral character (Ram 2003). Both the ambivalent findings about the effectiveness of aid and the poor record of official aid giving from the biggest Western economies underline that economic development depends above all on domestic efforts, institutions, and policies.

Still, there is some room for beneficial outside influences. The mere existence of prosperous and developed countries generates advantages of backwardness and opportunities for faster growth of less-developed countries (Barro and Sala-i-Martin 1995; Olson 1996; Bleany and Nishiyama 2002). They can borrow technology from the more developed countries and thereby grow faster than the Western pioneers of economic development grew. Japan until the 1960s and the East Asian tiger economies thereafter used these advantages of backwardness effectively. Currently, China, India, and parts of Southeast Asia do so. Catch-up opportunities are enhanced if poor countries invest in human capital for everyone—as China, South Korea, and Singapore have done to a much greater degree than India and Indonesia have (Drèze and Sen 1995)—if they follow an export-oriented development strategy, if they welcome FDI, and if prosperous Western economies provide open markets for poor countries and their products instead of protectionist obstacles. European and Japanese agricultural markets and Western textile and garment markets demonstrate the most persistent unwillingness of rich countries to provide a helping hand to poor countries.

The collapse of the World Trade Organization's meeting in mid-September 2003 was a tragedy for poor countries. According to *The Economist* and the World Bank, "a successful Doha round could raise the global income by more than $500 billion a year by 2015. Over 60% of that gain would go to poor countries, helping to pull 144 million people out of poverty. While most of the poor countries' gains would come from freer trade among themselves, the reduction of rich country farm subsidies and more open markets in the north would also help. That prize is now forgone" ("The WTO under Fire" 2003, 29).

As important as the provision of models for emulation is the avoidance of pressure from rich countries on poor countries to commit themselves to bad policies. Global labor standards are an important example of such pressure. Concerning the minimum-wage component of labor standards, the World Bank recognized this effect years ago:

> Those affected by minimum wage provisions in low- and middle-income countries are rarely the most needy. Most of the real poor operate in rural and informal markets in such countries and are not protected by minimum wages. The workers whom minimum wage legislation tries to protect—urban formal workers—already earn much more than the less favored majority. Sometimes the differences are extreme—an urban construction worker in Côte d'Ivoire earns 8.8 times the rural wage rate, and a steel worker in India earns 8.4 times the rural wage.... And inasmuch as minimum wage and other regulations discourage formal employment by increasing wage and nonwage costs, they hurt the poor who aspire to formal employment. (World Bank 1995, 75)

It has been estimated (Mitra 1998, 6) that in India less than 10 percent of the workforce is employed in the formal and privileged sector of the economy. More than 90 percent of the workforce stand no chance of benefiting from minimum wages or other labor standards. In essence, Western demands for higher wages in poor countries are nothing but an attempt to raise rivals' costs under the hypocritical guise of humanitarianism.

THE MEANING AND LIMITATIONS OF THE CAPITALIST PEACE

Earlier I referred to the wider concept of a "capitalist peace" instead of to the narrower concept of a "democratic peace." Fortunately, some crucial steps on the road to a capitalist peace exert a pacifying impact: prosperity, or high average income, contributes to the viability of democracy. A country achieves prosperity by economic growth. FDI is one helpful background condition for growth that also seems to promote democratization (Burkhart and de Soysa 2002). Export orientation, active foreign trade, FDI inflows, and economic openness are other useful determinants of economic growth (Dollar 1992; Edwards 1998; de Soysa and Oneal 1999; Bleany and Nishiyama 2002). As argued earlier, international trade by itself reduces the risk of war between trading nations. Thus, a beneficial means (namely, free trade) directly and indirectly (via prosperity and democracy) contributes to a desirable end: the avoidance of war between nations. Moreover, economic openness also reduces the risk of civil violence (de Soysa 2003) and of genocides or other political mass murders (Harff 2003), and the intervening variable of prosperity—in-between trade and war avoidance—also happens to reduce the risk of domestic instability and violence (Henderson and Singer 1999; World Bank 2003). The policy implications of the capitalist-peace strategy are simple: promote economic freedom and globalization. If the policy succeeds, one gets more prosperity, more democracy, less civil war, and less interstate war.

Ultimately, the capitalist-peace strategy rests on a policy of depoliticization. Under capitalism, material well-being depends less on political affiliations and more on market success. The capitalist peace depends on a universalistic ethic and its acceptance (Giersch 1995). Free trade and the principle of nondiscrimination between peoples or races and between domestic and foreign producers guide consumers to buy from the best and cheapest producers. Often, the cheapest producers in poor countries need their customers more than richer producers in rich countries, who can fall back on either capital income or social-security transfer payments, need theirs.

In applying the capitalist-peace strategy to contemporary problems, three conditions must be recognized.

First, a capitalist-peace strategy presupposes a minimal degree of state effectiveness. There is a need for the establishment of property rights, the enforcement of contracts, domestic stability, and the rule of law or, at least, substitutes for it, such as "market-preserving federalism" (Montinola, Qian, and Weingast 1995). Moreover, the democratization component of the capitalist-peace strategy requires overcoming arbitrary and autocratic rule. This statement obviously points to another difficulty. As Huntington suggested some decades ago, "authority has to exist before it can be limited" (1968, 8). Overcoming chaos, warlords, and state failure appears to be a prerequisite for the applicability of the capitalist-peace strategy. Analyzing how this prerequisite might be established is beyond the scope of this article.

Second, we have few reasons for optimism about the applicability of the capitalist-peace strategy to the Muslim world. Certainly, it does not look like a solution to the problem of international terrorism, although it might help in achieving something like containment of the problem—that is, in denying non-Muslim allies to Muslim terrorists and their sympathizers. My pessimism about the Muslim world derives from two sources. Muslim civilization so far has resisted democratization more consistently and persistently than other non-Western civilizations. Turkey is still the best example of a Muslim democracy, but Turkish democracy is strongly guided by the secularist armed forces, which makes the democratic character of the regime dubious. Moreover, even though Atatürk began the process of secularization in the 1920s, its success is still in doubt at the beginning of the twenty-first century.

Besides, some Muslim countries are rich in oil or other natural resources. Superficially, natural wealth might seem to facilitate the achievement of prosperity and growth, but it does not do so in these cases. Although we do not yet know why, "there is now strong evidence that states with abundant resource endowments perform less well than their resource-poor counterparts" (Ross 1999, 297; see also Lal 1998, 3). Perhaps rich resource endowments reinforce elite predatory behavior and rent seeking and thereby make institutional and economic development more difficult. In any event, the capitalist-peace strategy seems least likely to prevent violence and war within the Islamic civilization or between it and the rest of the world.

Still, it might work elsewhere, in particular Asia. As Bhalla (2002) has argued in more detail and more convincingly than anybody else, inequality among human beings has probably fallen since the 1970s. More important, global poverty has been reduced, too.[5] In 1980, approximately 43.5 percent of humankind had to survive on a single dollar a day or less in 1985 purchasing-power-parity terms. At the turn of the millennium the percentage was 13.1. This progress has been spread unevenly across the globe. Africa has done the worst. Asia was involved most in globalization and therefore has done best. Within Asia, the demographic giants China and India, where nearly 40 percent of humankind live, have been most important. As they opened up, they grew much faster than in previous decades. The degree of Asian progress is most vividly illustrated by some of Bhalla's data on middle classes. If one defines a middle-class person by a daily income between $10 and $40 in 1985 purchasing-power-parity terms, then the global middle class of 1960 was largely white. Only 6 percent of it was Asian. At the turn of the millennium, 52 percent of the global middle class was Asian, and its share is still growing.

The crucial question for the applicability of the capitalist peace is China. Taiwan and South Korea have recently demonstrated that Confucian civilization by itself is no permanent obstacle to democratization. In the long run, China's rise might upset the global balance of power. Historically, the rise and decline of nations have been associated with conflict and war (Organski and Kugler 1980; Gilpin 1981; Kugler and Lemke 1996), but the close FDI and trade links between China and the West, between China and the United States, even between China and Taiwan hold out some hope for "peace by trade." It is difficult to imagine better news than the eight-fold growth of Chinese exports between 1990 and 2003 (Hale and Hale 2003, 36). The strong economic-growth record of China promises that even the economic prerequisite for democratization might be achieved within two decades or so.[6] Therefore, the outlook for a capitalist peace between China and the West is not bad in the long run. Finally, in early 2004, it becomes conceivable that "trade trumps war" (Solomon 2004) even in the delicate relationship between India and Pakistan. If so, then the capitalist peace might spread to much of Asia.

Third, the typical limitations of social science analyses have to be kept in mind. Because social science propositions generally are probabilistic rather than deterministic—worse still, they are frequently weak rather than strong—one has to appreciate the risk of policy failure. Although I argue in favor of co-opting China into a peaceful democratic and capitalist world order, nobody can guarantee that the policy will work. Certainly, an incomplete transition to democracy and its attendant risks (Mansfield and Snyder 2002) cannot be ruled out in a country where democratization has not yet been seriously set in train. Still, even though in principle a capitalist-peace strategy may be risky, given the magnitude of American preponderance and the absence of powerful challengers, the opportunity to build a better world based on free trade, prosperity, democracy, and peace vastly outweighs the associated risks. For the next few decades, the United States will be so strong that it can easily concede greater relative gains to China, where hundreds of millions still have to survive on a dollar per day.

CONCLUSION

On the one hand, globalization promises to enlarge the market and therefore to increase the division of labor and to speed productivity gains and economic growth. On the other hand, it remains under attack from special-interest groups and misguided political activists. Critics of globalization not only forget both the benefits of free trade and globalization for developing countries and for their poor and underemployed workers and the benefits of free trade to consumers everywhere, but they know almost nothing about the international-security benefits of free trade. Quantitative research has established the viability and prospect of a capitalist peace based on the following causal links between free trade and the avoidance of war: first, there is an indirect link running from free trade or economic openness to prosperity and democracy and ultimately to the democratic peace; second, trade and economic interdependence by themselves reduce the risk of military conflict. By promoting capitalism, economic freedom, trade, and prosperity, we simultaneously promote peace.

Conceivable instruments to promote capitalism, economic freedom, free trade, and prosperity include advice about the institutional and legal foundations of capitalism and economic policies. Such advice is more likely to be persuasive if Western societies provide models for emulation to poor and conflict-prone countries. Open markets in rich countries for exports from poor countries generate credibility for free-market institutions and policies. They complement export-oriented growth strategies in poor countries. FDI by private enterprises and even donations from private Western sources to poor countries are more likely to have a positive effect on the growth path of poor countries than will official development aid, which tends to strengthen the state at the expense of free markets. The more capitalist the rich countries become, the more they provide an effective model for emulation to poor countries as well as a market and a source of technology and investment. By resistance to protectionism and to the creeping socialism of the welfare state, Western nations may simultaneously strengthen their own economies, improve the lot of the poor in the Third World, and contribute to the avoidance of conflict and war.

NOTES

1. Russett and Oneal (2001) refer instead to a Kantian peace, which is composed of three components: the democratic peace, peace by trade, and peace by collaboration in international governmental organizations (IGOs). In their research, the IGO element of the Kantian tripod is the weakest and least robust one. I do not know who invented the term *capitalist peace*. I have heard it spoken more frequently than I have seen it in print, but in any event it is a felicitous term.
2. Harff (2003), like Rummel (1994), has documented the relationship between autocracy and politicocide—that is, mass murder for political reasons—but her data cover only the period since 1955.
3. Actually, semirepressiveness is more closely correlated with political violence than with either autocracy or democracy. Although autocratic governments may provide the civil peace of the graveyard, this condition is obviously undesirable because autocracies sometimes murder millions of people.
4. There is a gap between theory and quantitative evidence. Theoretically, one expects a relationship between the level of economic freedom and growth rates. Empirically, however, the relationship between improvements in economic freedom and growth looks more robust than the relationship between the level of freedom and growth.
5. Similar in spirit but more cautious in its estimates and conclusions is the World Bank study *Globalization, Growth, and Poverty* (Collier and Dollar 2002).
6. Around the year 2015, the economic size of China may be equal to that of the United States in terms of purchasing-power parity (Maddison 1998). Because China's population then may be about five times that of the United States, Chinese income per capita will be about a fifth of U.S. income per capita. At this level of development, democratization was under way in Taiwan and South Korea.

REFERENCES

Adelman, Carol C. 2003. The Privatization of Foreign Aid. *Foreign Affairs* 82, no. 6: 9–14.
Barbieri, Katherine. 2002. *The Liberal Illusion: Does Trade Promote Peace?* Ann Arbor: University of Michigan Press.

————. 2003. Are Trading States More Peaceful? Paper delivered at the Second General Conference of the European Consortium for Political Research, Marburg, Germany, September 19.

Barro, Robert J., and Xavier Sala-i-Martin. 1995. *Economic Growth.* New York: McGraw-Hill.

Bauer, Peter T. 1981. *Equality, the Third World, and Economic Delusion.* London: Weidenfeld and Nicolson.

Beck, Nathaniel, Jonathan N. Katz, and Richard Tucker. 1998. Taking Time Seriously: Time-Series Cross-Section Analysis with a Binary Dependent Variable. *American Journal of Political Science* 42, no. 4: 1260–88.

Berggren, Niclas. 2003. The Benefits of Economic Freedom. *The Independent Review,* 8, no. 2: 193–211.

Bhagwati, Jagdish. 1991. *The World Trading System at Risk.* London: Harvester and Wheatsheaf.

Bhalla, Surjit S. 2002. *Imagine There's No Country: Poverty, Inequality, and Growth in the Era of Globalization.* Washington, D.C.: Institute for International Economics.

Bleany, Michael, and Akira Nishiyama. 2002. Explaining Growth. *Journal of Economic Growth* 7, no. 1: 43–56.

Boix, Charles, and Susan C. Stokes. 2003. Endogenous Democratization. *World Politics* 55, no. 4: 517–49.

Burkhart, Ross E., and Michael S. Lewis-Beck. 1994. Comparative Democracy: The Economic Development Thesis. *American Political Science Review* 88, no. 4: 903–10.

Burkhart, Ross E., and Indra de Soysa. 2002. Open Borders, Open Regimes? FDI, Trade, and Democratization, 1970–1999. Unpublished manuscript, Department of Political Science, Boise State University, Idaho, and Center for Development Research, Bonn, Germany.

Burnside, Craig, and David Dollar. 2000. Aid, Policies, and Growth. *American Economic Review* 90, no. 4: 847–68.

Collier, Paul, and David Dollar. 2002. *Globalization, Growth, and Poverty.* New York: Oxford University Press for the World Bank.

De Soysa, Indra. 2003. *Foreign Direct Investment, Democracy, and Development.* London: Routledge.

De Soysa, Indra, and John R. Oneal. 1999. Boon or Bane? Reassessing the Productivity of Foreign Direct Investment. *American Sociological Review* 64, no. 5: 766–82.

Dollar, David. 1992. Outward-Oriented Developing Economies Really Do Grow More Rapidly. *Economic Development and Cultural Change* 40, no. 3: 523–44.

Dollar, David, and Aart Kraay. 2002. Spreading the Wealth. *Foreign Affairs* 81, no. 1: 120–33.

Drèze, Jean, and Amartya Sen. 1995. *India: Economic Development and Social Opportunity.* New Delhi: Oxford University Press.

Edwards, Sebastian. 1998. Openness, Productivity, and Growth: What Do We Really Know? *Economic Journal* 108: 383–98.

Fearon, James D., and David D. Laitin. 2003. Ethnicity, Insurgency, and Civil War. *American Political Science Review* 97, no. 1: 75–90.

Flying on One Engine: A Survey of the World Economy. 2003. *The Economist* 368, no. 8342 (September 20): follows p. 54, separately numbered.

Gartzke, Erik. 2000. Preferences and the Democratic Peace. *International Studies Quarterly* 44, no. 2: 191–212.

Gartzke, Erik, and Quan Li. 2003. Measure for Measure: Concept Operationalization and the Trade Interdependence–Conflict Debate. *Journal of Peace Research* 40, no. 5: 553–71.

Gelpi, Christopher, and Joseph M. Grieco. 2003. Economic Interdependence, the Democratic State, and the Liberal Peace. In *Economic Interdependence and International Conflict,* edited by Edward D. Mansfield and Brian M. Pollins, 44–59. Ann Arbor: University of Michigan Press.

Giersch, Herbert. 1995. *Wirtschaftsmoral als Standortfaktor.* Jena: Max Planck Institute for Economic Research. Translated 2002. Economic Morality as a Competitive Asset. In *Method and Morals in Constitutional Economics: Essays in Honor of James M. Buchanan,* edited by Geoffrey Brennan, Hartmut Kliemt, and Robert D. Tollison, 444–69. Berlin: Springer.

Gilpin, Robert W. 1981. *War and Change in World Politics.* Cambridge: Cambridge University Press.

Gowa, Joanne. 1999. *Ballots and Bullets. The Elusive Democratic Peace.* Princeton, N.J.: Princeton University Press.

Gray, John. 1998. *False Dawn: The Delusions of Global Capitalism.* New York: New Press.

Greenaway, David, and Chong Hyun Nam. 1988. Industrialization and Macroeconomic Performance in Developing Countries under Alternative Trade Strategies. *Kyklos* 41: 419–35.

Haan, Jacob de, and Clemens L. J. Siermann. 1998. Further Evidence on the Relationship Between Economic Freedom and Economic Growth. *Public Choice* 95, nos. 3–4: 363–80.

Haan, Jacob de, and Jan-Egbert Sturm. 2000. On the Relationship Between Economic Freedom and Economic Growth. *European Journal of Political Economy* 16: 215–41.

Hale, David, and Lyric Hughes Hale. 2003. China Takes Off. *Foreign Affairs* 82, no. 6: 36–53.

Hansen, Henrik, and Finn Tarp. 2000. Aid Effectiveness Disputed. In *Foreign Aid and Development,* edited by Finn Tarp, 103–28. London: Routledge.

Harff, Barbara. 2003. No Lessons Learned from the Holocaust? Assessing Risks of Genocide and Political Mass Murder since 1955. *American Political Science Review* 97, no. 1: 57–73.

Hegre, Harvard. 2000. Development and the Liberal Peace: What Does It Take to Be a Trading State? *Journal of Peace Research* 37, no. 1: 5–30.

Hegre, Harvard, Tanja Ellingsen, Scott Gates, and Nils Petter Gleditsch. 2001. Toward a Democratic Civil Peace? Democracy, Political Change, and Civil War, 1816–1992. *American Political Science Review* 95, no. 1: 33–48.

Hegre, Harvard, Ranveig Gissinger, and Nils Petter Gleditsch. 2003. Globalization and Internal Conflict. In *Globalization and Armed Conflict,* edited by Gerald Schneider, Katherine Barbieri, and Nils Petter Gleditsch, 251–75. Lanham, Md.: Rowman and Littlefield.

Henderson, Errol A., and J. David Singer. 2000. Civil War in the Post-colonial World, 1946–92. *Journal of Peace Research* 37, no. 3: 275–99.

Huntington, Samuel P. 1968. *Political Order in Changing Societies.* New Haven, Conn.: Yale University Press.

———. 1996. *The Clash of Civilizations.* New York: Simon and Schuster.

Irwin, Douglas A. 2002. *Free Trade under Fire.* Princeton, N.J.: Princeton University Press.

Jones, Eric L. 1981. *The European Miracle.* Cambridge: Cambridge University Press.

Kapstein, Ethan B. 1999. *Sharing the Wealth: Workers and the World Economy.* New York: W.W. Norton.

Kasper, Wolfgang. 2004. Freedom and Economic Development: Applying the Lessons. Paper presented at the Mont Pelerin Society Regional Meeting, Sri Lanka, January 10–15.

Knack, Stephen. 2004. Does Foreign Aid Promote Democracy? *International Studies Quarterly* 48, no. 1: 251–66.

Krugman, Paul. 1996. *Pop Internationalism.* Cambridge, Mass.: MIT Press.

Kugler, Jacek, and Douglas Lemke, eds. 1996. *Parity and War.* Ann Arbor: University of Michigan Press.

Kuhn, Thomas S. 1962. *The Structure of Scientific Revolutions.* Chicago: University of Chicago Press.

Lakatos, Imre. 1968–69. Criticism and the Methodology of Scientific Research Programmes. *Proceedings of the Aristotelian Society* 69: 149–86.

Lal, Deepak. 1998. *Unintended Consequences.* Cambridge, Mass.: MIT Press.

Lindert, Peter H., and Jeffrey G. Williamson. 2001. *Does Globalization Make the World More Unequal?* National Bureau of Economic Research Working Paper no. 8228. Cambridge,

Mass.: National Bureau of Economic Research.

Lipset, Seymour Martin. 1994. The Social Requisites of Democracy Revisited. *American Sociological Review* 59, no. 1: 1–22.

Maddison, Angus. 1998. *Chinese Economic Performance in the Long-Run.* Paris: Organization for Economic Cooperation and Development.

Mansfield, Edward D., and Jon C. Pevehouse. 2003. Institutions, Interdependence, and International Conflict. In *Globalization and Armed Conflict,* edited by Gerald Schneider, Katherine Barbieri, and Nils Petter Gleditsch, 233–50. Lanham, Md.: Rowman and Littlefield.

Mansfield, Edward D., and Jack Snyder. 2002. Incomplete Democratization and the Outbreak of Military Disputes. *International Studies Quarterly* 46, no. 4: 529–49.

Mearsheimer, John J. 2001. *The Tragedy of Great Power Politics.* New York: W.W. Norton.

Mitra, Barun S. 1998. Democracy, Equity, and the Market. In *Democracy, Market, and Human Rights,* edited by Tibor R. Machan and Barun S. Mitra, 5–13. New Delhi: Liberty Institute.

Montinola, Gabiella, Yingyi Qian, and Barry R. Weingast. 1995. Federalism Chinese Style: The Political Basis for Economic Success in China. *World Politics* 48, no. 1: 50–81.

Mousseau, Michael, Harvard Hegre, and John R. Oneal. 2003. How the Wealth of Nations Conditions the Liberal Peace. *European Journal of International Relations* 9, no. 2: 277–314.

Muller, Edward N., and Erich Weede. 1990. Cross-National Variation in Political Violence. *Journal of Conflict Resolution* 34, no. 4: 624–51.

Olson, Mancur. 1996. Big Bills Left on the Sidewalk: Why Some Nations Are Rich, and Others Poor. *Journal of Economic Perspectives* 10, no. 2: 3–24.

Oneal, John R. 2003. Empirical Support for the Liberal Peace. In *Economic Interdependence and International Conflict,* edited by Edward D. Mansfield and Brian M. Pollins, 189–206. Ann Arbor: University of Michigan Press.

Oneal, John R., and Bruce Russett. 1997. The Classical Liberals Were Right: Democracy, Interdependence, and Conflict, 1950–1985. *International Studies Quarterly* 40, no. 2: 267–94.

———. 1999. The Kantian Peace: The Pacific Benefits of Democracy, Interdependence, and International Organizations, 1885–1992. *World Politics* 52, no. 1: 1–37.

———. 2003a. Assessing the Liberal Peace with Alternative Specifications. In *Globalization and Armed Conflict,* edited by Gerald Schneider, Katherine Barbieri, and Nils Petter Gleditsch, 143–63. Lanham, Md.: Rowman and Littlefield.

———. 2003b. Modelling Conflict While Studying Dynamics. In *Globalization and Armed Conflict,* edited by Gerald Schneider, Katherine Barbieri, and Nils Petter Gleditsch, 179–88. Lanham, Md.: Rowman and Littlefield.

Oneal, John R., Bruce Russett, and Michael L. Berbaum. 2003. Causes of Peace: Democracy, Interdependence, and International Organizations, 1885–1992. *International Studies Quarterly* 47, no. 3: 371–93.

Organization for Economic Cooperation and Development (OECD). 2003. *The Sources of Economic Growth in OECD Countries.* Paris: Organization for Economic Cooperation and Development.

Organski, A. F. K., and Jacek Kugler. 1980. *The War Ledger.* Chicago: Chicago University Press.

Peceny, Mark, Caroline C. Beer, with Shannon Sanchez-Terry. 2002. Dictatorial Peace? *American Political Science Review* 96, no. 1: 15–26.

Pei, Minxin. 1998. Is China Democratizing? *Foreign Affairs* 77, no. 1: 68–82.

Popper, Karl R. 1959. *The Logic of Scientific Discovery.* London: Hutchinson.

Przeworski, Adam, Michael E. Alvarez, Jose Antonio Cheibub, and Fernando Limongi. 2000. *Democracy and Development.* Cambridge: Cambridge University Press.

A Qualified Vote. 2003. *The Economist* 367, no. 8318 (April 5): 54.

Rajapatirana, Sarath. 2004. Trading to Prosperity and Freedom: Developing Countries in Perspective. Paper presented at the Mont Pelerin Society Regional Meeting, Sri Lanka, January 10–15.

Ram, Rati. 2003. Roles of Bilateral and Multilateral Aid in Economic Growth of Developing Countries. *Kyklos* 56, no. 1: 95–110.

Ratnapala, Suri. 2003. Moral Capital and Commercial Society. *The Independent Review* 8, no. 2: 213–33.

Rodrik, Dani. 1997. *Has Globalization Gone Too Far?* Washington, D.C.: Institute for International Economics.

Rosato, Sebastian. 2003. The Flawed Logic of Democratic Peace Theory. *American Political Science Review* 97, no. 4: 585–602.

Ross, Michael L. 1999. The Political Economy of the Resource Curse. *World Politics* 51, no. 2: 297–322.

Rowen, Henry S. 1996. China: A Short March to Democracy. *The National Interest* 45: 61–70.

Rummel, Rudolph J. 1994. *Death by Government.* New Brunswick, N.J.: Transaction.

Russett, Bruce M. 1993. *Grasping the Democratic Peace.* Princeton, N.J.: Princeton University Press.

———. 2003. Violence and Disease: Trade as a Suppressor of Conflict When Suppressors Matter. In *Economic Interdependence and International Conflict,* edited by Edward D. Mansfield and Brian M. Pollins, 159–74. Ann Arbor: University of Michigan Press.

Russett, Bruce M., and John R. Oneal. 2001. *Triangulating Peace: Democracy, Interdependence, and International Organizations.* New York: W.W. Norton.

Smith, Adam. [1776] 1976. *An Inquiry into the Nature and Causes of the Wealth of Nations.* Oxford: Oxford University Press.

Solomon, Jay. 2004. Trade Trumps War. *Far East Economic Review* 167, no. 2 (January 15): 14–17.

Survey: Asia. A Billion Consumers. 1993. *The Economist* 329, no. 7835 (October 30): follows p. 76, separately numbered.

United Nations Development Program (UNDP). 2003. *Human Development Report 2003.* New York: Oxford University Press.

Vanberg, Viktor. 2000. Globalization, Democracy, and Citizens' Sovereignty: Can Competition among Governments Enhance Democracy? *Constitutional Political Economy* 11, no. 1: 87–112.

Waltz, Kenneth N. 1979. *Theory of International Politics.* Reading, Mass.: Addison-Wesley.

Weede, Erich. 1975. World Order in the Fifties and Sixties: Dependence, Deterrence, and Limited Peace. *Peace Science Society (International) Papers* 24: 49–80.

———. 1996. *Economic Development, Social Order, and World Politics.* Boulder, Colo.: Lynne Rienner.

———. 2000. *Asien und der Westen.* Baden-Baden: Nomos.

———. 2002. The Transition to Capitalism in China and Russia. *Comparative Sociology* 1, no. 2: 151–67.

———. 2003. On Political Violence and Its Avoidance. Paper presented at the Second General Meeting of the European Consortium for Political Research, Marburg, Germany, September 19.

Weede, Erich, and Sebastian Kämpf. 2002. The Impact of Intelligence and Institutional Improvements on Economic Growth. *Kyklos* 55, no. 3: 361–80.

Wood, Adrian. 1994. *North-South Trade, Employment, and Inequality.* Oxford: Oxford University Press, Clarendon.

World Bank. 1995. *World Development Report 1995.* New York: Oxford University Press.
———. 2003. *Breaking the Conflict Trap.* New York: Oxford University Press.
The WTO under Fire. 2003. *The Economist* 368, no. 8342 (September 20): 29–31.
Zakaria, Fareed. 2003. *The Future of Freedom.* New York: Norton.

Acknowledgments: Reprinted from *The Independent Review,* 9, no. 2 (Fall 2004):165–86. ISSN 1086-1653, Copyright © 2004.

    A previous version of this paper was presented at the Mont Pelerin Society Asian Meeting, Sri Lanka, January 10–15, 2004. A long letter from John Oneal (University of Alabama) on his recent work is appreciated. Critical comments from Wolfgang Kasper (CIS, Sydney, Australia) and three reviewers contributed to the improvement of the paper.

About the Editors and Contributors

ABOUT THE EDITORS

Robert Higgs is Senior Fellow in Political Economy for the Independent Institute and editor of *The Independent Review*. He received his Ph.D. in economics from the Johns Hopkins University, and he has been a member of the faculty at the University of Washington, Lafayette College, and Seattle University, and a visiting professor at the University of Economics in Prague. He is the author of eight books, the most recent of which are *Depression, War, and Cold War: Studies in Political Economy* and *Neither Liberty nor Safety: Fear, Ideology, and the Growth of Government*, and the editor or co-editor of five earlier books, including *Arms, Politics, and the Economy: Historical and Contemporary Perspectives, Re-Thinking Green: Alternatives to Environmental Bureaucracy* (with Carl Close), and *The Challenge of Liberty: Classical Liberalism Today* (with Carl Close). A contributor to many scholarly volumes, he is also the author of more than 100 articles and reviews in the professional journals of economics, demography, history, and public policy and the author of many articles in the popular press. He was named to the Templeton Foundations Honor Roll for Colleges and Universities in 1989. He received the Distinguished Scholar Award from the Association of Private Enterprise Education in 1993; the Friedrich von Wieser Memorial Prize for Excellence in Economic Education from the Prague Conference on Political Economy in 2006; the Thomas S. Szasz Award for Outstanding Contributions to the Cause of Civil Liberties from the Center for Independent Thought in 2006; and the Gary G. Schlarbaum Prize for Lifetime Achievement in Liberty from the Ludwig von Mises Institute in 2007.

Carl P. Close is Research Fellow and Academic Affairs Director of the Independent Institute and Assistant Editor of *The Independent Review*. He is co-editor (with Robert Higgs) of The *Challenge of Liberty: Classical Liberalism Today* (2006) and *Re-Thinking Green: Alternatives to Environmental Policy* (2005). His research interests include environmental policy, the history of economic and political thought, and the political economy of propaganda. He received his master's degree in economics from the University of California, Santa Barbara.

ABOUT THE CONTRIBUTORS

Ted Galen Carpenter is the vice president of defense and foreign policy studies at the Cato Institute. He is the author of numerous books on international affairs, including *America's Coming War with China*, *The Korean Conundrum: America's Troubled Relations with North and South Korea* (with Doug Bandow), *Bad Neighbor Policy: Washington's Futile War on Drugs in Latin America*, *The Captive Press: Foreign Policy Crises and the First Amendment*, *Beyond NATO: Staying Out of Europe's Wars*, and *A Search for Enemies: America's Alliances after the Cold War*.

Stephen W. Carson, a software engineer, writes independently from St. Louis, Missouri. He is the author of more than sixty articles on political economy posted on the website of the Ludwig von Mises Institute. His movie guide, *Films on Liberty and the State*, is available at www.mises.org/content/film.asp/.

Michael T. Hayes is a professor of political science at Colgate University. He is the author of *The Limits of Policy Change: Incrementalism, Worldview, and the Rule of Law* and *Incrementalism and Public Policy*.

James L. Payne has taught political science at Yale, Wesleyan, Johns Hopkins, and Texas A&M. He is the author of *A History of Force: Exploring the Worldwide Movement Against Habits of Coercion, Bloodshed, and Mayhem*, *The American Threat: The Fear of War As an Instrument of Foreign Policy*, *Costly Returns: The Burdens of the U.S. Tax System*, *The American Threat: National Security and Foreign Policy*, *Why Nations Arm*, and *Overcoming Welfare: Expecting More from the Poor—and from Ourselves*.

Ralph Raico is a professor emeritus of European history at Buffalo State College. He is the author of *Classical Liberalism: Historical Essays in Political Economy* (forthcoming) and a book on the history of German liberalism, *Die Partei der Freiheit: Studien zur Geschichte des deutschen Liberalismus.* He is the recipient of the 2000 Gary G. Schlarbaum Prize for Lifetime Achievement in the Cause of Liberty.

Sheldon L. Richman is the editor of *The Freeman*, published by the Foundation for Economic Education, a senior fellow at the Future of Freedom Foundation, and a research fellow at the Independent Institute. He is the author of *Separating School and State: How to Liberate America's Families, Your Money or Your Life: Why We Must Abolish the Income Tax*, and *Tethered Citizens: Time to Repeal the Welfare State.*

R. J. Rummel is professor emeritus of political science at the University of Hawaii. He is the author of more than 100 scholarly articles and two dozen books, including *Lethal Politics: Soviet Genocides and Mass Murders 1917–1987, China's Bloody Century: Genocide and Mass Murder Since 1900, Democide: Nazi Genocide and Mass Murder, Death by Government, Power Kills: Democracy as a Method of Nonviolence,* and *Statistics of Democide.* He is the recipient of the 2003 Lifetime Achievement Award from the Conflict Processes Section, American Political Science Association. Many of his writings are available at http://www.2.hawaii.edu/~rummel/.

Edward Stringham is associate professor of economics at San Jose State University, president of the Association of Private Enterprise Education, editor of the *Journal of Private Enterprise*, research fellow at the Independent Institute, and editor of the books *Anarchy and the Law: The Political Economy of Choice* and *Anarchy, State, and Public Choice.*

Joseph R. Stromberg holds a Master of Arts degree in history from Florida Atlantic University. He has published in *The Freeman, Telos, The Agorist Quarterly, The Independent Review, Journal of Libertarian Studies*, and other journals, and has contributed to several scholarly volumes.

Jerry K. Sweeney, now retired, was a professor in and the head of the Department of History at South Dakota State University, Brookings, South Dakota. He is the author of *American Diplomacy: A Handbook: 1776–2000* and *A Handbook of American Military History: From the Revolutionary War to the Present.*

Erich Weede is a professor of sociology at the University of Bonn, Germany. He is the author of *Balance of Power, Globalization, and the Capitalist Peace* and *Economic Development, Social Order, and World Politics.*

Index

as nation builder, 142, 143 (table), 147
Nigeria occupied by, 147
Oman, intervention in, 151n.1
Portuguese alliance with, 169
Sierra Leone occupied by, 147
U.S. trade with, 234
Zimbabwe occupied by, 147
Great Depression, 23, 45, 53, 237
Great Leap Forward (China), 206
Great War. *See* World War I
Great White Fleet, 14–15
Greek-Turkish aid bill (1947), 29, 59, 62
Greer (warship), 25, 101
Grieco, Joseph M., 242
Gronna, Asle J., 18
Guam, x
Guatemala, 191, 202
Guffey Coal Conservation Act, 86n.21
Gulf War (1990–91), 35, 178, 187
gun control, 214–15
Gwartney, James, 226

Haass, Richard, 146, 147
Habibie, B. J., 180
Haiti, 129, 140–41
Hamowy, Ronald, 49, 85
Hanighen, Frank, 28, 80, 88n.39
    Merchants of Death, 21
Harding, William G., 20
Harper, F. A., 45, 87n.32, 89n.61
    "In Search of Peace," 74–75
Hartford Convention (1814), 9
Hartmann, George, 27
Hawaii, 8
Hayek, F. A.
    on democracy vs. autocracy/dictatorship in Germany, 207–8
    on economic control, 213
    as an *NIR* contributor, 84–85, 89n.58
    on property-rights violations and dictatorship, 216

The Road to Serfdom, 88n.45
on spontaneous order, 193
"Why I Am Not a Conservative," 89n.58
Hays, Michael, xvi
Hazlitt, Henry, 84–85, 87n.33, 88n.38
Hearst, William Randolph, 104
Hegre, Harvard, 242, 249
Henry George School, 69
Henry VIII, king of England and Ireland, 132
Herbert, Aubrey. *See* Rothbard, Murray N.
Higgs, Robert, 225, 232
high-violence societies
    democracy in, 127–31, 134–36, 165–66
    dictatorships, 134–36
    establishing stability in, 136
    evolution away from, 131–36
    good vs. bad guys in, 131
Himmelstein, Jerome L., 85n.5
Hitler, Adolf, 134
    appeasement of, 86n.15
    defeat of, 155
    as discredited, 166
    plans to conquer U.S., xv, 100–101
    rise of, 159, 207–8, 247
homeland security, 121
Hoover, Herbert
    anticommunism of, 59
    on Bolshevism, 46–47
    Depression policies of, 53
    on famine, 47
    on FDR, 101–2
    foreign trade/investment promoted by, 23
    on the Korean War, 30, 59, 87n.28
    New Deal opposed by, 23
    noninterventionism of, 58–59
    on WWI, 58
    on WWII, 59

WWI's contribution to, 247
See also Nazis; *and specific countries*
Wright, Frank Lloyd, 98

Yalta agreement, 70
Yom Kippur War (1973), 171
Yorkshire revolt (England), 132
Young Americans for Freedom, 84

Zakaria, Fareed, 249
Zelman, Aaron, 214–15
Zimbabwe, 147
Zink, Harold, 162–63, 164–65

INDEPENDENT STUDIES IN POLITICAL ECONOMY

For further information and a catalog of publications, please contact:

THE INDEPENDENT INSTITUTE

100 Swan Way, Oakland, California 94621-1428, U.S.A.

510-632-1366 · Fax 510-568-6040 · info@independent.org · www.independent.org